Praise for
How Risky Is It, Really?

"The perception (and misperception) of risk has profound effects on everything from environmental policy to foreign policy, from our health and consumer decisions to our sense of security and well-being. It is a topic at the frontier of research in cognitive science, economics, and political science. This book is a clear, balanced, and lively introduction to this crucial body of knowledge."

—Steven Pinker,
bestselling author of *How the Mind Works*

"How Risky Is It, Really? is going to change the way people think."

—Lester R. Brown,
President, Earth Policy Institute,
and author of *Plan B*

"Our problems with accurate risk assessment have serious consequences—we worry ourselves sick over trivialities, pay to protect ourselves from the wrong things, avoid something we deem risky by doing something riskier. In this clever, accessible, and surprisingly nonjudgmental book, David Ropeik tackles this subject, ranging from the realms of psychology and neuroscience to funny, winning self-reflection. It is both a field monograph about the foibles of one species as well as a self-help manual. Read this book, think about it, and you will be both safer and saner."

—Robert M. Sapolsky, Ph.D.,
author of *Why Zebra's Don't Get Ulcers*

How Risky Is It, Really?

Really?

DAVID ROPEIK

**Why Our Fears Don't Always
Match the Facts**

New York   Chicago   San Francisco   Lisbon   London
Madrid   Mexico City   Milan   New Delhi   San Juan   Seoul
Singapore   Sydney   Toronto

1 2 3 4 5 6 7 8 9 0   DOC/DOC   1 8 7 6 5 4 3 2 1 0

ISBN 978-0-07-162969-0
MHID 0-07-162969-6

McGraw-Hill books are available at special quantity discounts to use as premiums and sales promotions, or for use in corporate training programs. To contact a representative please e-mail us at bulksales@mcgraw-hill.com.

This book is printed on acid-free paper.

Library of Congress Cataloging-in-Publication Data
Ropeik, David.
  How risky is it, really? : why our fears don't always match the facts / David Ropeik.
     p. cm.
  Includes bibliographical references.
  ISBN-13: 978-0-07-162969-0 (alk. paper)
  ISBN-10: 0-07-162969-6 (alk. paper)
  1. Fear. I. Title.
  BF575.F2
  152.4'6—dc22   2009032688

To Toby, for her wisdom, patience, insight, and support.

To Rachel, Matt, and Ina, for their ideas and enthusiasm.

To Misha and Yuri, for waiting so patiently to go for their daily walk.

And to my friends and fellow travelers . . . may you make healthy choices.

CONTENTS

Acknowledgments ix

Introduction xi

CHAPTER 1 THIS IS YOUR BRAIN ON FEAR   1

The Amygdala to the Rescue: Hard-Wired to Fear First and Think
Second 2

The Fear Response Continues 7

Built-In Fears 14

CHAPTER 2 BOUNDED RATIONALITY: BECAUSE REASON ALONE CAN'T KEEP YOU SAFE   21

Mental Shortcuts for Making Decisions 23

The Framing Effect 26

Categorization: The Representativeness Effect 32

Loss Aversion 40

Anchoring and Adjustment 45

The Awareness/Ready Recall Effect 48

Innumeracy 52

Optimism Bias 56

CHAPTER 3 FEAR FACTORS: WHY SOME THREATS FEEL SCARIER THAN OTHERS   65

Principles behind Risk Perception Factors 68

Risk Perception Factor 1: Trust 70

Risk Perception Factor 2: Risk versus Benefit 81

Risk Perception Factor 3: Control 85

Risk Perception Factor 4: Choice 89

Risk Perception Factor 5: Is the Risk Natural or Human-Made? . . . 92

Risk Perception Factor 6: Pain and Suffering 96

Risk Perception Factor 7: Uncertainty 99

Risk Perception Factor 8: Catastrophic or Chronic 105

Risk Perception Factor 9: Can It Happen to *Me*? 109

Risk Perception Factor 10: Is the Risk New or Familiar? 114

Risk Perception Factor 11: Risks to Children 119

Risk Perception Factor 12: Personification 126

Risk Perception Factor 13: Fairness 130

Risk Perception Factors Redux 132

CHAPTER 4   THE WISDOM OR THE MADNESS OF THE CROWD?   135

A Conversation about Climate Change 135

Cultural Cognition 142

Chicken Little, Pollyanna, and Other Social Forces 156

And That's the Way It Is 166

CHAPTER 5   CLOSING THE PERCEPTION GAP   187

The Risk of Getting Risk "Wrong" as Individuals 187

The Risk of Getting Risk "Wrong" as a Society 198

Toward Healthier Individual Choices 214

Toward Healthier Choices as a Society 237

CLOSING THOUGHTS 259

Endnotes 263

Index 271

ACKNOWLEDGMENTS

This book is a woefully brief introduction to the wisdom and research findings of many people. To their work, I have added my experience as a journalist, my interpretations, clarifications, and emphases. For anything that accurately reflects their findings, they deserve the true credit. For any errors or omissions, I deserve the blame.

In addition to those already cited in this book, I am deeply grateful to Paul Slovic, a pioneer in research on the perception of risk; he has graciously supported my efforts to summarize the findings of that field and bring those insights to a wider audience. I am also grateful to other leaders in this field, including Baruch Fischhoff, Sarah Lichtenstein, and Melissa Finucane, whose findings have contributed significantly to my thinking and to the foundation for this book.

In the field of neuroscience, I am grateful for my informal editor, Caroline Davis, a graduate student who studies the amygdala in the lab of Paul Whalen at Dartmouth's Department of Psychology and Brain Sciences, and for guidance in the past from Joseph LeDoux and Liz Phelps of New York University.

I am grateful to many people who shared their time and thoughts: Sheldon Krimsky at Tufts, Steve Woloshin at Dartmouth, Daniel Kahan at Yale Law School, Matthew Adler at University of Pennsylvania Law School, John Evans at Harvard, George Lowenstein at Carnegie Mellon, Ellen Peters at the University of Oregon,

Jonathan Weiner at Duke, Dr. Matthew Friedman of the Veterans Administration, Robert Sapolsky at Stamford, Denis Mileti of the University of Colorado, Vivenne Parry of the BBC, and Marc Poumadere of L'Ecole Normale Superieure.

Thanks to Lester Brown for the push to write this. And thanks to all my friends and colleagues who showed sincere interest in this project—or at least faked it really well—and helped me with lots of ideas and encouragement.

INTRODUCTION

By the animal instinct that is awakened in us we are led and protected.
It is not conscious; it is far quicker, much more sure, less fallible, than
consciousness.

—ERICH MARIA REMARQUE, *ALL QUIET ON THE WESTERN FRONT*

The auditorium was jammed. The TV cameras were lined up down in front, aimed back at the crowd, ready to roll at the first loud voice. The moderator opened the floor to comments. Susan Napolitano leaped to her feet, her eyes wide and her face red.

"That school could give our children cancer! We demand that you close it and clean it up before our children have to go back there!" she screamed at the officials sitting at the head table. Stabbing her finger at them, she yelled, *"You* are not our children's parents! *You* will not decide whether they live or die!"

Sitting next to her, Susan's 10-year-old daughter, Stephie, looked up at her mom, a little embarrassed at and a little proud of her mother's public display of passion on her behalf. Stephie was a student at a public elementary school in a Boston suburb where trace amounts of the chemical trichloroethylene (TCE) had been found in the air of the library and one third-grade classroom. TCE is a confirmed carcinogen, but at the low levels found in the school, just a few molecules of TCE per trillion molecules of air, even the most aggressive public health experts said that there was no threat. The TCE levels were well within safety standards. There was no danger.

But that didn't matter to Susan. As reporters flocked around her after the meeting, she told them that she was convinced Stephie could get cancer if she attended the school, and she was willing to do anything necessary to get the school closed, even though that might mean taking kids who mostly walked to school and busing them to other classrooms around town, on sometimes icy winter New England streets, disrupting their education and spending tens of thousands of dollars from the school department's already tight budget to institute those changes. All to eliminate a risk that, according to the scientific evidence, wasn't a risk at all.

Susan stood there in front of the TV cameras and reporters, flushed with passion, with Stephie at her side. And as she talked about her fear of those trace amounts of TCE, she anxiously puffed away on her tenth cigarette of the night. And mother and daughter were also taking another big risk: both were significantly overweight.[1]

⚡

You've probably seen the same phenomenon in your family or friends, or maybe even within yourself, where the fears don't seem to match the facts. It happens to all of us. Sometimes we're more afraid of what the scientific evidence suggests are relatively small risks, but quite often, we aren't afraid enough of the risks that the evidence suggests we should worry about more. This sort of risk perception is often explained by blaming the media and politicians and marketers and poor risk communication. But that is simplistic, naive, and inadequate.

The first goal of *How Risky Is It, Really?* is to explain in much greater depth where our perceptions of risk actually come from. It's far more complicated than scary headlines and fearmongering politicians. Fascinating discoveries in neuroscience, psychology, sociology, anthropology, and economics help explain the underlying roots of the way we respond to risk, and why most of us at one time or another are more afraid of relatively smaller threats or less afraid of relatively big ones.

The second goal is to make the case that this phenomenon, which I'll call the *Perception Gap*, can be dangerous, a risk in and of itself. We often get risk "right," making judgments that work out for the best. But when we get risk "wrong," it can be dangerous. Susan was so afraid of trace amounts of chemicals in her daughter's school (for reasons to be explained in the chapters ahead) that she was willing—even *eager*—to subject Stephie to the greater danger of riding school buses on snowy streets, and to have Stephie's education seriously disrupted, to avoid a risk that the experts said was just not there. At the same time, Susan chain-smoked and was seriously overweight, but she didn't seem as concerned about these much greater hazards to her health (for reasons that will also be explained), which not only imperiled Susan but increased the chances that by the time Stephie got to high school, she might not have a mom.

This Perception Gap, the potentially dangerous distance between our fears and the facts, is a risk that we need to recognize so that we can reduce it. And that brings us to the third goal of this book: to propose ways to apply an understanding of where our fears come from, so that we can narrow the Perception Gap and make healthier choices for ourselves, our families, and society. As U.S. President Franklin Roosevelt suggested, we *do* have to fear fear itself. But Roosevelt was only half right. We have to fear both too much fear *and* too little. Both can be dangerous. But we don't have to be afraid of this disconnect between our fears and the facts if we understand *why* some risks feel scarier than others, and use that understanding to think about risks more carefully so that we don't end up doing what *feels* right and end up making things worse in the process.

In the framework of those three goals, here's a taste of what's to come.

THE RISK RESPONSE

The system by which we respond to risk is remarkable, a fabulous and complex mix of neural wiring and chemistry, subconscious psychological processes and instincts, and fact-based cognitive firepower. It's fascinating and powerful. It has to be. It's in charge of our survival. I'll call this system the *Risk Response*.

Notice that I said *system*—singular. This conflicts with the way most experts describe the human approach to risk perception. Many of the academics who study these things, and the reporters and bloggers and pundits who describe the academic research, talk about two separate systems. System 1 is a matter of reason and rational analysis of the facts. System 2 is a matter of emotion, instinct, and gut.

System 1 employs deliberative, conscious thinking. It's slower and it takes more effort, but many people argue that system 1 leads to more intelligent judgments, reducing the dangers of the Perception Gap. This is the system that Madame Marie Curie referred to when the famous scientist said, "Nothing in life is to be feared, it is only to be understood. Now is the time to understand more, so that we may fear less." *Homo rationalis*. Rational man. Reason to the rescue.

System 2 relies on feelings and instincts and gut reactions. It's faster, it happens largely subconsciously, and it has evolved as a powerful part of the Risk Response because we usually don't have all the facts we'd need to make a fully rational judgment, or all the time we'd need to go get all those facts, or all the intelligence we'd need to make sense of all the facts, even if we had them. As Ralph Waldo Emerson suggested, "Trust your instinct to the end, though you can render no reason." *Homo naturalis*. Natural man. Let your gut be your guide.

This widely accepted dichotomy is false. Reason and Emotion are not separate parts of the Risk Response. We are neither perfectly rational nor completely emotional and instinctive. As you will learn in the pages ahead, we are both, all the time. These are interwoven components of a single system. Sometimes we use one more than the other, but both are involved in any healthy person's judgment about risk. The view that these systems are separate leads to disagreements about which one is better and, in disputes over controversial risk issues, which system should win. All those disagreements do is impede progress.

Environmentalists blame system 1—a response to risk that's based solely on quantitative metrics and reason—for decision making that's too coldly rational, that ignores people's values and instincts. Businesses and regulators blame system 2—the emotional response—for making people irrationally afraid. These arguments delay acceptance of the evidence both from scientific research and from the real world, which makes a powerful case for a more holistic understanding of how people perceive and respond to risk. It is time to move past the system 1–system 2 argument and think about the way humans perceive risk as a single system with *several* key components, *all of which* play a role in the choices we make.

A simple label might help. When it comes to perceiving risk, people are neither rational nor emotional. We are *Affective*. Affectives are people who make risk assessments with both their head *and* their heart, cortex *and* gut, based on the facts *and* on their feelings and instincts and values and cultural views and personal experiences and life circumstances. Remember Susan Napolitano? She is an Affective. You are an Affective, and I am too. Even the most emotionless, coldly analytical Rationalist is an Affective. In fact, this book is about how we are *inherently* Affective. ("Affective" builds on the concept of "the Affect Heuristic," the findings of risk perception research that our judgments about risk are based both on the facts *and* on how we feel about those facts.[2])

Being Affective does not mean that we are solely emotional and instinctive. We don't just go with our gut and our feelings. We use the facts too. Susan Napolitano knew there was a carcinogen in the air her daughter was breathing. That was a fact. But it was an excessively scary fact to a mother, so Susan's emotions were part of her perception of the situation. Susan also undoubtedly knew the basic facts about the risks of smoking and of being overweight, but a different set of emotions made those threats feel less scary.

It's too simple to say that Susan was being emotional or irrational. And it is nothing short of arrogant to say that Susan was "wrong," a judgment often made by those who advocate purely rational decision making, which in itself irrationally disregards the overwhelming evidence that human animals are not, and cannot be, perfectly rational when it comes to threats to our survival. We have evolved a suite of tools to help us survive, and "thinking" is only one of them—and, as we will see, usually not the most powerful. Susan was neither right nor wrong. She was merely being human, doing what we all do when we assess risk—using *all* the tools we can, facts *and* feelings, to make choices about how to protect ourselves from danger.

Human risk perception, then, is a single system with several different facets, all of which contribute to the judgments we make about the things that threaten us. That part may seem obvious. What isn't as obvious are the specific psychological and neurobiological components of the Affective Risk Response system that determine *why* some risks feel scary and some don't, and *why* our fears so often don't seem to match the facts. Chapter 1, "This Is Your Brain on Fear," takes you deep into your brain to describe how and where the Risk Response begins. (*Hint:* It has nothing to do with conscious thinking.) Chapter 2, "Bounded Rationality," describes some of the fascinating mental shortcuts that humans have evolved to make decisions about risk, or about anything, when we don't have all the information we need, or all the time we need to get that information, or all the smarts necessary to understand the information. (*Warning:* There are lots of little quizzes you can take. They're fun, but you'll probably find that you don't think as rationally as you might believe. Then again, at least you'll know why!) Chapter 3, "Fear Factors," spells out in detail the psychological characteristics of potentially risky circumstances that make them *feel* more or less scary, the scientific evidence notwithstanding. ("Fear Factors" is rich with real-world examples. Some are entertaining, some are sobering, and most will be pretty familiar.) Chapter 4, "The Wisdom or the Madness of the Crowd?" explores social and cultural influences on risk perception. (This is where the media and politicians get their share of the blame.)

The idea of those first four chapters is to help you understand your fears and where they come from, which is the first goal of *How Risky Is It, Really?* The second goal is to make the case for how dangerous the Perception Gap can be, and the third goal is to offer ideas for how to close that gap. Those topics are the focus of Chapter 5, "Closing the Perception Gap," which offers some chilling evidence of the harms that can arise from the Perception Gap, and some suggestions for how we can narrow that gap in the choices we make both as individuals and as a society.

But before we move on, it's important to reinforce the point that worrying too much about a risk, or too little, can be risky all by itself.

The Dangers of the Perception Gap

We spend a lot of time and energy on the critical task of figuring out where danger lies. But in our focus on the risk at hand, we ignore the secondary risk that arises if the way we respond to danger feels right, but doesn't comport with the facts. The Affective Risk Response system includes a remarkable set of tools that we have developed in order to protect ourselves. But those tools evolved when risks were simpler—snakes and lions and starvation and the dark and bad guys with clubs and spears. In our modern world of more complex risks, the Affective Risk Response system can lead to perceptions and behaviors that feel right but that make things worse.

At both the individual level and the societal level, we need to pay more attention to the hidden risk of the Perception Gap, which can threaten us in three ways:

1. **The Perception Gap can lead to risky personal behavior.** After the September 11, 2001, terrorist attacks in the United States, a lot of people were so afraid of flying that they drove to distant destinations instead. Driving, because it offers a sense of control, *feels* safer, but it's a more dangerous way to travel. In the three months following September 11, the death toll on the roads rose significantly compared to what was statistically normal for that period. Many of those deaths were the result of a Perception Gap.

2. **The Perception Gap causes stress.** Worrying too much causes clinical stress, and the list of bad things that stress can do to your health is long and sobering. It is absolutely true that one of the things we should fear is fear itself. Fearing too much is bad for our health.

3. **The Perception Gap can lead to social policies that don't maximize the protection of public and environmental health.** We sometimes demand that the government spend money and resources to protect us from things that *feel* frightening, but which may not be the biggest risks. For instance, the U.S. government spends much more on cancer research than on research into heart disease, which is easy to understand given how much suffering cancer causes. Yet heart disease kills 20 to 25 percent more people than cancer every year. It's the number one cause of death in the United States—in most of the developed world, in fact. Wouldn't more lives be saved if the biggest threat, not the scariest, got the most resources?

Sometimes the Perception Gap shows up not in the inefficient way we spend our money, but in policies that protect us from one risk, and create others. For example, our worries about radiation led to regulations that limited the use of nuclear power. So instead we use more coal and oil. But that creates other risks. Burning fossil fuels produces carbon dioxide gas, which is changing the climate of the earth. And it produces microscopic air pollution particles, which contribute to lung and heart problems that kill tens of thousands of people around the world *each year*. Compare that to the World Health Organization's estimate of the overall death toll from cancer from the Chernobyl nuclear power plant accident for the *entire lifetime* of the 600,000 people exposed to radiation. The experts estimate that *that* death toll may reach 4,000.[3] Our fears have led to policy choices about power generation that may not have been the safest policies for human or environmental health.

This is an example of what is known as risk/risk trade-offs. Like our energy options, almost all risk issues involve these choices. But when we don't see those trade-offs because one threat has certain Affective characteristics that evoke more fear, the result is a Perception Gap that leads to policies that might not do us the most good.

So at both the individual level and the societal level, understanding the roots of our fears can help us judge risks more carefully and more thoughtfully, and that should help us make more informed and healthier choices for ourselves, our families, and society.

Nobody Can Decide What's Risky for You but You

One final thought: as mentioned earlier, there is a lot of argument over whether people who are too afraid of smaller risks or not afraid enough of bigger ones are being irrational. Susan Napolitano's fear of the negligible risk from the air in her daughter's school, for example, and her lack of concern about smoking and obesity, certainly seemed to fly in the face of reason. Her judgments were not good for her health. The people who blame too much emotion and lack of reasoning for people's irrational choices—businesspeople, political conservatives, regulators, scientists, engineers, and many academics—often claim, with no small amount of condescension and frustration, that Affectives like Susan who get risk "wrong" are, well, not the sharpest knives in the drawer. Affective thinking is described as "flawed" or "fallible." When Affectives' judgments about a risk don't match the facts, such judgments are called "blunders."

On the other hand, some people argue that too much cold rationality in decision making, often based on dollars and cents, inappropriately ignores our values and feelings. Environmentalists, consumer advocates, social activists, and political liberals hold that Affective thinking is fine. They argue that while some of our judgments about risk may not conform to all the scientific facts, they are based on a combination of the facts and our perspectives, informed by our feelings and instincts and experiences and cultural values, and that those are *all* valid parts of deciding how best to protect ourselves in a complex, risky world. They argue that there is nothing at all irrational about that sort of thinking.

Both views are right, and both sides are wrong. The position here is that *it doesn't matter*. It doesn't matter whether Susan's thinking is rational or irrational, good or bad, right or wrong. It simply *is*. This is how people perceive risk. This is how they behave. Period. We can understand this, and we can use that understanding to make wiser choices. Arguing over how people *should* perceive risk is really just a surrogate for an underlying clash of cultural worldviews that makes conflict over risk issues more intense and blocks progress.

That is why this book does not dare to tell you what you should be more or less afraid of. That's your business. I'll offer lots of examples of risks where people seem to be more worried than they need to be or less worried than they ought to be, given the scientific facts. But risk basically means the chance of something bad happening, and "bad" is in the eye of the beholder. These examples are only my view of things, meant not to illustrate how you should think about those specific issues, but merely to explain the hidden processes by which you and I think about risks in general. I'm not proposing what you should think about any individual risk issue, just explaining how such judgments arise.

The hope is that by *de*scribing some of the intrinsic ways in which we gauge the hazards we face, not *pre*scribing what we *ought* to think about this risk or that, this book can help you understand yourself a little better, keep your fears in perspective a little better, narrow the Perception Gap a bit, and make healthier choices for yourself and your family, and that we can start to come up with wiser solutions to some of the really big problems we face as a society.

CHAPTER 1

THIS IS YOUR BRAIN ON FEAR

Brain; An apparatus with which we think we think.
>—AMBROSE BIERCE

In general we are least aware of what our minds do best.
>—MARVIN MINSKY, THE SOCIETY OF MIND

 What's Your Risk Response?

Imagine that you are taking a walk in the woods. It's late in the afternoon. The path at your feet is dappled with light and shadow falling across narrow twisting tree roots. There is swampy ground on either side of the path.

Now imagine that, out of the corner of your eye, you notice that one of those long, thin, curvy lines at your feet just moved. It seemed to slither a little. Like a snake. Quick! What do you do!?

If you're like most people, you freeze, or scream, or jump back, or do something to protect yourself from the snake. You don't wait to figure out whether it really *is* a snake. You react instinctively, without thinking. The conscious awareness of your reaction seems to come *after* the reaction itself has already taken place. In fact, it does. By the time you become aware that you are afraid, your brain has already been hard at work, subconsciously perceiving that *you might die*, which triggers the Fight or Flight or Freeze response that will keep you alive. (This instinctive response to risk is more commonly known as the Fight or Flight response, but a lot of animals, including humans, Freeze at the presentation of a threat, so I've renamed it.) This automatic response sets off all sorts of physiological changes. Your heart speeds up. You breathe faster. Your blood vessels constrict in some areas and loosen up in others so the major muscles get extra blood and oxygen and energy. Your pupils dilate. Your digestive system gets shut down. You lose some of your peripheral vision, and the range of your hearing narrows. Without realizing it, you begin to make a facial expression of fear. All of these preconscious events happen in an instant! These are the first moments of the *Risk Response*, the first firings of a fantastic biological system that helps keep you alive.

THE AMYGDALA TO THE RESCUE: HARD-WIRED TO FEAR FIRST AND THINK SECOND

The cerebral cortex, the familiar outer layer of the brain where we do higher-order information processing like conscious thinking and reasoning, isn't even involved in this initial stage of our response to danger. Your brain's first reaction to potential danger happens subconsciously, in a section of specialized brain cells down near the brain stem, in the part of the brain known as the subcortex. The subcortex is the evolutionary part of the brain that was in place and protecting our ancestors long before modern humans evolved the cognitive cortex that gives us the power, as Ambrose Bierce said, to "think we think." It's an effective bit of adaptive neural design, set up more for speed and survival than for rational decision

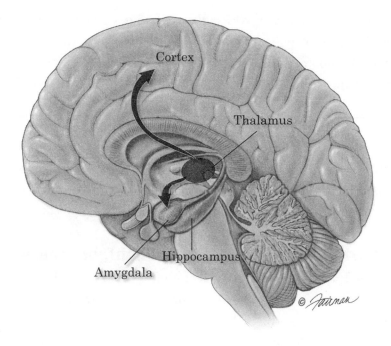

1.1 THE AMYGDALA

making. This is the first foundational truth about the human Risk Response: when it comes to perceiving and responding to danger, *human brains are hard-wired to fear first, and think second.*

Here is what actually happens in the first critical moments of a Risk Response. The raw visual data about that line on the ground speed from your eyes to a region in the brain called the thalamus, a group of unique cells deep in the middle of your brain that acts as a sort of relay station. The thalamus receives information from certain parts of the brain, or from the outside world via your external senses. It processes the information a bit—in the case of a snake, it quickly turns the raw optical information into a blurry line—then speeds that partially processed information on to other brain regions. This all happens in just a few thousandths of a second.

One of the areas to which the thalamus sends its data is the cognitive cortex, where we do our higher-order thinking and conscious decision making. But the thalamus also sends that picture of a blurry line to another area of the brain called the amygdala (pronounced ah-MIG-dah-la), shown in Figure 1.1. This is the part of the brain where fear starts. The amygdala is the star of the show. It doesn't get a lot of ink, but this one-inch-long area of unique brain cells, shaped kind of like an almond, is absolutely vital for keeping you alive.

The Triple F Response: Fight, Flight, or Freeze

For the fear response, as with real estate, location really matters. The thalamus is right next to the amygdala, but the cortex is further away. So when the thalamus sends its blurry picture of the line to both areas, the signal gets to the nearer amygdala first. Somehow—science does not yet know how—the amygdala can recognize information in the signal that suggests danger. It immediately sends out the alarm to the parts of the brain that control the automatic responses we use to protect ourselves. This is the Fight or Flight or Freeze response, what I'll refer to as the Triple F response, the first instinctive things that our bodies do to protect us.

Meanwhile, even as you are already starting to react, the message from the thalamus about that blurry curvy line is still on its way to the thinking cortex. The information that could mean *danger* hasn't even gotten to the part of the brain where you think. But the amygdala does not wait for a rational risk analysis from the cognitive cortex. It has already sounded the alert, and before you've thought about whether it's a snake or a stick—*before you are even consciously aware of the line on the ground*—you startle, freeze, jump, or scream.[1]

Finally, after the Triple F changes have started kicking in, the same visual information that the thalamus sent to the amygdala makes it to the cortex, which processes the data—simply put, it thinks things over—and sends its thoughtful interpretation of the information to a variety of areas in the brain, including the amygdala. But this new, more rational input arrives approximately 22 milliseconds *after* the amygdala has already received the first subcortical message from the thalamus and sent out the alert. The amygdala does not wait around to find out what the cortex "thinks." It sounds the alarm *before* the thinking, reasoning part of the brain has even had a chance to offer its opinion.[2]

This is a great system for survival: fear first, think second. If the line on the ground is a snake, you're safe. If it's a stick, maybe you're a little embarrassed about freaking out about a stick. But you're still safe!

Fear over Reason

The work involved in discovering this subcortical fear pathway was done on rats in laboratories. (And it was done using auditory, not visual, triggers, so it followed circuits from the ears to the thalamus, not the eyes. However, additional work suggests that the same early alert wiring system exists for inputs from the other senses as well.) But one of the wonderful things about research into various aspects of the Risk Response is how many examples there are in the real world that confirm what we've learned in the lab. Consider the personal observation of one of the great thinkers of all time, Charles Darwin, who observed in himself the impossibility of being perfectly rational about risk.

Darwin wrote " . . . our reason telling us that there is no danger does not suffice. I may mention a trifling fact, illustrating this point, and which at the time amused me. I put my face close to the thick glass-plate in front of a puff-adder in the Zoological Gardens, with the firm determination of not starting back if the snake struck at me;

but, as soon as the blow was struck, my resolution went for nothing, and I jumped a yard or two backwards with astonishing rapidity. My will and reason were powerless against the imagination of a danger which had never been experienced."[3] (By permission of Oxford University Press.)

Of course, had Darwin been directly exposed to the puff adder and stood there rationally considering the risk long enough to give the snake a chance to strike, he might have become the first winner of the Darwin Awards, the humorous acknowledgment of those who proved by the really dumb ways they accidentally killed themselves or destroyed their procreative capacities that it's better for the species to have them out of the gene pool. Most of the acts that win Darwin Awards are the result of outstanding stupidity, but conscious reasoning itself can be a form of stupidity if it delays your response to a risk when milliseconds matter.

So it's good for our survival that this hair-trigger system is set to go off when the amygdala senses the slightest possibility of danger. But it's not just triggered by information from our external senses.

 What's Your Risk Response?

After reading the following instructions, set the book aside for a bit. Okay, now take 30 seconds and recall *in as much detail as possible* a time in your life when you were really, truly, deeply *afraid*!

Welcome back. How did your recollecting go? Did you experience any sort of physical sensation along with your memory? Maybe a hint of sweaty palms? A quicker heartbeat, or perhaps some sort of feeling in your chest or your gut? A bit of a dry mouth?

In the classes I teach and the lectures I give, about a third of the participants in this informal survey report such sensations. These are physical Triple F responses, bodily changes triggered by the amygdala reacting not to the external sight of a snake or sound of an explosion, but merely to a memory that came from inside your head! If you experienced any kind of physical sensation along with your memory just now, you experienced what Darwin did, "the *imagination* of a danger," yet you reacted with a bodily manifestation of a Triple F response. Deep beneath your conscious mind, your amygdala was ready to protect you. (Interestingly, it's only *after* your brain senses all the physical sensations produced by the Triple F response that the conscious feeling of fear begins. Being consciously afraid is one of the *last* things that happens in the initial stages of responding to risk!)

THE FEAR RESPONSE CONTINUES

Okay, now what? The alarm has been sounded. Your autonomic Triple F response is underway. Let's say you have temporarily stopped dead in your tracks. Now let's suppose that the curvy line *is* a snake, and that it is coiled and hissing and looks like it's going to strike. What is the biological Risk Response, part two? Is the amygdala done? Hardly.

Not only is it effective at getting things going quickly, but the amygdala and the systems to which it is connected continue to protect you in several other ways. First, the amygdala turns up the volume on its connections with the outside world. It prompts the release of a neurotransmitter, a chemical signaling agent in the brain, called acetylcholine. Acetylcholine makes nerve cells throughout the brain and the body more sensitive and readier to fire. So when the amygdala sends out an alarm, it makes all your senses more acute. In essence, part of the initial Triple F response is a message from the brain telling the senses, "We're under attack! Pay closer attention!"

So now your sensory focus on the snake is sharper. And not only are you better at picking up sensory information in the first place, but the amygdala accelerates the speed at which that information travels after it enters the brain. It signals special cells in the thalamus, the relay station described a little earlier, to relay things faster. The faster the thalamus can process information and send it on to the amygdala, the faster the amygdala can sound the alarm, or keep sounding the alarm if the risky situation continues. This helps keep the senses on heightened alert, and that, in turn, does more to expedite faster relay of sensory input through the thalamus to the amygdala![4] It's a great reinforcing feedback loop for survival. But the amazing amygdala is not done yet.

Fear and Memory

Do you remember what you were doing on November 21, 1963? How about September 10, 2001? You probably don't. But you probably do recall where you were when John Kennedy was assassinated on November 22, 1963, or on September 11, 2001, the day of the terrorist attacks on New York and Washington, D.C. (or, if you're British, where you were when you heard about the tube bombings on July 7, 2005, or if you're Spanish, where you were on March 11, 2004, when terrorists killed 191 and injured more than 1,800 in a series of train bombings). Those were powerfully emotional events, and the more emotional the nature of what you are experiencing, the more strongly that memory will be encoded in your brain, and the more readily it will be recalled, especially if the emotion is fear. This is another adaptive feature of the brain's risk-response system, a trait that helps us survive. If you make it through the first encounter with that snake, it's pretty handy for you to remember the trail and the location in as much detail as possible, so that you can avoid getting yourself in the same mess again.

And guess what empowers this hyper memory for fearful situations. Yup, that tiny clump of unique nerve cells down near the brain stem called the amygdala. Here's how. In addition to triggering that release of acetylcholine as part of the Triple F response, the amygdala also triggers a flood of the stress hormone norepinephrine into the brain. Norepinephrine increases the amygdala's ability to remember the event that started everything in the first place.[5] It acts like a Marine drill sergeant shouting, *"Remember this in case it happens again!"* The next time you hit that trail, your amygdala will remember, and it will be more prepared to protect you.

Memories that are stored in the amygdala are called *implicit*. They are representations of things that happened that we *cannot* consciously recall. (*Explicit* memory is the kind that we *can* consciously recall, like the memory of that scary time you summoned up for our little experiment a while ago.) What good is a memory that you can't consciously recall? Consider the patient of French physician Dr. Edouard Claparede, a young woman who could not form new memories—or so it seemed. Every time Dr. Claparede met with her, he had to introduce himself again. She couldn't remember having met him previously. But on one of these occasions, Dr. Claparede hid a pin in the palm of his hand, and when he shook hands with his patient, he deliberately stuck her with the pin. She winced, but they continued with their conversation, then bid each other adieu. The next time Dr. Claparede met with his patient, she still didn't remember him. *But she wouldn't shake his hand!* Her ability to form new *explicit* memories of meeting the sicko doctor with the pin was still impaired, but her amygdala's ability to form new *implicit* memories of danger was there to protect her.[6]

Explicit memory, the kind that you can consciously recall, is obviously important for self-protection as well. And the amygdala pitches in here too. Explicit memory is formed and recalled by the hippocampus, a part of the brain right next to the amygdala. Along with the release of acetylcholine and norepinephrine, a Triple F response prompts the release of stress hormones called glucocorticoids, which do the same thing to the hippocampus that norepinephrine does to the amygdala. They facilitate better formation and faster recall of memories, in this case explicit memories. This probably happened when you experienced that scary situation that I asked you to recall a while ago. The amygdala caused a flood of glucocorticoids to rush into the brain, some of which made it to your hippocampus and helped it do a better job of recalling memories of what had happened.

(This part of the fear memory process works only if the levels of stress hormones in the hippocampus don't get too high or stay elevated for too long. When the stress is too severe, or when it lasts longer than a few hours, the hormones have the opposite effect. Instead of helping the hippocampus, high levels of glucocorticoids impair the formation and recall of explicit memory, sometimes permanently. There will be much more on this when we talk about the negative impacts of stress in Chapter 5, "The Perception Gap.")

The amygdala's powerful influence on learning about danger isn't done yet. Another result of the Triple F response is the release of the neurotransmitter glutamate. The brain sends signals by squirting neurotransmitters from one nerve cell—we'll call it Cell 1—into a tiny space, a synapse, sometimes triggering responses in Cell 2 on the other side. Glutamate is an important neurotransmitter for memory. If Cell 1 squirts only a little glutamate into that synaptic space, Cell 2 has a sort of ho-hum response. Add a bit more glutamate, and you get a bit more response. But at some point, when enough glutamate is pounding on the door, Cell 2 doesn't just respond. It metaphorically screams, "Eureka!" and undergoes several important changes that sensitize it to that unique signal the next time it comes around. Cell 2 "learns." It remembers. So the next time you're exposed to that stimulus, the low level of glutamate that wasn't enough to trigger the Eureka response the first time around is now enough to do the trick. Cell 2 has learned. This is good for survival, because the *second* time you encounter that risk, Cell 2 doesn't need as much of a signal from Cell 1 to prompt the explicit memory that says, "Be afraid!" Where does the amygdala enter this process? It facilitates this learning by increasing the amount of glutamate squirting into the synapses of the hippocampus, that vital area for explicit memory.

⚠️ **What's Your Risk Response?**

You can try this on a friend. Tell him that you are going to change his brain. (You can be a little smug about this. It really will work!) Ask him to help you pick out something really sharp, something that could cut him or poke a hole in him. Ask him to offer you the inside of his wrist. Apply the sharp object to his skin gently, briefly, and nonthreateningly. Ask him how that felt. Your pal probably will report that it wasn't too bad, that he didn't feel all that threatened.

Now ask him for his wrist again, and this time press *harder and longer.* Ask him how he felt about *that.* Wait a second or two, then try it a third time, and press even *harder,* making clear that you're building up to drawing blood. (*Please* make sure that you don't actually cut your friend's wrist!)

Now, if he's still your friend, ask him how that third poke felt. If you've done things right, raising the threat with each successive poke, your pal started feeling at least a little nervous. You may now proudly pronounce that you have changed his brain, and you can tell him how. Poke 1 carried only a weak stimulus, not enough to pose a threat, so the amygdala didn't stimulate the release of any stress hormones or extra glutamate. Poke 2 upped the danger a bit. Poke 3 hopefully made the danger clear and present enough to kick the amygdala into risk-response mode. It prompted the release of stress hormones and extra glutamate. That did the trick. The extra neurotransmitter prompted that "Eureka" moment down at the level of the synapses in your friend's hippocampus, making the signal strong enough to trigger a response and causing the synaptic connections between the neurons involved in the response to grow permanently stronger and more sensitive. Ta-da! You have changed his brain! Your pal has learned that you and that sharp object are a potentially threatening combination. You have created a fear memory.

To prove your point, after you've explained the process, ask him for his wrist one more time. Chances are your friend may hesitate just a bit. That's fine. In fact, that's your proof. You don't need his wrist. You just need to show that his response this time was different from what it was when you asked for his wrist the first time. That hesitation is the manifestation of the physical changes in his brain that represent his newfound fear.

Now put the sharp object away and go buy him a coffee, a beer, or a burger.

Fear and Energy Levels

And we're not done yet. There is still another positive reinforcement loop in this remarkable system that helps us learn about danger. The Triple F response prompts the release of lots of glucose—sugar, brain fuel—to supply the body and the brain with energy. After all, it takes energy to Fight or Flee, or even to tense up and Freeze. It also takes a lot of energy to think and learn. (No other organ in the body needs as much energy as the brain. The brain is about 3 percent of your body's weight and uses 20 percent of its energy.) The cellular mechanics of memory, all those changes prompted by glutamate or those stress hormones, are energy-hungry operations. A well-fueled hippocampus works better at encoding memories than one with less fuel. So the extra glucose released as part of the Triple F response improves the ability of the hippocampus to form explicit memories of fear-inducing events.

Glucose helps the hippocampus recall memories too. Let's imagine that you really like that trail where you encountered the snake, and you've been back there 10 times in the last few weeks—with no snakes. It's time for your late afternoon hike again, and you hit the trail. Only it's been six hours since you last ate. You're a little sleepy. Your hippocampus is a couple squirts of glucose short of full capacity, so your explicit memory of the encounter with the snake sleeps away in the background. Ah, but remember our backup system, the *implicit* memory formed in the amygdala itself.

You come upon the section of the path with all those curvy lines at your feet, and the eyes send information to the thalamus, which processes the information into crude images of long curvy lines and sends those images to the amygdala. The amygdala says to itself, "Hey! This is the place with the snake! *Alert, alert, alert!*" It triggers a Triple F response. That releases glucose, some of which quickly tops up the tank in the hippocampus, which improves the ability of the hippocampus to summon up that explicit memory of the encounter with the snake, information that may help keep you alive.

The amygdala-driven biological Risk Response is a fabulous guardian angel. It protects us in so many ways. It is constantly vigilant. It goes off quickly. It can turn itself up by heightening our sensory ability to detect danger. It triggers chemical and physical changes in the brain that strengthen learning about and memory of risky situations. And it helps protect us in one more remarkable way. It apparently comes with a built-in library of risks that evolution has taught us to be afraid of.

BUILT-IN FEARS

Were you afraid of the dark when you were a kid? Not every child is, of course, but many are. A lot of adults are too. There is a reason why so many of the scary and suspenseful scenes in books and movies are dimly lit. Fear of the dark is common. Whether nyctophobia is genetic is for others to argue. But it would certainly make sense that we have evolved to be afraid of the dark. For most of human history, the dark was a time when we were *in* the food chain, not at the top of it.

The dark is just one of several items that appear on most lists of top ten things that people are afraid of. Some fall into the category of "it could kill me": snakes, spiders, heights, enclosed spaces, and being underwater. (Note how many of these threats were frequently used in the TV program *The Fear Factor*.) Some fall into the category of social rejection or isolation: fear of public speaking, fear of intimacy, and fear of failure or social rejection. Social fears may be linked to survival too. Humans are social animals. We depend on the tribe to help protect us. Anything that means that we are less accepted by the tribe means that we are less protected, less safe.

The fact that these fears are so common suggests that they may somehow be at least partly built into the human animal. By now it shouldn't surprise you to learn that the biological roots of some of these fears can be found in the amygdala.

Because fears of spiders and snakes are so common, they've been popular fear factors for researchers investigating the workings of the amygdala. In one study, subjects were shown flashes of nine pictures in a three by three grid. One of the nine was a picture of a snake or a spider, while the other eight were pictures of flowers or mushrooms. Various configurations of the grid were flashed, with the snake or spider popping up in different locations. The subjects were also shown grids that featured eight pictures of snakes or spiders, with one picture in the grid showing either a flower or a mushroom.

All the subjects had to do was hit a button as soon as they detected a picture that "didn't belong"—the single snake or spider in a field of flowers and mushrooms, or the flower or mushroom in a field of snakes and spiders. Subjects were way faster at hitting the button when the one standout picture was of a snake or a spider in a field of flowers or mushrooms than when it was the other way around. They were faster at detecting something that could be a threat. And another fun fact from this study: for one phase, subjects who were either spider-phobic (arachnophobes) or snake-phobic (ophidiophobes) were identified. (In most surveys, spiders rank higher on the scary scale than snakes.) The people who were more afraid of spiders hit the button even faster when the "doesn't belong" image was that of a spider than when it was that of a snake. The ophidiophobes were quicker on the draw for snakes.[7]

To locate the biological roots of these fears, PET scans were done of subjects' brains, and these scans showed more activity in the amygdala than in other areas when pictures of snakes were flashed in front of study subjects.[8] And when scientists studied monkeys in which they had purposely damaged one particular tiny group of cells of the amygdala, the monkeys showed much less fear of snakes.[9] It appears that those few precious cells in that one section of the amygdala somehow "know" to be afraid of snakes.

Scary Faces!

There is something else that triggers an instinctive Risk Response in people worldwide: angry faces and scared faces. This makes sense. An angry face looking at you is innately threatening. It also could be signaling social rejection, one of those common fears. And a fearful face means that somebody else's amygdala just went off, so maybe yours should pay attention too.

In a study using that grid technique in which one picture differs from the other eight and subjects had to respond as soon as they became aware of the picture that didn't belong, subjects were much faster at picking out the angry face in a field of neutral and positive faces than the other way around (in grids where the single "doesn't belong" image was neutral or positive in a field of angry or fearful faces.) It even worked when the pictures of the faces were shown upside down![10]

And where in the brain does this propensity to respond to angry or fearful faces reside? Yup. The amygdala. In another study, subjects lay in an MRI machine that could observe areas of blood flow in the brain in real time, showing which part of the brain is more active (consuming more energy). That is known as functional MRI, fMRI for short. The subjects were shown pictures of faces that were either fearful, angry, or neutral. The amygdala "lit up" faster and more dramatically—suggesting a greater sensitivity— when the subjects saw fearful faces than when they saw angry ones, and they responded faster and more strongly to angry faces than to neutral ones.[11]

In another investigation, scientists used fMRI to watch the amygdalas of subjects who were shown a sequence of pictures of fearful, happy, or neutral faces. The researchers flashed the fearful faces so fast, surrounded by longer-lasting pictures of the neutral faces, that the subjects reported seeing only neutral faces. This is called masking. Then they did the same with the happy ones: masked them by flashing them so fast that subjects said that they saw only the neutral ones that came before and after. But the fMRI revealed that the subjects' amygdalas had a much more powerful response to the "hidden" fearful faces than to the "hidden" happy ones. Their conscious brains might not have been aware of the threat, but the instinctive part of the biological risk-response system, always on the lookout for danger, picked up the signal.[12]

And then there is Patient S.M. She lost most of her amygdala on both sides of her brain early in life. When she was shown a range of emotional faces—happy, sad, angry, disgusted, and fearful—she could identify all the emotions *except fear!* She couldn't even *draw* a fearful face, even though she recognized and drew faces with the other emotions just fine. (Interestingly, she and two other patients with amygdala damage could recognize and draw an *angry* face, but they found such faces trustworthy and approachable.)[13] Our ability to recognize fear in others' faces is apparently rooted in the amygdala, this wondrous ancient bunch of special brain cells where the Risk Response begins.

Studies with S.M. have found that somehow the amygdala can even recognize scary *music!* Researchers played S.M. happy, scary, sad, or peaceful music, and asked her to describe the emotional content of each. She recognized the happy music as happy and the peaceful music as peaceful, but she couldn't identify the sad music as sad or the scary music as scary.[14] (They didn't use the themes from *Jaws* for scary or *The Sound of Music* for happy. The music was composed specifically for the experiment. You can hear samples at www.brams.umontreal.ca/plab/research/Stimuli/Gosselin(march%202001)/Gosselin_March_2001_stim.html.

From Snakes to Nukes

The neural architecture and chemistry of the biological risk-response system is fascinating. It does a brilliant job of protecting us in so many ways. It is constantly scanning inputs for any possible threat. It leaps into action at the first hint of danger. It has the ability to heighten our senses and to speed the flow of information into the system. In other words, it can turn itself up from Orange alert to Red. It has multiple reinforcing feedback loops that magnify our ability to remember dangerous circumstances, so that we can constantly add to the library of fears with which we are probably born.

It's pretty autocratic too. It takes nearly complete control of your brain when you are initially threatened. Then, when the messy and time-consuming democracy of thinking tries to elbow its way into the Risk Response, the autocratic amygdala and associated systems dominate with their faster signaling pathways, powerful neurotransmitters, and dominating memory systems. As Joseph LeDoux, a pioneer in this field, put it, "While conscious control over emotions is weak, emotions can flood consciousness. This is so because the wiring of the brain at this point in our evolutionary history is such that the connections from the emotional systems to the cognitive systems are stronger than the connections from the cognitive systems to the emotional systems."[15]

But this system does seem to have one gaping dangerous flaw. Effective as it is with simple threats, obvious threats, threats that don't take a lot of complicated thinking to figure out, how does a system that can make us subconsciously flinch away from a snake figure out what to do about something like radioactive waste from nuclear power plants? It makes sense that we might have evolved some instinctive fears, like the common fear of the dark. But we haven't been around long enough as modern humans to have built-in fears for most of the new risks we now face, dangers that are not as obviously threatening as that menacing guy running at you waving a club or that thin curvy line on the ground at our feet. Genetically modified foods? Climate change? Carpal tunnel syndrome? The bogeymen of the modern world are a little more complex than "Lions and tigers and bears, Oh My!" as Dorothy exclaimed of the perils she faced in *The Wizard of Oz*.

So if the amygdala is not already programmed to recognize a lot of the threats that we now face, how do we make the decisions that we need to make to protect ourselves? And how do we make those decisions *quickly* when we need to, if the response isn't already encoded in the alert system? What protects us then? Is this where the powerful cognitive cortex takes over and leads us to careful, thoughtful, rational decision making? How can that be? We've already established that cognition takes time, and despite Mick Jagger's promise, when it comes to survival, sometimes time is *not* on our side. Are there instincts at work here too, neural tools that operate below the cognitive radar, subconsciously empowering us to make quick judgments about what to be afraid of and how afraid, if at all, to be?

Yes, there are. Working alongside the powerful amygdala-based biological system of the Risk Response are several other subconscious processes that involve many other areas of the brain and help us meet the challenge of staying out of harm's way. These systems process information and form quick initial judgments about whether that information implies danger, sort of the way the thalamus converts raw external sensory data into a blurry, half-processed first image to quickly send to the amygdala. And although they take a little cognitive processing, these systems can make sense of information pretty quickly.

⚠ What's Your Risk Response?

To give you a taste of how these other systems kick in to help protect us, here is a list of words. Which ones, if any, give you a sense of danger, what the academics call "an aversive response"?

Airplane	Chemical
Ice	Gun
Hospital	Dog
Alcohol	Pretzel

At face value, *airplane, chemical, ice, gun, hospital, dog, alcohol,* and *pretzel* are all words that seem neutral. None of these words screams *danger.* But perhaps a few of them caused you some alarm. Maybe you slipped on the *ice* once and broke your arm. Or maybe you were attacked by a *dog.* Or maybe you once almost choked on a *pretzel.*

Or maybe some of these words evoked pleasant feelings. Perhaps you were really happy to travel on an *airplane* to that *hospital* where you received treatment with a therapeutic *chemical* that healed you. Or maybe you remember that great time you had with your friends at the shooting range with that fabulous antique *gun,* after which you went out and enjoyed some *alcohol* on *ice* and some delicious salty *pretzels.*

The point of this exercise is to show that words themselves don't elicit fear. It's their meaning that makes them feel threatening or not. So now we have to understand where that meaning comes from. What is it about vaccines or artificial sweeteners or lead that makes them frightening to some of us? What qualities make mad cow disease or mercury or melanoma menacing? Why does nuclear radiation scare us, but solar radiation doesn't? Why is cancer scarier than heart disease, if heart disease is far more likely to kill us?

What are the qualitative characteristics of risks, and what are the processes by which we make judgments and decisions, that give certain circumstances aversive properties? And why do some of us find things frightening that others don't? For that, it's time to move on from the neurosciences to the psychological study of how people make decisions about things. It turns out that even the thinking we do, the cognitive processing of information as opposed to the instinctive reactions of the amygdala, is also a combination of reason and affect, of *Homo rationalis* AND *Homo naturalis.*

CHAPTER 2

BOUNDED RATIONALITY

Because Reason Alone Can't Keep You Safe

The man who insists upon seeing with perfect clearness before he
decides, never decides.

> —HENRI FREDERIC AMIEL, SWISS PHILOSOPHER

Intuition is reason in a hurry.

> —HOLBROOK JACKSON, BRITISH JOURNALIST

 What's Your Risk Response?

Answer the following questions with a yes or no:

1. Do you think bioterrorism is a serious threat to public health?
2. Do you think pesticides are a serious threat to public health?
3. Do you think that people using their cell phones when they drive creates a serious threat to public health?
4. Now the most important question: Did you have all the facts you needed to make a fully informed, analytical, reasoned decision about any of the first three questions?

I have posed these questions to thousands of people at various speaking engagements and in educational settings. Most people usually answer no to the questions about bioterrorism and pesticides and yes to the question on cell phones and driving. The only question that gets a *unanimous* answer is Question 4. Nobody thinks they have all the facts necessary to answer any of those other questions.

The same is probably true for you. You voted yes or no on the first three, but then had to admit that you didn't know everything you needed to know in order to vote intelligently. So how did you judge the risk of bioterrorism, or pesticides, or cell phones and driving? Can you name the six Category A agents that the Centers for Disease Control (CDC) say are the highest-priority bioterror threats? Probably not. (They are anthrax, botulism, plague, smallpox, tularemia, and viral hemorrhagic fever—these are considered the worst threats because they can all be easily disseminated, they all spread from person to person, and they all kill *a lot* of people.) Have you ever read any of the studies on farm workers exposed to *high* amounts of pesticides? Probably not. The workers suffer little harm. So the risk to the public from the *low* doses of pesticides to which we are exposed is not that great. Did you know that you are four times more likely to be injured or killed by using your cell phone while you drive than to be injured by that jerk driving next to you using his cell phone?[1] Probably not. Nor did you have all the time you needed to go get all those facts. And, if you're like most people, and like me, you don't have all the background knowledge and intellectual ability you would need to fully understand those facts, even if you had the time to look everything up. So there are lots of limits on our ability to be perfectly rational and make decisions based solely on the facts.

Still, you did have a sense about the dangers of each respective threat, and so, even without complete information, you felt you had enough to go on to make a choice. When you were called upon to decide, you used what you knew, and somehow that was enough.

This is how life is most of the time. Living from one moment to the next forces us to make judgments and decisions when we don't have all the facts, or enough time to get all the facts, or the intelligence necessary to understand all the facts. This concept is called *bounded rationality,* the process by which we make judgments and decisions without perfect knowledge. The subconscious mental tricks we use to make choices and judgments under conditions of bounded rationality play a huge role in how we respond to risk. The Risk Response is, after all, a matter of judgment, not some cold, hard, fully factual logical analysis. That sort of perfect rationality is a myth, an ideal. In real life, rationality is bounded, limited. It can take us only so far. So the first part of the Risk Response to understand is the fabulous subconscious tool kit that we use to make judgments and decisions about anything, including how to keep ourselves safe, when the conditions of bounded rationality make perfect, fact-based, fully informed reasoning impossible.

MENTAL SHORTCUTS FOR MAKING DECISIONS

At first the phrase "bounded rationality" may sound offensive. It sounds like your ability to be rational, to be intelligent, to make fully informed decisions is bounded: limited and flawed—you dummy. But Herbert Simon, who came up with the concept, clearly didn't intend it that way. He wrote, "Theories of bounded rationality, then, are theories of decision-making and choice that assume that the decision-maker wishes to attain goals, and uses his or her mind as well as possible to that end . . . theories that also take into account in describing the decision process the actual capacities of the human mind."[2] We use our minds "as well as possible" to make judgments about anything, including risks. But if we don't have all the facts, what else do our minds use to decide? What are the "actual capacities" you used to choose yes or no for those questions I posed earlier?

You probably applied some of the same mental tools we all use to process limited information in the limited time available to make a decision. We use these tools to sort and analyze and compare and categorize what we know, filtered through the context of our immediate circumstances, what we have experienced in the past, and our general life situation, such as our health and wealth and family circumstances and lifestyle preferences. These mental shortcuts also mix in our religious and political and social and other cultural norms. Using *all* those inputs, *in an instant* we come up with a judgment! It is absolutely remarkable how quickly these hidden mental processes help us sort through vast amounts of information and make the judgments we constantly have to make, including judgments about circumstances that might involve risk. (The academics call these mental shortcuts *heuristics* and *biases*.)

These mental processes are vital for our very survival. Think how long most decisions would take if we had to think—really carefully, analytically, consciously think—about all the relevant details that apply to each choice we face. Our lives would come to a screeching halt. Not even the most powerful information processor known, the human brain, could do all those calculations quickly enough to get us through 10 minutes of a normal day. And we would need a practically endless supply of candy bars, because the brain is such a huge energy consumer. It takes a lot of glucose to power the brain: 400 calories a day in a person who burns a total of 2,000. Intense activity can increase energy demand in the brain as much as 50 percent. Thinking takes energy, so we have developed a set of mental shortcuts to reduce our rate of CPT (calories per thought) and to quickly facilitate decision making by cutting cognitive corners.

The research that discovered these processes of decision making, which are mostly applied subconsciously, initially focused on economics. It was done by psychologists who were trying to figure out why people made choices about money that seemed, well, less than rational.[3] Economists, big fans of perfect rationality, couldn't understand why people made all sorts of decisions about money, the result of which was that they ended up with less of it. The rational choice should be *more* money, right? So psychologists did a number of ingenious experiments involving choices about money, and they uncovered patterns of decision making which explain things that, in economic terms, seem just plain dumb. These decision-making processes play a key role in the Risk Response, so we need to understand them.

Here's a simplified version of one of the experiments that was done.

 What's Your Risk Response?

Let's say you've been meaning to get a lamp for your desk, and two stores have the lamp you've been looking for. One of them is right next to your home and sells it for $50. The other sells it for $45, but it's a 10 minute walk away. Do you walk the extra 10 minutes to save the five bucks?

Now let's say you've been shopping for a new car, and the one you like is available at two dealers. One is right next to your home and is selling the car for $20,000. The other is selling it for $19,995, but the dealer offering the five-dollar discount is 10 minutes farther away. Do you go the extra 10 minutes now?

Most of the people who would travel the extra distance to save five bucks on the lamp pass on the opportunity to save the same amount of money on the car. Huh? Economists would say that's irrational. Five bucks is five bucks. Well, not always. Psychologists Daniel Kahneman and Amos Tversky, along with many others, helped figure out what goes into such decisions. They discovered several mental tools that people use to make choices, and how other-than-economic values and conditions of bounded rationality led to predictably irrational judgments and behavior. It turns out that we use these mental shortcuts for all sorts of decision making—about money, about risk, about pretty much anything.

This is the second part of the risk response. The first part is the architecture and wiring of the brain itself. If the brain subconsciously "sees" a snake or a spider or an angry face, the amygdala already knows what to do. But when the brain is faced with a situation that takes a bit more analysis, or a risk that the amygdala doesn't have the built-in tools to recognize, like a lot of the risks we face in our more complex modern world, these mental processes kick in to help us quickly judge whether we are in danger. They help us make sense of things "as well as possible," as Simon put it, in order to make a choice. Most of the time they work pretty well. But it's also easy to see how they can contribute to a potentially harmful Perception Gap, not only on choices about money, but also between our fears and the facts, that can threaten our health. So let's consider a few of these subconscious decision-making tools in more detail.

THE FRAMING EFFECT

How you see things, and how you think about them, depends to a large degree on how they are presented.

 What's Your Risk Response?

Let's say you're the mayor of a city of one million people. You are facing a crisis. An infectious disease is killing some of your citizens. Most of the deaths have come in one

neighborhood that is home to 5,000 people, although there
have been several deaths in other parts of the city as well.
Your city council has authorized a sum of money to fight the
disease, and you have two choices for how to spend it.

- Plan A will save the lives of 1,000 people in that
  neighborhood of 5,000 where most of the cases are.
  That's 20 percent of the people who live in the area
  that's most affected, one person out of every five.
- Plan B will save 2,000 people, but out of the entire city
  of one million. That's 0.2 percent, or one person out of
  every five hundred.

What would you do? Which seems better, Plan A or
Plan B? Pick one before you read on.

Now consider the same choice, just framed a different
way:

- Plan A will save 1,000 people.
- Plan B will save 2,000 people.

Now which one do you choose?

In most groups that are asked the first question, a majority
chooses Plan A, to save 20 percent of those who are at highest risk.
It's really interesting to see the lightbulbs come on when you ask
the question the second way, which simply removes the percentages
and highlights only the choice of how many actual people might
be saved, making it easier to see that if you choose Plan A, you are
condemning 1,000 people to death. The lightbulb now shines on
the facts in a new way. Rationality is now *un*bounded by how the
choice was *framed*.

Sometimes, as in the previous example, framing comes from which information is presented or omitted, like putting the percentages in or leaving them out. Sometimes the issue is which information is prioritized, or which comes first, such as whether the first aspect of a choice is the positive or the negative. ("You could win a million dollars in the lottery, although the chances of winning are really low," versus "The chances of winning the lottery are really low, although you could win a million dollars.") Sometimes the framing comes from simple semantics. Death tax or estate tax? Oil drilling or energy exploration? Pro-life or pro-choice? Even at this simple level, framing powerfully influences how we use information to make judgments. People were asked to taste samples of beef labeled "75 percent lean" and samples labeled "25 percent fat." After trying both, a majority of the people tasting them judged the beef labeled lean to be less greasy and better tasting even though the information about the fat content of both samples was identical.

Framing plays a big role in the way we make judgments about risk. Consider three news stories on a national study of human-made chemicals in our blood. All the stories contained pretty much the same information. But note how each one emphasizes different things. Here is a paraphrased excerpt of how one major newspaper reported it:

Encouraging Trends in Study of American Chemical Exposure

An extensive review of the levels of Americans' exposure to potentially harmful chemicals offers encouraging findings, and some surprises.

The federal study showed, for example, that nonsmokers' exposure to cigarette smoke is going down. It's only a quarter of what it was in 1991.

There is positive news about mercury too. Levels of mercury in children were lower than expected, far below federal safety limits. But the news on mercury was mixed. Concentrations in women of childbearing age were higher than expected, though still within safe limits.

Now here's a paraphrased version of how a wire service reported the same study. (The paraphrased headline was written by a regional newspaper.)

Study Finds Exposure to Questionable Chemicals Higher Than Expected

Americans' bodies contain surprisingly high amounts of mercury and a potentially dangerous chemical commonly found in soap and cosmetics, according to a landmark federal study on environmental poisons in the body.

The study measured levels of 24 environmental toxins in people's blood and urine, providing information that could be used to pinpoint pollutants that cause disease.

And here is the paraphrased version from another national newspaper.

Study Measures American's Exposure to Environmental Toxins

Most Americans carry measurable amounts of manmade chemicals, including plastics, pesticides, and heavy metals, in their blood and urine, according to a government study.

Many of the substances widely found in Americans' blood have been shown to cause brain damage, birth defects, cancer, and other toxic effects in animals. But the levels found in the average person, according to the federal analysis, are far below those at which those problems occur in humans.

Each story was accurate. However, each one framed the study differently, and each would probably evoke a different risk response, based not on the facts, but on how those facts are framed. If you read the first version, you might get a sense that things aren't that bad—even "encouraging." If you read the wire service version, you might worry more about those "questionable" chemicals. The third version might leave you somewhere in the middle.

Or consider two stories about mad cow disease that ran a few days after the first sick cow in the United States was discovered. After the flurry of news about the discovery itself came stories about what the risk might be for the meat-eating public. The evidence from years of study in Europe showed that the brain and spinal cord of sick cattle were the tissues that carried the disease from cows to humans, not the meat. But a few days into the coverage, there were stories about whether the meat of the cow, the stuff we eat in steaks and hamburgers, might also be a risk. Here is a bit of the story by the *Wall Street Journal*:

Scientific Data Offer No Proof of Beef Safety

After last week's discovery of the first case of mad-cow disease in the U.S., government officials sought to reassure the public. White House spokesman Scott McClellan said President Bush had been eating beef, and U.S. Department of Agriculture Secretary Ann M. Veneman said she'd serve it for Christmas.

Ms. Veneman even told CNN that beef from infected cows such as this one "should be entirely safe to eat" because its brain and spinal cord had been removed. Those tissues are known to be most infectious in cattle stricken with bovine spongiform encephalopathy, or BSE.

But while federal officials' safety message was emphatic, the scientific evidence behind those claims isn't as certain.

Steaks and hamburgers made from beef muscle haven't been shown to be dangerous, but some leading experts in Europe and the U.S. say the risks of meat from sick cattle remain unknown, and new studies have implicated muscles in other species.[4]

Here is the same story from the *Washington Post*, paraphrased:

Most Scientists Agree; Muscle Meat Is Unlikely to Transmit Mad Cow Disease

American officials continue to say that, despite the discovery of a cow infected with Mad Cow disease on a Washington farm, American beef is safe to eat. That claim is based on carefully acquired evidence from Europe, where the disease was rampant in cattle, showing that muscle from sick cows does not transmit the disease.

The European research found that brain and spinal tissue are the likely vectors between cow and human. Eating brain or spinal cord tissue from an infected cow is how scientists believe about 150 people worldwide contracted Bovine Spongiform Encephalopathy, or BSE, the human version of mad cow disease since the first human case appeared in Britain in 1996. But muscle meat alone—beef—appears safe.

The headline and story in the *Wall Street Journal* are alarming, suggesting that muscle meat *might* be a risk. The *Washington Post*, reporting the same information, said no, beef is almost certainly not a risk. The *Wall Street Journal* story cites a few skeptical scientists first, and 18 paragraphs into the story tells the reader that the overwhelming scientific consensus is that muscle meat from animals with mad cow disease is safe. The *Washington Post* cites the overwhelming scientific consensus first, and gives less notice to the critics. Both stories, read to their conclusions, contain pretty much the same information overall.

The risk of eating meat was framed quite differently in these two reports. The risk response of a reader of the *Wall Street Journal* might have been to swear off beef and burgers, whereas a *Washington Post* reader might have felt reassured. The same facts, framed differently, can produce a very different Risk Response.

The issue here is not the news media (much more on them later) or how we get our information about risk, but how that information is framed when we get it. The Framing Effect has a lot to do with how we see the risks we face and is one of the mental shortcuts that sometimes leads to a Perception Gap between what feels right and what the facts actually say. Another such shortcut is the way we tend to categorize information into patterns.

CATEGORIZATION: THE REPRESENTATIVENESS EFFECT

⚠ What's Your Risk Response?

Imagine that there is a professional athlete outside your room right now. Is the athlete bigger than you, the same size, or smaller?

If you're like most people, you guessed that the athlete is bigger. But you don't know if the athlete is a football player or basketball player (or even *a horse*), or if he or she is a golfer, a tennis player, a skater, or a soccer player, each of whom is more likely to be your size, or even smaller. You used the mental shortcut of *categorization,* what some people call stereotyping and what the academics call *representativeness.* You applied what you already knew about athletes in general to the specific choice you were facing. You categorized partial information based on representative patterns that you already had in place to help you make your decision.

Many of the risks we face, even new ones, fit into categories that are already familiar to us. Perhaps you've heard about the risk of bisphenol A (BpA), the chemical that used to be in Nalgene and baby bottles. It's a component of many plastics, and it has been associated with disrupting healthy fetal development in lab animals exposed to trace amounts. Suppose you wanted to make a judgment about the risk of BpA. You'd certainly want some key facts, like:

- **Have you been exposed to BpA?** Probably.
- **How have you been exposed?** Through food mostly. BpA is used in lots of food containers, including the lining of metal cans, and trace amounts leach into what we eat.
- **How much BpA have you been exposed to?** Probably a few parts per trillion. One part per trillion is like one person out of a population 160 times greater than everybody currently alive on the earth.
- **At the levels to which you have been exposed, what can it do to you?** Most of the evidence suggests that at the levels to which most of us have been exposed, BpA doesn't do much to adults or kids, but if it is passed by pregnant women to their developing children, it might interfere with healthy fetal development.

Knowing these details will certainly inform your judgment about this risk. But BpA also fits into the broad risk category of "chemicals," and many of us have learned things about chemicals and the risks associated with them—and not good things. What came to your mind when you read the word *chemicals* in our little word association quiz at the end of Chapter 1? Many people associate chemicals with words like *dangerous, toxic, deadly,* or *cancer.* What comes to mind when you think of "the chemical industry"? Many people say "no trust" or "pollution" or "Love Canal" (an infamous toxic waste dump) or "Bhopal" (a release of deadly chemicals in the worst industrial accident in human history). Those are risky images.

So when you hear about the risk from BpA, or *any* chemical, subconsciously out come the mental files you have labeled "Chemicals" and "Chemical Industry," and you sort the new information about BpA (or trichloro-whatever) against the background information you already have on the general topic, which carries a lot of risky associations. In the end, your perception of the risk of BpA isn't based just on the facts about that one chemical, but on what you know about the whole category to which it belongs—which obviously might contribute to a Perception Gap between your fears and the specifics of the risks of BpA.

I had a conversation with a friend of mine the other day that offers another illustration about how categorization can color our judgments. "I was talking with a friend, one of my old colleagues from Greenpeace," Peter told me. "She was deep in the fight back when we were working hard to kill nuclear power. I wanted to provoke her, so I asked, 'What do you think about nuclear fusion?' She used all the old arguments about accidents and the waste. But of course they don't apply, because what I was talking about was fusion, not fission. So I pointed that out. And she stood there, and stood there, and got all red in the face, and finally she blurted out, 'Well, I'm *still* against it!' I asked why. She said, 'Well, . . . it's . . . it's still *nuclear*!'"

The Fallacy of the Small Sample

Here is another version of categorization that frequently colors how we perceive risks, the problem that arises when a description of a risk begins with, "A study says . . ." You know, when that new study comes out that says that people who put their left sock on first have higher rates of dandruff. Wait. Wasn't it just last week that you read another study that claimed that people who put their *right* sock on first have elevated rates of dandruff?

Let's call this form of categorization the Fallacy of the Small Sample. We tend to infer that what is true of small samples, including individual scientific studies, is true for the entire category. In 1998 the British medical journal *Lancet* published a study that investigated a possible association between kids who developed autism and their vaccination with MMR vaccine, a vaccine against measles, mumps, and rubella. If you read the journal article itself, it's hard to understand all the fuss it caused. The authors say that *others* had made the association between MMR vaccine and autism, especially the parents of the autistic kids who were being studied. The study authors specifically conclude, "We did not prove an association between measles, mumps, and rubella vaccine and the syndrome described."[5]

But at the news conference announcing the article, the lead author, Dr. Andrew Wakefield, suggested that just such a link existed and advised parents to give vaccines for the three diseases separately. Not much happened at first, but when some parents of autistic kids cited Wakefield's work a couple of years later, the story took off. In the worldwide explosion of concern that followed, what was all but ignored was the fact that Wakefield et al. studied all of 12 kids. *Twelve!*

Massive research since then has conclusively shown that there is no association between MMR vaccines and autism, although a small group of parents fiercely insist that there is such a link. But even if Wakefield and his collaborators *had* found an association,

12 kids shouldn't be enough evidence to convince anybody of any-thing. Much more evidence would be needed before the connec-tion could be reasonably inferred. That's how science works. Each finding is another brick in the wall of evidence. One brick does not a wall make.

But that's not how things work in the world of Bounded Ra-tionality. We have to make judgments and choices day after day, moment by moment. We can't wait around for 10 more years of sci-entific studies before deciding whether to have our kids vaccinated. We have to assess risk *now*. So we have learned to categorize the partial information that we have, and one of the ways we do that is to jump to the conclusion that what is true for a small sample might be true generally.

This can lead to a Perception Gap that creates its own danger. In the United Kingdom, the number of two-year-olds getting the recommended double shots of MMR vaccine fell from 92 percent to 75 percent in 2008. In 2007, England had its largest outbreak of measles in 20 years—730 cases—and its first death in 14 years, a 13-year-old boy. In 2006 and 2007, more than 12,000 cases of measles were reported in children in Europe, mainly in Germany, Romania, Switzerland, Italy, and the United Kingdom. (Ten co-authors of the 1998 Wakefield paper issued a retraction, and the editor of *Lancet* says that the journal should not have published the paper.)

That's a troubling legacy from an initial study of just 12 people. You could blame all this on Dr. Wakefield. You could certainly blame it on the parents of autistic kids who have been vocal about their concerns and who, for totally understandable reasons, are even more ready to categorize small-sample hints into large-pattern conclusions. You could blame the media, which continue to give the upset and suspicious parents a lot of attention despite over-whelming scientific evidence that the MMR vaccine is not linked with autism.

But really you have to blame human nature, what Herbert Simon called "the actual capacities of the human mind." The Fallacy of the Small Sample is simply one of the mental shortcuts we have developed in order to use partial information to make quick judgments about staying safe.

Problems with Probability

We also use categorization in ways that create *problems with probability*. We have expectations in our minds of how statistical patterns are supposed to work out, and we categorize the evidence at hand against those expectations.

 What's Your Risk Response?

Here are two sequences of coin flips. Which one seems more likely?

A. H T H T H T H T H T H T H T
B. H H T H T T H T T T H H H T

Both A and B include equal numbers of heads and tails. The likelihood of each pattern is the same. But most people choose B because it displays the randomness that we expect. Sequence A is too smooth, too even. Coins are just not supposed to alternate that regularly, right? I mean, what are the odds of that happening? Well, they're about the same as the odds of Sequence B, 50/50 for each coin flip. The coin doesn't remember what it did last time. But we do, and we project our expectations of probability patterns onto what's supposed to happen next.

We wouldn't expect the coin to come up H H H H H H H T T T T T T T, either. It's supposed to be random, like anything governed at least in part by chance. Like, say, the incidence of a given disease—cancer, for example. A lot of people get cancer, 1.3 million per year in the United States alone. (Not including the three kinds of skin cancer. That's another 1 million all by itself.) But those cases are supposed to be spread out over any given community. We expect them to occur randomly.

So just as when we see all those heads and tails in a row, H H H H H H H T T T T T T T T, when a cluster of cases of some specific kind of cancer shows up, we get suspicious. Something is violating the probabilities that we expect. We look for the cause, the hidden threat, because that's not how chance is supposed to work. Clusters grab our attention because they don't fit our expectations of the randomness of chance. They don't categorize the way they're supposed to.

Actually, that kind of categorization effect has led to some important advances in public health. Because people wondered what caused a cluster of rare cancers in seven gay men in Los Angeles in 1981, we learned about a disease that came to be known as AIDS. When scientists investigated a cluster of shipbuilders who developed mesothelioma, a rare form of lung cancer, the findings helped alert us to the dangers of asbestos. In fact, the science of epidemiology itself—the study of patterns of public health—got its start when English physician John Snow investigated a suspicious cluster of cholera deaths in one neighborhood in London in 1854, and figured out that only the people drinking water from one local well were getting sick.[6]

But sometimes a cluster is nothing *but* chance. Sometimes the coin flips, or the dice roll, or the diseases appear in unexpected bunches, and there is nothing more at work than the laws of probability. Sometimes four kids in the same neighborhood can have brain cancer and, as anomalous as that is statistically, it's still only a matter of tragic chance that those four kids live close to each other. Yes, chance is random. But it's not always smooth and even.

We are right to expect that in the long run, the probability is that a coin will come up heads and tails about the same number of times, that after we spend a month at the craps table, 7 will have shown up 16.67 percent of the time, and that out of 36,000 spins of the roulette wheel, the little ball will have settled into 0 pretty close to 1,000 times. But in the short run, when the coin comes up heads five times in a row, we have trouble remembering that the next flip is still a 50/50 shot. What are the odds that somebody rolling dice who just rolled 7 five times in a row is going to do it again? It's 16.67 percent, just like the odds for all the other rolls. Could that roulette ball that landed in 0 five consecutive times possibly do it *again*? I mean, the odds against that must be . . . almost exactly the same as for every other spin of the wheel.

The probability problem in this case is the blurring of time. We categorize evidence from short-run clusters of events against our expectation of the long-term likelihood of those events. So when people living along a major river experience serious "hundred-year" floods—floods so severe that they're supposed to happen only once every hundred years—three years in a row, they figure that the chances of a hundred-year flood next year must be lower, despite the fact that next year's weather hasn't gotten the memo yet.

Categorization in its various forms is one of the important mental shortcuts that we use to make the judgments and choices that we are constantly called on to make. When we have to decide things in a hurry, which is often the case with risk, and the amygdala needs a little help figuring out whether something is dangerous enough to sound the alarm, Categorization helps us quickly take the partial information we have and make sense of it so that we can make a snap judgment about how to stay safe. Another of these mental shortcuts is called Loss Aversion. Simply put, nobody likes to lose.

LOSS AVERSION

 What's Your Risk Response?
Here are two scenarios, and each offers you a choice.

- **Scenario 1.** The first option in this scenario is a gamble that offers you an 80 percent shot at winning $4,000 and a 20 percent shot at winning nothing. The other option is to pass on the gamble and go for the sure thing in Briefcase Number 1, which is open and contains $3,000. What'll it be? The sure money, or a gamble on getting more?
- **Scenario 2.** Okay, let's say that you went for the gamble in Scenario 1, and you won! You now own $4,000. (Congratulations!) Now here's a second choice. This time you can take a gamble that offers you an 80 percent chance of *losing* the whole $4,000 and a 20 percent chance of keeping it. Or you can take the sure thing, which in this case would require you to hand over $3,000! So your choices are a sure loss of $3,000 or a gamble with an 80 percent shot at losing all your money but a 20 percent shot at losing nothing. Now what? Do you choose a sure loss, or do you choose the gamble that at least offers you a shot at holding on to all your money?

When Kahneman and Tversky ran this experiment, four out of five people took the sure $3,000 in the first scenario. They passed on the gamble. "Let's not take chances," they said. "Let's grab the sure cash." They were *risk-averse*. But when the same people were offered the choices in Scenario 2, 92 percent of them chose to gamble. Why? Because Scenario 2 offers a 20 percent shot of not losing anything. Nearly all the study subjects were willing to gamble this time, risking the whole wad, in the hope of *not losing*. They were no longer risk-averse. They were *loss-averse*.[7] Losing stinks in almost every scenario, and not just when it involves money.

The Endowment Effect

Here's one type of Loss Aversion that isn't about cash as much as it is about *value*. It's called the *Endowment Effect*. Researchers asked some college students how much they'd be willing to pay for a chocolate bar. The average price was 90 cents. The students were then given the candy bar, and the researchers asked them at what price they'd *sell* it. The average selling price was $1.83. Now that the students owned the candy bar, it was worth more. The very fact that you own something—a car, a lamp, your time, your *health*—makes that commodity worth more than if you don't own it. Ownership adds value. So when you give something up, not only do you lose the commodity, but you affectively experience loss. That's why giving something up carries more weight than getting it in the first place.[8]

(The same thing has been tested with basketball tickets, wine, lottery tickets, hunting permits, clean air, and even *time*! Test subjects were willing to pay a worker less for *that worker's time* than the subjects wanted to be paid if they did the work themselves and had to give up *their own* time.)

As the Greek philosopher Epicurus observed, "Riches do not exhilarate us so much with their possession as they torment us with their loss." Loss aversion is one of the reasons why people hold onto stocks and other investments as they go down, longer than the experts say they should. Selling for less than you paid means confirming the loss, and the aversion to loss outweighs the economic logic of selling off assets that are likely to go still lower.

Need more proof? Let's look at sports. A careful (obsessive) analysis of baseball found that when there is a runner on base and a ball is hit to the center fielder, if the runner tried to move ahead more than one base, he succeeded 98 percent of the time. Yet only 40 percent of runners in that position try.[9] You're not into baseball? Faced with the gamble of whether to go for it on the fourth down, football coaches are massively loss-averse. In a study that makes you wonder what economists do with all their spare time, economist David Romer of the University of California at Berkeley found that of 1,100 situations where going for it was warranted statistically, coaches decided to punt nine times out of ten. Put in Romer's economist-speak, "Examination of teams' actual decisions shows systematic, overwhelmingly statistically significant, and quantitatively large departures from the decisions the dynamic-programming analysis implies are preferable." In the language of bounded rationality, football coaches are loss-averse.[10]

Loss aversion is a powerful factor in how we respond to health risks. This is not surprising if you think about it. Loss of health is about survival. Dying is much worse than being thrown out trying to stretch a double into a triple or turning the ball over on downs.

Here's an example to tie this to the Risk Response.

 ## What's Your Risk Response?

Say you are suffering from a condition that has a lot of different symptoms. You are offered a choice between two drugs. Drug A is guaranteed to eliminate *half* of your symptoms. However, if you take Drug B, you have a 50/50 shot at eliminating *all* of your symptoms, but there is a 50/50 chance that there will be no relief at all. Which drug do you want?

A majority of you are likely to choose Drug A, because it offers a sure shot at *some* relief, and Drug B, although it offers the promise of a total cure, also carries a 50 percent chance of *losing* the sure relief that you can get with Drug A. You have been offered the certainty of some relief, and you don't want to lose it. Here's another one.

Experimenters asked groups of doctors, students, and patients to choose between two different treatments for 1,000 imaginary people with cancer. They were told that if they chose Treatment A, one patient out of ten would *die*. Treatment B, on the other hand, would produce a *survival* rate of 90 percent. A majority of patients, students, and doctors chose Treatment B.[11]

Why? Isn't that irrational? It's easy to see that the choices are statistically equivalent. But it's also easy to see how framing the choice in terms of loss or gain makes the two choices *feel* different. One choice is framed in terms of life, the other in terms of death. To the doctors, patients, and students in the study, and to you and me, death = *loss*. The power of the Framing Effect here is Loss Aversion. Loss has a more powerful influence on how we see risks than an equivalent gain.

This is a particularly important mental process when it comes to risks, because most risk choices involve trade-offs: pros and cons, risks *and* benefits. Because of Loss Aversion, we often pay more attention to the risk side of many trade-offs. Let's take mercury. Humans become exposed to mercury largely through eating certain types of fish, mostly ocean fish. The danger is that a pregnant woman might pass some of that mercury to her fetus in the womb. At high enough levels, *in utero* exposure to mercury can cause mental deficits in attention, language, verbal memory, and IQ in children, although these effects are relatively mild. (Direct exposure to mercury can also be dangerous to children up to age one, before the blood-brain barrier is fully formed and some mercury can still get at brain tissue, but not a lot of kids under age one eat large amounts of those specific species of fish.)[12]

Because we are loss-averse, *especially* when the health of our children is concerned, many people are worried about the risk of mercury. It is heavily covered in the press. The "loss" side of the story is clear. But the "gain" side doesn't get as much attention. Fish are good sources of nutrients for a healthy heart. And that goes for everybody, not just unborn or newborn children. Furthermore, the nutrients in fish contribute to healthy cognitive development in unborn and newborn children, precisely the group that is at risk from the harms of mercury, by providing the kinds of fats that the developing brain needs to insulate the neural wiring system. In fact, a study published in *Lancet* found that the benefits of the nutrients in fish for the neural health of the developing fetus outweighed the harm that mercury could do to the neural health of the developing fetus. That's as apples-to-apples a risk/benefit trade-off as you can get. The study said that kids born to mothers who ate *less* than about three-quarters of a pound of seafood per week were at *higher* risk of having lower verbal IQ scores and "increased risk of suboptimum outcomes for prosocial behaviour, fine motor, communication, and social development scores. For each outcome measure, the lower the intake of seafood during pregnancy, the higher the risk of suboptimum developmental outcome."[13] According to that piece of research, in a straight trade-off between the harmful mercury in the fish and the healthy fats in the fish for the brains of developing children, the fats win.

But in most news stories about mercury, the benefits side is almost always brief, and is lower in the report than the risk side of the equation, the "loss" aspect, which is likely to carry more affective weight with the reader and get the story more attention. The *Lancet* study got a little bit of coverage in the news, but not much. Do you know how the *New York Times* reported it? According to its archives, it didn't.

This is not a discussion of whether mercury is dangerous. At certain levels, to certain populations, it certainly is. Nor is this a discussion about whether, if you are pregnant or could become pregnant in the next couple of years, you should eat fish. That's your call. (Most neutral experts recommend that those women avoid fish species that are potentially higher in mercury.) Instead, mercury is discussed here because it offers a great example of how we often pay more attention to the risk side of risk/benefit trade-offs because we are inherently loss-averse. Almost every risk issue involves some kind of trade-off, and the risk side is usually going to fuel the fires of our fears more than the benefit side is going to dampen those flames. Loss aversion is just an intrinsic characteristic of the way humans respond to risk.

ANCHORING AND ADJUSTMENT

A lot of the information that we get about risks involves numbers. We're not very good with numbers. Most of us are, as some have called it, innumerate. (Count me among them.) But even when we do understand the numbers, a mental shortcut called *Anchoring and Adjustment* can throw us off in how we use those numbers to estimate risk. Simply put, we tend to make estimates based on a starting initial value, the anchor, and adjust from there.

In one experiment, one group of people was first asked to spin a Wheel of Chance, just to see what number would come up. It landed on 65, as the experimenters had secretly rigged it to do. That was the anchor. Then the group was asked to estimate what percentage of the countries in the United Nations was from Africa. They guessed 45 percent. A second group of people got their shot at the Wheel of Chance, and, as it had been rigged to do, the wheel stopped (anchored) on 10. That group estimated that only 25 percent of the nations in the United Nations were African.[14] The members of each group had one number planted in their heads at the outset and adjusted from there, and their judgment was influenced by where the anchoring value had been set. (To save your having to go look it up, the answer is 28 percent; 53 of 192 United Nations member states are African.)

 What's Your Risk Response?

You can try this on some friends. Show one or two of them the following equation for only a few seconds, then ask them to write down the product:

$8 \times 7 \times 6 \times 5 \times 4 \times 3 \times 2 \times 1$

Then show another friend or two the next equation for only a few seconds, and ask them for their total:

$1 \times 2 \times 3 \times 4 \times 5 \times 6 \times 7 \times 8$

The chances are pretty good that the friends who saw the first equation will offer a higher answer than those who saw the second, since the early numbers in the first equation—the anchors—are higher. (To spare you a visit to the calculator, the answer is 40,320.)

Relating anchoring and adjustment to the Risk Response, in another experiment, one group of subjects was asked to rank the frequency of death from 40 causes, and to estimate the actual numbers of victims for each cause. But first these subjects were told that 50,000 people a year die in motor vehicle accidents. A second group of people was asked to do the same exercise, but first that group was told that 1,000 people a year in the United States die from electrocution—a lower anchor. Each group ranked the risks pretty much the same way. Lung cancer and traffic accidents rated higher than bee stings and lightning strikes. But the first group, given a higher anchoring number to start with, estimated that many more actual people died from each cause than the second group did. In some categories, the first group estimated as many as five times more victims for a given cause of death than the second group, which had been "anchored" to the lower number.[15]

Now let's apply the Anchoring and Adjustment Effect to the Risk Response in real life. There are efforts underway around the world to increase electricity production from nuclear power in order to cut greenhouse gas emissions and reduce global warming. But critics say that nuclear power creates dangerous waste that we haven't figured out how to store safely, and creates materials that can be used to make nuclear weapons. They also say that there could be accidents at nuclear power plants, like the one at Chernobyl.

⚠ What's Your Risk Response?

Let's say that you are trying to figure out where you stand on this issue. You do some research. Imagine that you see a news article about the issue of nuclear power safety that talks about the health effects of the Chernobyl accident. The article begins this way: "More than 5,000,000 people lived in areas contaminated by radioactive fallout from the Chernobyl nuclear accident. Considerable controversy remains over the lifetime death toll among all those exposed, with estimates ranging from 4,000 to more than 100,000."

Now imagine that instead, you saw an article that presents the story this way: "To date, authorities believe that 56 people were killed by radiation from the Chernobyl accident. Considerable controversy remains over the lifetime death toll among all those exposed, with estimates ranging from 4,000 to more than 100,000."

Do you know everything that you need to know in order to make a fully informed, rational estimate of the number of people who will eventually be killed by radiation from the Chernobyl accident? No. Do you have all the time you need to go out and research everything that you would need to know to make this estimate? No. And if you're like most people, you don't have the background in nuclear physics, biology, genetics, epidemiology, and the other sciences that you'd need in order to make sense of all the research available on the health effects of Chernobyl. Your ability to be perfectly rational is bounded and limited.

So you take the information you've been given, and you subconsciously apply the mental shortcut of making numerical estimates by anchoring on the initial number and adjusting from there. Both articles are factually accurate. But the first article, with the anchoring number of 5,000,000 in the first sentence, is likely to lead you to think that the ultimate death toll from Chernobyl will be higher than you would think if you had read only the second article, with the anchoring number of 56 in the first sentence. The first article might make you a bit more worried about nuclear power. The second would probably cause you to worry a little less.

Like the earlier discussion of mercury, this is not an argument for or against nuclear power. It is offered only as an example of one of the mental processes by which we make sense of quantitative information in order to judge what we should be afraid of, and how afraid, or not, we should be.

THE AWARENESS/READY RECALL EFFECT

In late October 2002, few people in the Washington, D.C., area felt safe. A mysterious sniper was shooting random victims at random sites at random times. The uncertainty had everybody jumpy.

The sniper killed someone in a gas station, and people began hiding behind their car doors as they fueled up. He killed someone in the parking lot of a Home Depot, and for days people drove miles out of their way to avoid that area. He shot a 13-year-old outside a middle school, and parents started keeping their kids indoors as hundreds of schools across the region canceled outdoor sporting events and field trips. Many more schools from outside the Washington, D.C., area canceled plans to send their kids to visit the nation's capital.

But beyond the danger itself and beyond the frightening uncertainty of where the sniper would strike next and whom he might target, something else was feeding the fear. The risk of being shot by the sniper was all anyone was paying attention to. Newspaper headlines declared, "Fear Sinking into Local Lives," "Kids Face a Fearful World," "Dread Reckoning," and "Region Paralyzed by Fear." At stores and malls, offices and restaurants, church meetings and bus stops, everywhere people got together, they talked of little else. Educated people, smart people, people who *knew* that their chance of being a victim was practically zero were afraid. Maybe they could escape the sniper. But there was no escaping the awareness of the threat.

The greater our awareness, and the more readily information about a risk can be recalled, the greater our concern. The Awareness/Ready Recall Effect is connected to the Categorization shortcut described a few pages back. You'll remember that when we get a bit of partial information, in order to make sense of it, we subconsciously pull out the mental files on things that seem to fit the same pattern, and we apply the partial information in a way that's consistent with what we already know about the general category. The Awareness/Ready Recall Effect is a matter of how easily we can open those mental files. It's not what we do with the information once the files are open, but the ease with which the files can be opened and the background information brought to mind in the first place. It was *easy* for people in the Washington, D.C., metropolitan area in October 2002 to bring instances of the sniper's actions to mind. That ready awareness fueled a huge Perception Gap between the low risk of being shot and the high level of fear many people felt that they might be next.

The Awareness/Ready Recall Effect works for quickly judging the frequency or probability of something because it's easier to remember frequent events than infrequent ones. So if something comes to mind quickly, that's a clue to your amygdala that whatever triggered that memory is also more likely. To demonstrate this effect, here's a question for you: *Does the letter* R *appear more frequently as the first letter in words, or as the third letter?*

Most people judge it more likely that *R* will be the first letter of a word than the third, because its easier to recall words that start with *R* (like *recall*) than words in which *R* is the third letter (like *words*). In fact, *R* is more often the third letter in English words. But the Awareness/Ready Recall Effect provides a mental shortcut that influences how we estimate likelihood.

Sometimes we recall things readily not because they happened frequently, but because they were vivid, dramatic, or frightening, and that makes our memory of them stronger. I have a friend in Vienna with whom I recently conducted some business in China. There was a banquet thrown by our Chinese hosts at the end of our meeting, at which a special local liquor was served, and all were expected to join in the toast. I looked over at my friend, and his face was white and his eyes were darting around frantically. His hand holding the glass with the liquor was trembling. As he drank it, he looked terrified. I asked him later what was wrong, and he told me that years ago at a Chinese banquet, the round after round of toasts with this particularly intense beverage had left him seriously poisoned and hospitalized. His vivid memory and his ready recall of that event fired up his amygdala to sound the alarm here years later.

An example of the Awareness/Ready Recall Effect is people's fear of nuclear power. A surprising number of people fear nuclear power because they think, incorrectly, that a nuclear power plant can blow up like an atomic bomb. Even when you explain why that can't happen, images of Hiroshima and Nagasaki come so readily and so powerfully to mind for some people that these images still affect their response to the risk of nuclear energy.

Another example of this was Hurricane Rita, which struck the Gulf Coast of Texas in 2005. Thankfully, hurricanes in that area are infrequent. Still, roughly half the people in the Houston area evacuated, a much higher number than many emergency managers had expected. Why? Because Hurricane Katrina had devastated nearby New Orleans just four weeks earlier, and the dramatic images depicting the danger from big hurricanes were fresh in everybody's mind.

Obviously the news media play a big role in the Awareness/Ready Recall Effect. It will be pretty easy to recall information if you just heard it on the news an hour ago, or if it's on the news *constantly,* like the sniper in Washington, D.C. When there is a plane crash in the news, some people become more afraid of flying. The statistical likelihood of *their* plane crashing is the same as it was before the plane crash that made the news. But the ease with which they can recall a plane crash is up, and so is their concern.

But it's not just the news. Information comes to us from a wide range of sources. We learn in school, on the job, and from our friends. We remember what we have experienced ourselves. We learn from books and from movies. A lot of people in America in early 1979, for example, were talking abut a new risk that they had just learned about, the risk of a meltdown at a nuclear power plant, depicted in the movic *The China Syndrome.* Twelve days after the movie was released, the partial meltdown accident at the Three Mile Island plant in Pennsylvania took place. That accident, combined with the already heightened awareness of the risk of such accidents, contributed to a metaphorical explosion in public fear of nuclear power.

So the more readily we can recall some background information similar to a risk that we may be facing at the moment, the more concerned about that risk we are likely to be. And that Awareness/ Ready Recall Effect, like Framing and Loss Aversion and all the other mental shortcuts we use to quickly make sense of partial information, will have even more influence on our perceptions if the risk is being described using numbers—not because we understand numbers, but because most of us don't.

INNUMERACY

If someone asks, "What's the risk of _____?" that person is often looking for a number—the odds, the numerical probability. The risk is one in a million, three in a thousand, or something like that. The only problem is, even when we have that number, our rationality will be bounded, because a majority of us are not very good with numbers.

 What's Your Risk Response?

1. Which is more likely, 1 in 100, 1 in 1,000, or 1 in 10?
2. Let's say you buy an "I'm Feeling Lucky!" lottery scratch ticket. One player in 1,000 wins. So if 1,000 people (including you) buy that ticket, what percentage of those folks are going to feel lucky *after* they scratch off the ticket?
3. Let's say you buy an "I Am Going To Be Filthy Stinking Rich!" lottery ticket. One percent of the "investors" in

this game win the big prize. If 1,000 people play this game, how many people end up filthy stinking rich?

4. If you take one die from a set and roll it 1,000 times, how many times would it come up on an even number (2, 4, or 6)? (For the answers, see the endnotes.[16])

If one train leaves Cleveland heading for Chicago going 65 miles per hour, and another train leaves Chicago heading for Cleveland going 45 miles an hour . . . no, never mind about that one.

Does the word *equation* make you sweat? Do percent signs make your brain hurt? When it's time to figure out the tip at a restaurant, do you

A. Pull out a calculator?
B. Make sure the check lands in front of somebody else?
C. Take a shot at figuring out 15 percent of $39.18, only to learn that you got it wrong when your friend uses her calculator?

A lot of us are not particularly good with numbers. Some people say this is because we're not taught math well. Others say it is because the news media butcher statistics. Still others say it is because math makes their brain hurt. There is truth to all of these. But for this discussion, the cause of innumeracy doesn't matter. What matters is that numbers are a large part of how we learn about risk, and if we don't handle numbers well, our risk response is more likely to be based on our feelings than on the facts, and to result in a Perception Gap.

How well did you do on our little quiz? In one study of well-educated people, more than 80 percent (8 in 10) of whom had greater than a high school education, about 1 in 5 (20 percent) got the first question wrong. They couldn't tell that if they were 1 person out of 10 who might die, their chances of dying were greater than if they were only 1 person out of 100 at risk, which is a greater risk than only 1 person out of 1,000.[17]

How did you do on the question about that single die? In the study, 55 percent got it right. This means that nearly half the well-educated participants couldn't even figure out that over 1,000 rolls of a cube with an equal number of odd numbers and even numbers, the chances are pretty good that evens and odds are each going to come up about 50 percent (half) of the time.

And those questions were the easy ones. The study subjects didn't do much better at converting percentages to proportions. Question 2 asked you to convert 1 in 1,000 to a percentage, 0.1 percent. Only 2 in 10 (20 percent) of the subjects got the answer correct. Question 3 asks you to convert 1 percent of 1,000 into a whole number, or 10. About 60 percent (6 in 10) of the subjects got that one right.

Risks are often presented as proportions or percentages, which are statistical ways of describing the probability that some individual or group will be affected, out of the entire population to which that individual or group belongs. Statistical probability is an important part of understanding a risk you might be facing so that you can make a thoughtful choice. In fact, as Peter Bernstein so wonderfully explains in his aptly titled book *Against the Gods: The Remarkable Story of Risk,* when French mathematicians Blaise Pascal and Pierre de Fermat solved "The Problem of the Points"[18] in 1654, it was the first time that people gained the power, using mathematics, to predict the future and trump fate—the Gods. But if we struggle to understand that 1 in 5 and 20 percent are the same thing, or if we have trouble understanding whether one in a thousand or one in a million is the bigger risk, then our rationality is bounded not by a lack of information, but by a lack of ability to understand information, and our risk-response judgments will have to rely on more affective mental shortcuts.

That's just what research has found. Several studies have first measured how numerate the test subjects were with some standard numbers questions like the ones with which we started. Then the researchers challenged the subjects to make judgments about health risks based on mathematical information. The more numerate subjects made more precise numerical judgments of their actual risk. The less numerate subjects made judgments based more on emotion and mood, which resulted in a wider Perception Gap between their fears and the actual risks that they faced.

Just because you studied math in school doesn't mean that you're numerate. It turns out that the ability to understand and work with numbers is independent of education level. It's a scary fact, but even the doctors on whom we depend for sound medical judgments aren't as good with numbers as we would hope. A study presented doctors with the results of two randomized trials of ways to treat a group of 1,000 people for high blood pressure.[19] The first trial showed that the treatment reduced mortality among study subjects from 7.8 percent among those who weren't being treated to 6.3 percent among those who were. So with the treatment, 1.5 percent fewer people died, or 15 fewer actual people per thousand. That's called *absolute* risk—just the actual number of victims.

The doctors were then told that the second randomized trial showed a 20 percent reduction in the mortality rate. This compares the 7.8 percent death rate to 6.3 percent: 6.3 is 20 percent less than 7.8. That's called *relative* risk, measuring one group relative to another.

The outcomes are the same. A 20 percent *relative* reduction in deaths, from 7.8 percent to 6.3 percent, equals an *absolute* reduction of 15 people per thousand. Yet when the doctors were asked which study they'd use to decide how to treat their patients, 4 out of 10 chose the second study. They probably felt that 20 percent sounded bigger than 15 out of a thousand. Whatever the reason, the study demonstrates that doctors, experts on whose judgments our health often relies, can get numbers wrong too.

It's pretty clear how innumeracy can contribute to a Perception Gap. There is much more on this in the pages ahead, including some valuable tips on how we can use numbers more effectively as we make our judgments about risk. But we'll get to that later. If I told you now, your head might explode.

OPTIMISM BIAS

- Bill, 17 years old: "Yeah, I know smoking can kill me. But a lot of people smoke and don't die. My father smoked a pack a day 'til he was 80. It won't happen to me."
- Suzanne, 49: "Sure, using my cell phone while I drive is risky. But I'm a good driver."
- Two guys overheard at a fast food restaurant: "What are you gonna get?"
  "I'm going for it! The Super Whammo Extra Double Triple Cheeseburger, Mega Monster Fries, and a Mountain O' Milkshake."
  "Dude, eatin' like that'll kill you!"
  "Nah. Not *me*!"
- The Little Engine That Could: "I think I can. I think I can. I think I can."

We all do it. People who are warned to evacuate cities that are about to be hit by hurricanes choose to stay. Motorists don't wear seat belts. People have that one last glass of beer or wine before driving home. Then there are people who eat fugu (puffer fish).

And hitchhikers. And those wackos on Shark Week who swim in open water with great white sharks. Our response to risk is often to deny it. We don't think it can happen to us because, in many circumstances, we are optimists.

Students expect higher scores on exams than they actually get. Newlyweds think that their marriages will last longer than the average marriage lasts. Most people think that they'll live longer, healthier lives, with more professional success and less likelihood of being robbed or assaulted or getting in a motor vehicle crash, compared to others. You know that vacation you're planning? Sorry, but you probably think you'll have a better time than you actually will. You know that project at home that you're thinking of doing that you think you can wrap up in two weeks? Better allow more time.[20]

Rose-colored glasses are pervasive when it comes to risk. Consider an ABC News poll taken five years after the September 11, 2001, terrorist attacks in the United States. Respondents were asked, "How concerned are you about the possibility there will be more major terrorist attacks in the U.S.? Does that worry you a great deal, somewhat, not too much, or not at all?"

The answers were:

A GREAT DEAL	SOMEWHAT	NOT TOO MUCH	NOT AT ALL
29%	45%	17%	8%

Nearly three people in four said they worried either some or a lot that a major terrorist attack will happen again in the United States. But they were also asked this: "How concerned are you about the chance that *you personally* might be the victim of a terrorist attack?"

And the answers were:

A GREAT DEAL	SOMEWHAT	NOT TOO MUCH	NOT AT ALL
10%	25%	35%	29%

So while 74 percent were a great deal or somewhat worried that a terrorist attack could happen again, only 35 percent said that they were worried that it would happen *to them*.

We are to be forgiven for a rose-colored-glasses view of things. From where each of us sits, we are right to figure, "It won't happen to me." After all, most Americans *won't* be injured or killed by the next terrorist attack. (The official death toll from the September 11, 2001, attacks in the United States is 2,998.) Even in terrible storms like Hurricane Katrina in 2005 (official death toll 1,836) or Hurricane Andrew in Florida in 1992 (death toll 65), most people survive. Most drivers *don't* crash. Most fugu eaters live to taste puffer fish again another day. Most people who swim near sharks are *not* attacked.

But none of us really knows when it will be *our* number that comes up. And if nearly everybody who gets married thinks that his marriage will last forever, and only 6 in 10 marriages do,[21] some of those optimists will have sad surprises ahead, and the only people who can really be optimistic are the ones who run wedding chapels and divorce lawyers. In other words, individually we may be right to figure that it won't happen to us. But without the ability to see whether the rosy future will actually be ours, the statistics suggest that we need clearer lenses.

You may recall that just a few pages ago, we were talking about loss aversion. Doesn't that conflict with Optimism Bias? Not really. Loss Aversion most often colors our risk response to a choice that we face in the short term. Optimism colors our views of how things will turn out further down the road. It turns out that the rose-colored view of down-the-road results shifts toward realism as the future turns into tomorrow. Those students who thought they'd do better on the tests they were going to take in several weeks weren't so sure the night before the exam.

This may be because as the time of the test or the wedding or the jump into shark-infested water draws near, our minds are no longer imagining the future and filling in the blank spots that we can't predict with all sorts of optimistic images, with what Daniel Gilbert, in his entertaining book *Stumbling on Happiness*, calls the "illusion of foresight." Down the road, the details are fuzzy, and we get to optimistically imagine the ones that make the future look bright. But as we sit down at the desk to start the test, or we stand at the altar and it's time to say, "I do," or we stand on the back of the boat and it's time to jump in with the sharks and there are those fins circling in the water, now we are doing what Gilbert calls "nexting"—foreseeing the *immediate* future with more sobering clarity and detail, and our optimism about an imaginary tomorrow is tempered with the realism of the facts of now.[22]

This could help explain why people in Florida, where hurricanes are more frequent, are more prepared for these storms, and readier to evacuate, than people in areas that are hit by hurricanes less frequently. In Florida, thinking about hurricanes is reality-based "nexting." In Rhode Island or Massachusetts, where hurricanes are rare and the next hurricane is far enough off in the future that it is more imaginary, Optimism Bias can paint a rosier picture of how things might turn out.

Our degree of optimism depends on more than just temporal proximity. It depends on several circumstances, and on the nature of the risk itself. A pioneering study in the field of risk perception, "Judged Frequency of Lethal Events," found that we optimistically *under*estimate the likelihood of some causes of death, but we pessimistically *over*estimate the likelihood of some others, in part because of "memorable characteristics of the different causes of death, such as sensationalism or vividness." In other words, something about the nature of certain ways of dying grabs our attention. This also means that those same causes of death will probably get more attention from the news media, which in turn will make us more aware of them, strengthening the Awareness/Ready Recall Effect.

The people in that study overestimated the likelihood of killers like tornadoes, floods, and botulism. (In 1978, the year the study was done, the second-largest outbreak of botulism poisoning in U.S. history killed 2 and sickened 32 in Clovis, New Mexico, and made national news for days. And that came on the heels of lots of news coverage of the largest U.S. food poisoning outbreak ever, in Michigan, the year before. So awareness was high.) At the same time, the study subjects underestimated causes of death like diabetes, stroke, and heart disease, three of the five leading causes of death in the United States. But these are not headline grabbers, not causes of death that you hear about in the news every day. As the authors of that study note, "Silent killers" indeed.[23] With less awareness of these major threats, people are more optimistic.

There are other characteristics of risks that also determine how optimistic we are. A study of college students in New Jersey by Neil Weinstein[24] asked students to rate the likelihood that they would experience any of 42 different events, some positive, some negative, compared with the likelihood that others might experience those outcomes. Here are a few:

> *You'll like your job.*
> *You'll own your own home.*
> *You'll travel to Europe.*
> *You'll go five years without a night in the hospital.*
> *You'll have an alcohol problem.*
> *You'll get divorced.*
> *You'll get a sexually transmitted disease.*
> *You'll have gum problems.*

The students were predictably optimistic that they would get a good job, own a home, travel, and stay out of the hospital. And they were also optimistic that they would *not* turn into alcoholic divorced ex-spouses with mystery rashes and problems chewing their food. That's not surprising. The students were also asked to rate each event for certain characteristics that made their optimism stronger or weaker. These characteristics provide interesting evidence of how some of the Bounded Rationality mental shortcuts we talked about earlier can affect how optimistically we respond to risk.

For each of the positive and negative events, students were asked, "Have you or anyone you know had any experience with this?" In the case of *positive* events, if the students could recall any personal experience with the event, they were more optimistic that it would happen again. But in the case of the *negative* outcomes (divorce, bad gums, and so on), just as the Awareness/Ready Recall Effect would predict, the more easily the students could summon up an example of somebody who had experienced that negative event, the *greater* they predicted were their chances of the same thing happening to them, or happening to them again. This time, the students weren't optimistic. They were pessimistic, because their Ready Recall of a negative event cautioned them against too much hope.

They were also asked to categorize their chances compared to certain types of people, certain stereotypes, which shows how the Categorization Effect interacts with the Optimism Bias. Sure enough, the more they envisioned a person who owned a home, liked her job, traveled to Europe, and stayed out of the hospital—a category of person that they would *like* to be—the more optimistic the students were about their own likelihood of fitting into that category. In the case of the negative events, the more they could envision a drunk divorcee with a rash and bad gums—a negative type of person that they would *not* want to be—the *lower* they rated the likelihood that they would experience those negative events.

What's Your Risk Response?

Want to know how much of an optimist you are? Take the Life Orientation Test.[25] It's used as a quick measure of where someone falls on the continuum between optimism and pessimism. There is no cutoff, just a continuum. You'll have to judge for yourself how optimistic you are about your results.

Rate each of the following questions on the following scale:

0 = strongly disagree, 1 = disagree, 2 = neutral, 3 = agree, 4 = strongly agree

1. In uncertain times, I usually expect the best.
2. If something can go wrong for me, it will.
3. I'm always optimistic about my future.
4. I hardly ever expect things to go my way.
5. I rarely count on good things happening to me.
6. Overall, I expect more good things to happen to me than bad.

Total your answers for questions 1, 3, and 6, and compare it with the total of your answers for questions 2, 4, and 5.

On to the Personality of Risk

Optimism Bias is a great place to move our story forward, because the studies of optimism help to illustrate some of the other psychological elements that we're about to get to that contribute to the Risk Response. These are the personality traits that make some risks feel scarier than others, qualitative Affective characteristics of the situation that make our fears go up or down. We'll call them Risk Perception Factors. And Weinstein's optimism study tested for a couple of these characteristics as well.

One Risk Perception Factor is the issue of control. The more control you feel you have, the less afraid you are. Less control = more fear. Weinstein's subjects were asked to rate their optimism about positive or negative events in terms of "controllability." You can probably guess the result. The more control the students thought they had over whether or not the event would happen, the more optimistic they were that the positive events would happen and the negative things wouldn't. That makes sense until you look at the list of events. It contains lots of outcomes over which people don't really have much control. Staying out of a hospital for five years? Living until age 80? Your home doubling in value in five years? Being fired? Having a heart attack? Anybody who thinks that she can completely control any of those outcomes is wearing *really* pink lenses. Nonetheless, the more the students felt that they had at least some sense of control, the more optimistic they were.

Control is just one of more than a dozen unique characteristics that make some risk situations feel riskier than others. While the mental shortcuts of Bounded Rationality help us to make decisions and judgments about anything, including but not limited to risk, now we're heading into the specific psychological factors that speak directly to the Perception Gap about risk. These factors will help explain why you're more afraid of some things than you need to be, and not as afraid of some things as you should be.

CHAPTER 3

FEAR FACTORS

Why Some Threats Feel Scarier Than Others

There are nights when the wolves are silent and only the moon howls.
—GEORGE CARLIN

I've spoken before of the additional deaths on the roads in the United States following the September 11 attacks. Here is that story, made tragically personal.

The family matriarch was turning 80 in October. Her children, grandchildren, and great-grandchildren were all looking forward to gathering at her home in the Midwest to celebrate. For most of them, it was a short drive. But one daughter, Sarah, lived in New England, more than a thousand miles away.

Flying didn't worry Sarah. She had flown home to see her mom many times. But this was October 2001. Air travel had just resumed following the attacks on September 11. The wrenching images of those planes flying into buildings were still ominously clear in Sarah's mind.

So she decided to drive. "I know it's a long trip," she told her mother on the phone, "but it just feels, well, safer. At least behind the wheel I feel like I have some control. Don't worry. You know I'm a good driver."

Sarah never made it to her mother's birthday celebration. She was killed in a crash a few hundred miles from home.[1] She was just one of hundreds of people killed in the deadly increase in motor vehicle crashes in the months following September 11.

Here are the details. One analysis estimates that 317 more people died in motor vehicle crashes in the United States in the three months after the September 11 attacks than would have been expected for those three months.[2] A second analysis puts the increased motor vehicle death toll for October to December 2001 at 725.[3] A third analysis, done by a group with more expertise in motor vehicle risk than the other two, estimates the extra death toll on American roads for those three months at 1,018.[4]

Despite overwhelming statistical evidence that flying is safer than driving, something that many of the drivers who were killed may well have known, those people made choices based more on their Affective perceptions than on the statistical evidence, and the resulting Perception Gap killed them.

We humans like to think we're pretty smart. After all, we have more cerebral cortex than any other species. Dogs can smell better, and elephants can hear better, but when it comes to thinking, our three pounds of gray matter up there puts us at the top of the evolutionary tree. We proudly presume that, with such superior mental firepower, we can rise above our animal instincts and figure things out in a perfectly rational way. Just give us enough information, and we have the neurons to figure out the objective truth. We assume that, since we have the remarkable capacity to reason, that reason is how we make our choices, or at least, how we should.

For such a smart species, that's pretty dumb. There is overwhelming evidence from both careful scientific research and everybody's real lives that reason and rationality are only part of how we make up our minds, especially when it comes to choices like the one Sarah faced—choices about threats to our health. Remember, the amygdala fires up a Risk Response before the rational cortex can contribute its reasoned input. And given the wiring and chemistry of the brain, even after the initial response, affect is generally more powerful than reason. Risk perception is far more than just a factual affair. It's a matter of feelings too.

But where do our feelings come from? What makes one threat more threatening than another? Why are we more afraid of some dangers when the facts suggest that those dangers are not all that dangerous, and we are not particularly afraid of some hazards that are in fact far more hazardous? And why is it that most of us seem to be afraid of the same things, for the same basic reasons?

In addition to the mental shortcuts we have developed for handling decision making under conditions of Bounded Rationality, humans have also developed a sort of psychological shorthand for quickly sensing what's scary and what's not. Since the 1970s, research into the psychology of risk perception has been done in many countries, across many cultures, at different times, when different threats were getting a lot of attention, and a pattern has emerged across all those people in all those different circumstances. We share a well-identified set of psychological factors—Risk Perception Factors—that are strongly associated with whether we are more or less afraid. Think of it this way: risks have personality traits that help us to instinctively judge their *character,* even while we are consciously considering the facts. There is evidence from neuroscience that these affective characteristics also help the amygdala make its rapid judgment about whether we are in danger and whether to sound the alarm.

One of these Risk Perception Factors, as Sarah's story illustrates, is the issue of control. The more control we feel we have, the less afraid we generally are, whether we actually *have* that control or only *think* we do. Conversely, the less we feel in control, the more afraid we are likely to be. It made complete sense that more people would prefer to drive than fly in the wake of the September 11 attacks. Driving affords some degree of control, so, despite the statistics, it *feels* safer.

PRINCIPLES BEHIND RISK PERCEPTION FACTORS

There are a number of these Risk Perception Factors, and we'll explore them in greater depth in the rest of this chapter. But first, you need to understand a few general concepts that apply to all of them.

The same factor can make the fear either go down or go up. For example, more control = less fear. Less control = more fear. The first important principle is that each Risk Perception Factor can cause us to be either more afraid or less afraid.

A second principle: there are many Risk Perception Factors, and more than one is usually involved in most situations. Take the risk of heart disease. You know that you can diet and reduce your risk, which gives you a sense of Control, and that will reduce your fears. But another Risk Perception Factor is Pain and Suffering; the more pain and suffering a risk involves, the more afraid we're likely to be. Let's say you watched a friend die of congestive heart failure, a kind of heart disease that causes a person to slowly suffocate over a couple of years—an awful way to die. So while the Control factor is making you less afraid of heart disease, the Pain and Suffering factor makes you more afraid.

A third important principle: Risk Perception Factors are just one part of the system. They make our fears go up or down, but so do Optimism Bias, and Anchoring and Adjustment, Categorization, and the other general mental shortcuts we use for deciding things under conditions of Bounded Rationality. And so do the amygdala and all those biological risk response mechanisms. And so do many social and cultural forces, which we'll get to in Chapter 4. And let's not forget the cognitive, thinking, reasoning cortex. It's not as if we don't use the facts *at all*. Risk Perception Factors are just one part of the human system of Affective risk perception, which is a complex interaction of several conscious and subconscious components.

A fourth key principle about these Risk Perception Factors: for more than 30 years, research on people all around the world has found that while these factors are generally true for all of us, each of us is also unique, and our perceptions will also depend on what we have learned and experienced; our current life circumstances; and our religious, political, and cultural norms. Remember the example of reacting to that snake on the ground that we used earlier? I used that example once in a talk I gave to farmers and dairy industry people in Japan. When I asked them what they would do if they saw what might be a snake on the ground, one of the farmers said he would try to capture it, cut off its head, and make its blood into soup. This fellow had an amygdala just like you and me, but in his personal context, a snake meant something different than what it meant to Charles Darwin. Risk Perception Factors are true for people in general, but we all bring our own individual perspectives to bear on how we respond to risk.

Here is an important example of how our personal characteristics interact with the Risk Perception Factors. Let's say you are a reasonably affluent white male in the United States, between 20 and 60 years old, healthy, professionally successful, and a member of whichever political party is currently in power. You probably have a general sense that you can control things, certainly more than if you were a poor, unemployed immigrant from a non-English-speaking racial minority. As a result of your greater general sense of control, you are generally less afraid of most things than white women or nonwhites of either gender. Researchers believe that the factor of Control helps explain what they call "the white male effect," but it obviously applies only to people with certain individual characteristics. So,

- Risk Perception Factors can make our fears go up or down.
- Usually more than one Risk Perception Factor is involved in our overall perception of a threat.

- Risk Perception Factors are only one input into the overall system of Affective risk perception.
- Risk Perception Factors appear to be universal, but our perceptions also depend on our experience, education, lifestyle, and other factors that make each of us unique.

Back in 2005, when the possibility of a global epidemic of avian flu was raising a lot of concern, a friend of mine, well educated and politically liberal, said, "I used to think that bird flu might be a serious threat. But now that President Bush says it is, I'm not so sure." Huh? We begin our journey through the fascinating world of these Risk Perception Factors with what is probably the most important one of all: Trust.

RISK PERCEPTION FACTOR 1: TRUST

Humans are social animals. Our individual prospects depend to a significant degree on the prospects of the group(s) to which we belong and how well we get along with these group(s). Survival means being acutely sensitive to who is on our side and who is not. So it isn't surprising that trust matters so much in how we go about protecting ourselves. And it isn't surprising to find that the instinct for trust is intimately connected with the neural processes deep in the subconscious parts of the brain that help keep us safe.

Few forms of trust are more basic than that between a mother and her newborn child. Scientists studying this bond have discovered that it is strengthened by the hormone oxytocin, which is released when the baby stares up at mom during breast feeding. It turns out that staring lovingly at your boyfriend or girlfriend can also trigger the release of oxytocin, as can warm physical contact like touching and hugging. Oxytocin reduces stress within arguing couples, helps us recognize faces, and even helps us look at a face (in fact, just a pair of eyes) and identify the mood that person is in. The stuff is magic.

Based on the evidence that oxytocin is involved in social bonding, researchers tested its impact on trust. And since trust is so important to risk perception, it's not surprising that they found evidence for some of its roots deep in the chemistry and construction of the brain. Nor should it surprise you at this point that the part of the brain where they found oxytocin had a strong effect on trust was—drum roll, please—the amygdala.

 What's Your Risk Response?

Let's say researchers give you $100, and this option: you can either keep the money, or you can give it to an anonymous trustee who will either invest it and double it to $200 and then return half of the hundred dollars profit to you ($50) along with the original $100 or keep all the original $100 for herself. So by giving it to the anonymous trustee, you can go from $100 to $150 or lose the $100 and end up with nothing. Would you trust that anonymous investor? (Remember Loss Aversion from Chapter 2, where in a similar experiment, most people decided to avoid the gamble and take the sure cash.)

An hour before the start of this actual experiment, half the volunteers were given a sniff of a spray that contained oxytocin. The others got a snort of a placebo spray. More of the volunteers who had sniffed the hormone trusted the anonymous investors and gambled with their money.[5]

A later experiment by another group took this investigation a step further. The second experiment involved only the volunteers from the first round who had chosen to invest with the trustee, had been burned, and had lost their money. They were asked if they wanted to try again. This would be like getting another spam e-mail from the Nigerian investor and sending him $5,000 again, right?

The whole group was given some new cash. Half of the burned volunteers got a fresh whiff of Eau de Oxytocin, and half got a sniff of Eau de Placebo. Those who sniffed the oxytocin were more trusting and ready to invest with an anonymous trustee *a second time* than were the placebo-exposed subjects. And as each volunteer was asked, "Do you want to try this again?" the response was timed. The ones who got the sniff of trust spray responded *faster* than those that didn't. It was as if their ability to be wary and mistrustful had been turned off or at least turned down.[6]

It shouldn't be surprising that oxytocin affects the part of your brain so intimately involved in keeping you safe, the amygdala, since trust has a lot to do with survival among social animals who depend on each other for safety and protection. Show someone an untrustworthy face, and the amygdala is one of two areas that become more active than anywhere else in the brain.[7] An untrustworthy face sets off the same sort of response in the amygdala that a snake or a spider does!

But we have to be just as good at recognizing whom we *can* trust, so the system needs fine-tuned control. That's where oxytocin has its effect on the amygdala. In the second set of those gambling experiments with the volunteers and the trustees, the one that just used the volunteers from the first round who had trusted the investors and had been burned, the researchers used *f*MRI to watch the activity inside the brains of their subjects as they made their choices. As the levels of oxytocin in the exposed volunteers went up, activity in the amygdala went down! It turns out that the amygdala is loaded with receptors for oxytocin, and the oxytocin binds with those receptors in a way that diminishes the amygdala's ability to be wary. It turns down what appears to be the amygdala's default setting, to be cautious about whom to trust, and reduces its ability to send out the message, "Warning! Warning! I don't trust this guy." Like I said, the stuff is amazing!

This is so important for our perception of anything, including risk, that it's worth summarizing. The ability to accurately know whom we can trust, and whom we can't, is vital for survival and powerfully influences how we make judgments and behave. The neural tools for making these vital judgments are, to a significant degree, *subconscious,* and they are intimately connected with the fundamental brain architecture and chemistry that helps us sense and respond to danger, and stay alive. These fundamental biological underpinnings deep in the self-preservation systems of the brain suggest why trust plays such a powerful part in our Risk Response—as we learned from how the public reacted when mad cow disease broke out in Japan and Germany.

The first mad cow that was born and raised in Japan (i.e., not imported) was found in late 2001. Not to worry, said Agriculture Minister Tsutomu Takebe. The food supply in Japan is safe, he promised. He also offered his assurance that there were no more sick cows. None. *Oops!* The second cow was found just a couple days later.

Don't worry, Minister Takebe promised. We have rules that ban the kind of cow-feeding practices that cause the disease to spread in cattle, he said, the kind of ban that has been adopted in the rest of the world. But the news media soon reported that the "ban" was only a set of *voluntary guidelines* for the cattle industry. The media also reported that government *health* officials, who wanted to make the feed rule mandatory, were defeated in a power struggle with *agriculture* officials, including Minister Takebe, who wanted to keep controls more flexible and agriculture industry–friendly. *Oops #2!* Trust dropped further.

Then the Japanese news media reported that, months earlier, the Japanese government had suppressed a European Union document that found that Japan was at high risk for mad cow disease. The government knew that the risk was high, and covered it up. Big *Oops #3!* Trust was all but destroyed. Yet after all these false promises and revelations, Minister Takebe fired a subordinate, but did not resign, and he continued publicly munching meat in an effort to reassure the public.

The actual physical risk to the public was infinitesimal. The Japanese found only a few sick animals, and a decade of experience with the disease in the United Kingdom showed that even with tens of thousands of sick cows, fewer than one hundred people in Great Britain, out of a population of 59 million, had gotten the human version of the disease. But fear ran high because trust in the Japanese government's ability to keep food safe had been destroyed. A lot of amygdalas in Japan were screaming, "Alert! Alert!" Within days, sales of beef dropped to practically zero. Stores posted signs promising that *their* meat was safe. Many restaurants specializing in beef had to close. Six months later, beef sales in Japan were still off 40 percent.

To further illustrate the importance of trust, contrast the Japanese experience with what had happened less than a year earlier in Germany.

In November of 2000, German Agriculture Minister Karl-Heinz Funke declared confidently that Germany was *immune* from mad cow disease. There's that *absolute* assurance of safety again! Promising zero risk means that if just one sick cow comes along, instead of people saying to themselves, "No sweat. The risk is low," they say to the government, "You're supposed to protect me, but you lied. I don't trust you. I'm more afraid." But Minister Funke made that mistake in Germany, and the same result followed as later occurred in Japan. People freaked out, and beef sales dropped to near zero.

But compare the German response to that of the Japanese. Within a matter of weeks, Funke was kicked out and replaced by Renate Kuenast, a member of the environmentally progressive Green Party, who promised to make the agriculture ministry more aware of consumer concerns. And Chancellor Gerhard Schroeder said, "The crisis has made it compellingly clear that we have to make several organizational, and not just personnel, changes." He proposed new laws to move German agriculture away from industrial practices and toward organic farming. Unlike in Japan, where beef sales stayed so low for so long that they depressed the gross domestic product of the country in the quarter following the outbreak, in Germany sales were back to normal in a few weeks. Why? In part because the German government responded to the mad cow threat with concrete actions that helped restore trust and eased public concern, saving their economy hundreds of millions of dollars.

Whom Do You Trust?

It makes sense that if we don't trust the people or organizations that are supposed to protect us, our fears will rise. But trust also depends on who is doing the communicating about a risk. This explains why my liberal friend felt differently about the risk of avian flu after she heard what then-President George W. Bush had to say. This also explains what a conservative friend said to me recently: "Maybe I'd worry more about climate change if it wasn't Al Gore up there trying to win his second Nobel Peace Prize or another Academy Award." We worry more about a drug when we learn that the doctor recommending it was paid by the drug company to do the original studies that said that the drug is safe. We worry more about the risk of chemicals if an environmental organization is describing the danger than if it's being described by a chemical company. Why? It's not because we understand the science of climate change or pharmaceuticals or industrial chemicals. It's a matter of which communicator we trust.

Sometimes it's not about trusting the communicator or the organization that's supposed to protect us. Sometimes it's a matter of whether we trust the person or organization *that created the risk in the first place*—like a company selling a product. In the 1980s, women who had had breast implants containing silicone sued Dow Corning, a silicone manufacturer, claiming that the material was causing the medical problems the women were having. As part of one lawsuit, it was revealed that Dow Corning had not fully reported studies the company had done indicating a possible connection between silicone breast implants and inflammation. Word of that "hidden study" made major news. The resulting mistrust of the company helped fuel so many lawsuits that Dow Corning filed for bankruptcy and ended up paying billions of dollars to women, even though its product was not at fault.

Trust in the Food and Drug Administration (FDA), which was perceived to have contributed to the creation of the risk by approving the implants in the first place, had also been badly damaged. The FDA ordered the breast implants off the market. Governments around the world spent tens of millions of dollars researching the risk of silicone, coming to the same conclusion that had been reached years earlier when the substance was studied before it was approved in the first place—that while there are plenty of medical risks with breast implantation, silicone is not one of them.

But the Perception Gap had been created, in part because of mistrust. Tens of thousands of women suffered physical pain and suffering because they chose to have their implants removed. Thousands more suffered from fear and stress. And a lot of lawyers got rich riding the Perception Gap to a multibillion-dollar class action settlement.

Or consider a more modern case. When it came to light that the Merck pharmaceutical company *may* have known about dangerous side effects from its pain medication Vioxx but failed to report what it knew before bringing the drug to market, the fears that followed were as much about a lack of trust in Merck as they were about the drug itself. Indeed, the Vioxx issue shook people's trust in the entire pharmaceutical industry, raising public concerns about many of that entire industry's products and practices.

Or consider the public's Risk Response when it was reported in 2005 that the Guidant Corporation had withheld information that there might be a defect in one of its heart defibrillators, a defect that may have killed a 21-year-old man. Guidant had some preliminary evidence that *a few* of its devices *might* be failing. The company wasn't even sure. And even if there was some bug the company hadn't quite figured out, the failure rate of the device because of this *possible* defect was lower than the rate at which the defibrillators fail just by random chance (since no machine can be absolutely guaranteed not to fail), and patients accept that random error rate before having the devices implanted. The company also knew that sounding an alarm about the suspected failure might scare people into taking defibrillators *out* of their bodies, an operation more likely to cause side effects, including fatal infections, than the device itself was likely to fail. So statistically, sounding the alarm could be worse than saying nothing. And it would hurt sales too.

So the company said nothing. But when the press reported that Guidant had withheld the information, even though the risk of this one device failing was very low, the corporate secrecy damaged trust and created a huge and dangerous Perception Gap. Thousands of people with all kinds of defibrillators and pacemakers, from every manufacturer, had operations to remove the devices from their bodies. The sales of these remarkable machines, which save a lot of lives and improve the quality of many more, plummeted and stayed low for several months. If you are in the world of business and reading this, the lesson about the risk of keeping secrets and damaging trust cannot be louder, in the direct lingua franca of commerce: cash. At the time the news broke, a rival company had an offer on the table to purchase Guidant for $25 billion. Within a few weeks, it dropped its bid to $21 billion. Guidant's CEO was gone from his job several weeks later.

So our Risk Response depends on how much we trust the sources of the risk, the communication about the risk, or the people or agencies that are supposed to protect us from the risk. But there is one more area where trust is important: trust in the *process*.

Consider the proposed National Institutes of Health high-security biological laboratory at Boston University (BU).

This lab would study the most deadly pathogens known, like the Ebola virus and the Marburg virus. Such laboratories are known as BL4 facilities. (BL stands for bio lab; the "4" is the highest level of safety bio labs are required to have.) Boston University held a public meeting early in the development process to address the public's concerns. Those concerns were passionate, but reasonable. People at the meeting asked, "How safe will I be?" "What if there is an accident?" "Even if every safety precaution is taken in the lab, how will these deadly germs get delivered? You mean to tell me that the FedEx guy is going to be delivering Ebola on our local streets?"

The proponents sat at the head table and listened, and they respectfully told each speaker, "We will note your concern." But many of the citizens asked their questions again, eager for not just an acknowledgment, but for an actual answer. The proponents from Boston University told the citizens that the purpose of the hearing wasn't to answer questions, but just to allow people to voice their concerns, which naturally made several people in the audience furious. One man yelled, "How can we trust you people to keep us safe?" The Boston University officials protested that the law governing such hearings did not allow them to discuss the details of the project, but they failed to offer to stay around after the formal hearing, outside the constraints of the law, to address people's concerns more fully.

Those few angry citizens who didn't like the way they had been treated started an opposition campaign that got plenty of media coverage. Opponents charged that BU was being secretive and was interested only in gaining the money and prestige of the lab, even at the expense of its neighbors' safety; matters of trust, not about the safety of the lab itself. Their opposition led to lawsuits and expensive delays, and ultimately a special panel of national experts had to be convened by the National Institutes of Health to investigate how the whole thing had been handled. At the first hearing of this special panel, the woman who had led the local opposition complained that she and her neighbors felt the decision to build the lab had been made with no real concern for local input. She said, "You know, if I hadn't been treated the way I was treated at the beginning, we wouldn't be here today." It wasn't the safety of the lab alone that had upset her. It was her lack of trust in the process that was making decisions about her safety, a process in which she felt she had no input.

Dishonesty. Keeping secrets. Not admitting mistakes. Making promises like "No Risk" that are impossible to keep. Failing to acknowledge people's affective response to risk. Failing to be open, when possible, and share decision making with people who are affected, when possible. These are just a few of the ways in which people and organizations, especially businesses, can, and regularly do, damage trust. It's stunning, really, how often these mistakes are made, given the importance of trust and the huge political and economic consequences to governments and companies that so regularly seem to get this wrong. You'd think they would learn. And not only from failures. There are success stories out there to teach them too.

Years ago, Finland committed to nuclear power as its principal source of electricity. It also committed to disposing of the high-level nuclear waste from Finnish nuclear plants, in Finland. The Finnish government reasonably assumed that siting a nuclear waste dump would not be easy. What community would want to be the final repository of some of the most dangerous material known?

So the Finns set up a process for siting such a dreaded facility, a process specifically designed to build trust.

> **STEP 1.** Develop a list of possible sites that could host such a facility based on the science, looking at factors like geology, hydrogeology, and climate.
>
> **STEP 2.** Invite representatives of all the possible locations to present their concerns and perspectives. Promise to pay all participants for their involvement in seriously considering the proposal, no matter what the outcome.
>
> **STEP 3.** Give those local communities *veto power* over the final decision. Potential communities could just say "No," even though Finland would be in trouble if all the potential host communities refused.

The process truly shared decision-making power with local residents. It built trust in the government. It was far different from the process by which the U.S. Congress and Department of Energy chose Yucca Mountain in Nevada as a possible high-level nuclear waste repository nearly 40 years ago, a choice that was essentially imposed on the local community by federal officials. Opposition to the facility had been relatively low-key up to that point, but when the choice of Yucca Mountain was made, opposition grew significantly. Now, decades and several billion dollars later, the facility has been abandoned by the Obama administration because of that opposition. In Finland, in part because of the process by which site selection was done, two communities actually ended up competing to host the site, trusting the site-selection process in which they had a significant voice.

The way we respond to risk is far too complex a process to say which factors matter most. But it is safe to say that some factors matter more than others. I start with Trust because it plays such a key role in how we view the world, and it has so much to do with why we're more afraid of some things than others. Now, let's move on to another important Risk Perception Factor, the issue of trade-offs between the Risks and the Benefits.

RISK PERCEPTION FACTOR 2: RISK VERSUS BENEFIT

My wife and kids say I play the lottery too much. I know they're right. Still, every once in a while I'll buy a scratch ticket or lay down a few dollars on the Megabucks, hoping to win. Hope. That's all I'm buying, of course, because I'm pretty sure that I'm tossing my money away. Still, as I hand over my cash in exchange for what in a few moments will be a worthless piece of paper or cardboard, at that moment the benefit of the hope outweighs the risk of the loss. Then I lose, and I sheepishly admit to my wife and kids that they're right.

Humans are intuitive economists. We weigh the value of trade-offs all the time, sometimes consciously, but a lot of the time sub-consciously: trade-offs about money, about how to spend time, or how to accomplish some task; trade-offs between the risks and benefits of a given choice or between one risk and another. Un-like classical economists, however, we don't weigh these choices in strictly quantitative, dollar-based terms. You may compare the price of one possible car purchase against another, or the miles per gallon that each car gets, or the resale value, but when it comes time to choose which car to actually buy, you will also have thought about which car looks better, which one handles better, and which one announces, "The person driving this car has an environmental conscience" or "The person driving this car has *made it*!" If in the end the car you like costs more and gets lower fuel economy, you'll figure out some way of convincing yourself that those other factors didn't matter as much as you thought they did when you started your comparison shopping. So values other than money help us subconsciously calculate the pros and cons of various options and play a big role in the choice we ultimately make.

It's the same with risk. We intuitively weigh the trade-offs between risks and benefits, and we often play down the risk in order to enjoy the benefit, sometimes in ways that create dangerous Perception Gaps. We dramatically increase the risk of killing ourselves, or somebody else, for the benefit of that one last drink before we leave the party. We take on the risk of dangerous jobs for the benefit of higher pay. We risk contributing to global warming for the benefit of those few extra degrees of indoor heating in the winter or air-conditioning in the summer. When we use our mobile phones while we're driving, we risk injury and death for the benefit of staying connected. These aren't conscious quantitative analyses. They are below-the-radar judgments that compare qualitative risks and benefits. And whenever a choice involves both risk and benefit, the greater the benefit, the more we play down the risk in our mind. The smaller the benefit, the greater the risk is likely to seem.

Consider the drug Tysabri. When it was approved in 2004, it was considered the breakthrough drug for treatment of multiple sclerosis (MS). But in February 2005, when its manufacturers, Biogen and Elan, discovered two cases of a rare brain disease among the thousands of users of the drug, a side effect that had not shown up in premarket testing, they pulled Tysabri from the market.

The clamor from patients to get it back started immediately. When the FDA held hearings a year later about whether to reapprove the drug, it had to take the unprecedented step of extending the hearings an extra day to let all the people testify who begged to have access to the benefits of this medicine, fully aware of and willing to accept its risks.

As mentioned, Risk Perception Factors work both ways. The same factor can make us either less afraid or more. The Risk versus

Benefit factor is no exception. The greater the perceived benefit, the smaller the risk will seem. But if there is little perceived benefit, the associated risk will feel bigger:

- Consider proposed waste disposal facilities, which often meet fierce resistance. People in many areas don't want a trash dump or an incinerator anywhere near them. So their waste is trucked several states away, usually to poorer communities that see the trade-off differently and accept the facility, willingly reaping the tax revenue from literally being dumped on.

- Consider different international views of nuclear energy. In Austria, resistance is fierce, all about the dangers. But in neighboring Hungary, nuclear energy is seen as producing benefits for economic growth, energy independence, and lower carbon emissions, and it has much wider public and government support.

- Consider spraying pesticides to kill mosquitoes. There are several communities in my state of Massachusetts that oppose such spraying until the first case of eastern equine encephalitis shows up in late summer. "Triple E," as it is called, is a regional disease that is worse for horses than for humans, but it kills a person or two every few summers, often children. When Triple E shows up, resistance to spraying goes down because the fear of Triple E is so great that the risk/benefit trade-off of spraying has changed.

In many cases, these risk/benefit trade-off decisions make sense. When there is no Triple E around, even though the risk of spraying to forestall an outbreak is low, why take it, when there is no immediate benefit? That's perfectly logical. In places with malaria, the benefit of DDT, the most effective pesticide against the mosquito that spreads the disease, outweighs the risk of using a chemical that some think may harm human health. The trade-off to spray makes sense. In places without malaria, it doesn't.

But sometimes the risk/benefit trade-offs we make do not appear to make much sense. Consider the person who adds to his or her blood alcohol level before getting behind the wheel of a motor vehicle. Or the person who is 100 pounds overweight who mentally plays down the risk of heart disease for the benefit of that second juicy Whammo Awesome Mega Burger. The point is not to judge, but merely to observe that how we perceive risk is more than just a matter of the statistical or scientific facts about drunk driving or DDT or obesity. It's a matter of perspective, and that perspective is powerfully informed by how we compare the risks versus the benefits.

The Risk versus Benefit perception factor plays a huge role in the personal decisions we make and the decisions we make together as a society. And it plays a huge role in the Perception Gap because, at our peril, this kind of Affective risk response doesn't fully consider all the trade-offs. Mostly we want what we want, driven by really basic needs and desires that are often rooted deep in our genetic imperative to survive, and we do the risk/benefit mental gymnastics necessary to get it. The fundamental drive to nourish ourselves is a big part of why we want that extra-large serving of ice cream, or that large order of fries, or that large steak, so we ignore how eating poorly raises the risk of obesity and heart disease/diabetes/stroke/various forms of dietary-related cancer. To be attractive (and increase our chance of mating), we want that glowing, healthy tan, and we ignore the damage that too much sun does to our skin, from aging and wrinkles and damage to our immune system to disfigurement and fatal skin cancer. We want all the protections and comforts of modern living, and we ignore at the peril of our very species the unsustainable demands we are putting on the limited biological system on which we depend. And to survive, we want protection from the things that threaten us, like terrorists or hazardous waste, so we don't think about how the billions of dollars spent on those relatively lower risks could save a lot more lives and protect a lot more human and environmental health if society spent that money on relatively larger threats.

So if there is a benefit, we play down any associated risk in order to get it. If there is a risk, we play down potential benefits in order to protect ourselves. Again, this is not to judge, but to observe an important Risk Perception Factor and how it contributes to our Affective Risk Response in ways that feel right, but that sometimes lead to choices and behaviors that can actually increase our risk.

Here's another one. If you think you can do something to protect yourself from a risk, you will be less afraid. If you don't think you can do anything to keep yourself safe, no matter how small the actual risk, your fear will be greater.

RISK PERCEPTION FACTOR 3: CONTROL

Perhaps you've had the experience where you've been driving for several hours and you suddenly wake up and realize, steering wheel in your hand, that you don't remember the last few seconds because the trees you were driving past were more awake than you were. So you say to your partner over in the passenger seat, whom you know to be a reliable driver, "Hey, I've gotta sleep. Let's switch."

You pull over, go around and get in the passenger seat, and suddenly you're not so sleepy. Those brake lights on the car ahead of you seem closer than they did when your foot was near the brake pedal. Suddenly those huge trucks in the next lane look closer and bigger than they did when you had the wheel in your hand. Your amygdala is wide awake, signaling your senses to be more alert. You are no longer in control of what's happening, so you are more afraid.

Remember when the U.S. government suggested that one way of preparing for a possible biological or chemical terrorist attack was to have plastic and duct tape available to seal off a room for a few hours? And everybody laughed? Well, not everybody. Stores ran out of the stuff. Millions of people bought it. One fellow interviewed on TV looked sheepish as he walked out of Home Depot, his arms loaded with rolls of plastic, and said, "I know it seems stupid, but at least it gives me the feeling that there's something I can do." A person in Connecticut enclosed his entire house in plastic and duct tape. No word on whether he suffocated by "taking control." Desire for control is why, when anthrax spores were sent through the U.S. mail in late 2001, people went out and bought gas masks, even though the spores are too small to see (unless you get an envelope full of them), so by the time you know you need to put your mask on, it's too late.

Desire for control helps explain why, when H1N1 "swine" flu broke out in the spring of 2008, people in affected countries rushed to buy face masks long before the disease was widespread. Desire for control helps explain why demand for both H1N1 and "regular" flu vaccine was so high in late 2009, even though the "regular" flu season wasn't at all unusual. Back in 2004, when production of influenza vaccine ran into trouble and supplies to the United States were cut in half, people waited in line for hours to be vaccinated at clinics and drugstores before the supplies ran out. The *New York Times* reported that an elderly woman fainted after standing in line for so long, hit her head on the ground, and died. Some people traveled to other countries where the supplies were better. Doctors' offices had trouble attending to patients because they were swamped by demands for flu shots. But was it really the vaccine itself that people wanted, or a sense of control?

Normally, when flu vaccine is plentiful and demand is low, the public health challenge is to get *more* people vaccinated. Why? In part, because the availability of the vaccine gives people a sense of control. We know that if the flu season starts to look bad, we can always go get vaccinated. But in 2004, headlines in early October announced that there might not be enough for everybody, and suddenly we no longer had the same sense of control over the risk from influenza. Mind you, there was no evidence that the flu season was going to be bad and no sign of some new pandemic strain of flu, like bird flu or swine flu, that could actually pose an out-of-the-ordinary risk. All we had was the out-of-the-ordinary possibility that we might lose an important way to keep ourselves safe. Doctors reported patients pleading for vaccine, saying that they "felt helpless."

If you doubt the emotional importance of control here, consider this: the U.S. government scrambled and came up with more vaccine, so in the end, there was only a temporary shortage. When the news media reported that supplies would be adequate, demand dropped right back to the low levels of normal years, and by the end of that flu season, the *Boston Globe* reported that up to 4 million doses of flu vaccine had gone unused and had to be thrown out. People's sense of control went up and their worries went down.

The evidence that Control is a powerful Risk Perception Factor, rooted deep in the human animal, is emphatically supported by evidence of the permanent psychological damage people suffer when they experience acute fear and stress. Many studies find that people who have a sense of control *during* a traumatic experience are less likely to develop post-traumatic stress disorder (PTSD), or develop less serious PTSD symptoms.[8] People traumatized by flooding who said that they had no sense of control during the event were more depressed afterward than people who were similarly traumatized but said they felt some sense of control while they were afraid.[9] The more psychotherapy for earthquake survivors gives them a sense of control over their lives, the more successfully those survivors recover from their PTSD.[10]

And there's plenty of evidence that this powerful Risk Perception Factor can contribute to a dangerous Perception Gap. Desire for the safe feeling of control is why people in the Washington, D.C., metropolitan area drove miles out of their way to avoid a location where the sniper had shot somebody the day before, raising their risk of an accident with each extra mile driven. In the weeks after the September 11 attacks, and again 10 months later around the July 4 holiday weekend, the number of people buying guns accelerated. I have nothing against guns, but it's safe to say that guns purchased to provide a sense of control against the danger of terrorist attack are more likely to hurt someone in an accident than to protect the gun owners from a terrorist. Al Qaeda is probably not coming to their house.

Or we buy hands-free devices for our cell phones so we can keep both hands on the wheel while we drive and chat, because that gives us at least the *belief* that we have more control (as if we ever keep both hands on the wheel anyway). And our fear goes down. Only, the risk doesn't. The danger created by talking on a mobile phone while you're driving has practically nothing to do with your hands. It's the mental distraction, and that's just as bad whether you have one or both hands on the wheel. But with that cool *Star Trek*–looking device in your ear, you have a feeling of control, and you think you're safer, so you take fewer precautions, and your actual risk is either the same, or perhaps even higher. Consider, then, the public health implications of the way a sense of control has skewed our view of the actual risk in several U.S. states and more than 50 countries around the world that have adopted laws banning the use of handheld cell phones by drivers, but permitting them to drive mentally distracted, as long as their hands are free.

Control. The more we think we have, the safer we feel. The less we think we have, the greater our fear. But sometimes our fears are based not so much on how much we think we can influence events as they occur. Sometimes it's a matter of whether we've chosen to take the risk in the first place.

RISK PERCEPTION FACTOR 4: CHOICE

As long as we're using the example of cell phones and driving, let's talk about the Risk Perception Factor of Choice. The issue here is not whether you feel safer because you can control what's actually happening. It's whether the risk is something you've chosen to do in the first place or whether you are at risk because of the actions or decisions of others. Maybe you have had this experience: you're driving along on the highway, talking on your cell phone. Let's say it's a hands-free device. Several factors have led you to play down the risk in your mind. There's the protective glow of Optimism Bias—it won't happen to me. There is the benefit you are getting from being able to talk to someone when you want to. And there is a sense of control because you have the wheel in both hands.

Suddenly you notice that the car in the lane next to you is weaving closer and closer, then back in its lane, then closer again. And it's speeding up and slowing down, speeding up and slowing down. And you look at the driver, and he is holding a cell phone to his ear, gabbing away. That selfish b_____rd! Putting *you* at risk! Man, you think, they ought to ban cell phones and driving! But are you hoping the government bans *yours?* Or *his?* Statistically, the risk of injuring yourself by using a cell phone while you drive is four times higher than the risk of being injured by someone else doing it. But that doesn't matter much. The feeling of risk here does not come from what you have chosen to do yourself. It comes from the risk that the other driver is imposing on you. The involuntary nature of the risk makes it feel more threatening than the same risk if you have taken it by choice.

What's Your Risk Response?

You know those long brochures in tiny print that come in over-the-counter medicines, with all the details about possible side effects? Do you ever read them? Most people don't. But suppose drug companies proposed getting rid of those informational inserts because they waste paper and ink and money and energy, and besides, nobody ever reads them anyway. How would you feel about that?

Most people I ask say they want that informational brochure, and when I ask them why, they say they want it because it gives them the information they need in order to understand and consider the risks and benefits of the product. They can decide for themselves whether to take it, or how to take it. Never mind that most people who feel this way never read the label. Just the fact that it's available gives them the feeling of choice, which reduces their sense of risk because the actions they take will be of their own accord.

Not long ago, the U.S. government announced that it was safe to eat meat and milk from cloned animals. The Consumer Federation of America (CFA) came out against it. But if you look at the basis for the CFA's concern, it wasn't about the cloned meat and milk products themselves. The CFA just opposed selling those products without labels. Its official statement said, "Putting cloned milk and meat on the market with no identifying label information eliminates the option to avoid the products." "The option." The risk concerned them because of a lack of choice.

Remember, Risk Perception Factors can make fear go up or down. The more involuntary a risk feels, the more worrisome it is likely to be. But if we *do* have a choice, we are willing to jump off bridges head first with only a thick rubber cord around our legs, or chat on the phone while we drive, or even host a high-level nuclear waste dump in our community.

Remember the example of the siting of a nuclear waste facility in Finland? The communities that were selected as scientifically feasible all had veto power. The choice was theirs. Most said no, but two were interested in learning more about the risks and the benefits, and in the end, those two communities competed to host a facility that would permanently store some of the most dangerous material known to humans.

The community of Eurajoki won. Two reactors had been operating there for decades. That surely contributed to the acceptance of the facility, along with the proposed tax benefits and all those new good-paying, long-term jobs. The Finns trust their government and are strongly pro-nuclear, which also helped. But choice had a lot to do with the perception of the risk too. Being able to say, "Yes, we want it" made a huge difference, compared with the people near Yucca Mountain, Nevada, whose resistance to the U.S. government's proposed nuclear waste storage facility dramatically increased when Congress narrowed the list of candidate sites to one, Yucca Mountain, and the risk was imposed on them.

Imposed risk is often a big factor in opposition to the siting of controversial facilities. In a Boston suburb a few years ago, some members of a church fought the placement of a cell phone tower in the steeple of the church. They opposed it on the grounds that radiation from the tower would be dangerous to churchgoers. That fear was not supported by the scientific evidence, which pretty conclusively shows that radiation from cell phone towers isn't powerful enough to cause harm to anyone on the ground, even right at the base of the tower. The concerned members of the congregation argued against it because there was a day-care center in the church, so they thought the radiation could threaten children, also not true, according to what experts say about radiation from cell phone towers. But when the opponents were asked what upset them the most, it was the fact that they hadn't been given a say in the decision to put the tower in the steeple in the first place. The agreement had been made by church leaders without any input from the church-goers, some of whom then rose up in opposition.

So church leaders scrapped the deal with the mobile phone company. They held a series of meetings with churchgoers to get their thoughts on whether to proceed. And after those meetings, the churchgoers somehow saw things differently. Instead of worrying about the radiation, now they were pleased about the tens of thousands of dollars the mobile phone company would pay to rent the steeple. Of course, they had known about that income before, back when they opposed building the tower, but the benefits now outweighed the risks because now they had a say in whether the tower would go in. Now the risk was voluntary, a matter of choice. So their perspectives changed, and what was unacceptable, with a risk that outweighed the benefits, was now acceptable, with benefits that outweighed the risks.

It's amazing how these Risk Perception Factors work, isn't it?

RISK PERCEPTION FACTOR 5: IS THE RISK NATURAL OR HUMAN-MADE?

West Nile virus was starting to show up in a California community, and a debate arose over what to do. One of the options was to spray an insecticide that kills mosquito larvae, which reduces the spread of the disease. The idea of spraying caused controversy, but in the end, the question wasn't whether to spray, but what spray to use.

The choices were between a natural insecticide that had a slightly higher toxicity to humans, or a synthetic product with a slightly lower toxicity. (In either case, the risk to people was extraordinarily low.) The community chose the natural one, even though that product was slightly more dangerous. People felt more comfortable using something natural.

Anybody who's gotten poison ivy or food poisoning, or who has seen those shows where lions and hyenas kill and eat their prey, knows that sometimes nature is not nice. But when it comes to the judgments we make about risk, a natural threat is generally less worrisome than one that's human-made. Consider the laws in many countries governing medicines. The development, testing, sale, and advertising of pharmaceuticals are tightly controlled. These are human-made biologically active substances, and we want them kept safe. But if you wanted to, you could grab a handful of leaves from any bush, grind them into a powder, put it in a jar with a nice New Age–looking label, call it Leaves of Love—Nature's Libido Enhancer, and sell it tomorrow in natural product stores and natural food stores (and possibly a few porn shops). There are far fewer controls on natural and herbal remedies than there are on human-made drugs, although both are bioactive and most of the human-made drugs are only manufactured versions of some natural substance to begin with. Why haven't we demanded the same controls on herbal and natural drugs? In large measure, it's because we just don't worry as much about risks from natural sources as we do about risks that are human-made. And that can cause a dangerous Perception Gap.

A 1994 study of Ayurvedic herbal medicines found that one sample in five purchased from local stores in Boston contained enough lead, mercury, or arsenic that somebody using the medicine as directed would get a higher dose than U.S. safety standards deemed safe. And not just a little higher. Some of these natural products, used as directed, would expose a user to 10,000 times as much of these toxic heavy metals as federal rules allow.[11] (Why didn't environmentalists scream and yell about that as much as they do about much lower levels of mercury in seafood? Maybe because the product was sold in *natural* food stores?)

There are numerous cases around the world in which natural and herbal remedies have caused all sorts of health problems (as well as terrific benefits, of course). In 2008, the British Medicines and Healthcare Products Regulatory Agency (MHRA) put out a blanket warning cautioning the U.K. public about using unregulated herbal medicines, citing problems with contaminated products, mislabeled products, and just plain dangerous but untested products. "The problem," the agency said, "is that consumers have to guess whether these *unlicensed* products contain the ingredients that are declared, and have reliable information about their use." Because we are less afraid of natural risks, we have not pushed for regulation of these substances, and we are at greater risk as a result.

This Risk Perception Factor plays a key role in a large number of environmental risk controversies. Lots of plants contain known carcinogens or toxins at much higher levels than the pesticides the plants are sprayed with, but we worry about the pesticides. Soybeans are really high in estrogen, and too much of that hormone can raise the risk of breast cancer and birth defects, but many people are much more worried about human-made chemicals in the environment that have the same effect. Or consider genetically modified food.

It scares a lot of people. It's the process of cutting and splicing single genes from one organism into another to produce food with beneficial properties—taste, shelf life, or resistance to pests. We used to do this the old-fashioned Gregor Mendel way. We'd mix all the natural genetic material from different species and see what we ended up with. If we came up with a redder tomato or a plumper chicken, we'd breed that one. Lord only knows what *else* had changed inside the tomato or the chicken and how those traits could spread to other organisms, but no matter. It was done the natural way.

Genetic engineering replaces that shotgun approach with the precision of scientifically changing only one gene. We know precisely what trait is supposed to show up in the new plant or animal, and we can test the new organism to see if it produces allergies or environmental damage or other hazards. Yes, those traits could spread to other plants and animals, but so could the new traits of organisms that we hybridized the old way—the natural way. The real problem for some people is that genetically modified organisms are human-made—from the lab, not the farm. On the Greenpeace Web site under "What's Wrong with Genetic Engineering," the very first thing mentioned is, "Genetic engineering enables scientists to create plants, animals and micro-organisms by manipulating genes in a way that *does not occur naturally*" (my emphasis).

Again, I'm not arguing for or against genetically modified food, or saying that you should or shouldn't be afraid of pesticides or not eat soybeans. These are just interesting examples of risks where the Natural or Human-Made factor plays a big role in our Affective perceptions.

Here is another one. Are you worried about radiation from cell phones or cell phone towers or microwave ovens or power lines or nuclear power plants? Some people are. Yet many of these same people don't protect their skin from the sun when they spend more than half an hour outside. That's a radiation risk, and a much greater threat than all those other ones. But the sun is natural, so the risk from solar radiation doesn't scare people the same way human-made radiation does.

Or how about radon, a naturally occurring radioactive gas formed from the breakdown of uranium in rocks and soil. It seeps up into our homes and has been called the second leading cause of lung cancer in the United States, after cigarette smoke. A 1997 Public Broadcasting System documentary about nuclear power included an interview with a woman, Linda, who lived near the Three Mile Island nuclear power plant in Pennsylvania. She believed the accident at the plant in 1979 had released radiation and caused cancer in her neighborhood, although all the scientific evidence showed that this wasn't the case. Linda continued to monitor cancer deaths in her neighborhood nearly two decades after the accident.

It turns out that this region is known geologically as the Reading Prong, a formation of underground rock particularly rich in uranium, which produces radon. So Linda has Three Mile Island in the neighborhood and monitors radiation from the plant. But listen to what she says about whether she has had her house tested for radon. In particular, listen to *why*.

"I have not had my house tested for radon. And perhaps I will someday. But I don't look at it as . . . it's not a, it's not a manmade thing. Radon is part of . . . it seeps in through . . . it's in the dirt. It seeps into our homes. And we've been building homes for many, many, many, many, years. Am I . . . you know . . . where's my thinking wrong here?"

Linda is a clear example of what this chapter and this whole book are about. The facts are pretty clear. She ought to have her home tested for radon. But she is suffering a potentially dangerous Perception Gap because of her Affective Risk Response, in this case because she is less afraid of risks that are natural and more afraid of risks that are human-made. Like we all are.

RISK PERCEPTION FACTOR 6: PAIN AND SUFFERING

 What's Your Risk Response?

Let's say that you are going to die tomorrow. That's the bad news. The good news is, you get to decide how. You will be given three choices, one at a time.

1. Presuming that you have to die tomorrow, and that you can die either *being eaten alive by a shark or from*

heart disease, which way do you choose to go?

Most people facing that choice vote for heart disease. A few vote for death by shark attack. When asked why, they say something like, "It will be quicker." One journalist who voted for death by shark explained, "At least my obituary would be on the front page."

2. Presuming that you have to die tomorrow, and that you can die either *burning alive in a fire or from heart disease,* which way do you choose to go?

Nobody ever votes for burning alive.

3. Presuming that you have to die tomorrow, and that you can die *either of cancer or from heart disease,* which way do you choose to go?

The overwhelming majority of people to whom I pose this choice vote for death by heart disease rather than cancer.

Statistically, these answers don't make sense. The much greater risk in all three cases is heart disease. In the United States, roughly 20 percent more people die of heart disease than of cancer each year. Worldwide, cardiovascular diseases kill twice as many people as cancer. Shouldn't you be more afraid of what is more likely to kill you? But the questions weren't framed in terms of likelihood. All three are framed to get you to think about the affective *nature* of the death, and the greater the Pain and Suffering, the greater the fear. This is why some people vote for death being eaten alive by a shark. "Quicker" means less Pain and Suffering. (The journalist was probably thinking about Risk versus Benefit when he voted for dying in an awful way so his obituary would make Page One.)

Remember Susan Napolitano, from the Introduction, the overweight smoker worried about nondangerous levels of chemicals in the air in her daughter's school? What was she really worried about? She was worried that chemicals *"could give our children cancer!"* And Linda, the woman worried about Three Mile Island? What was she really worried about? She was monitoring local deaths caused by cancer. It would be easy to dismiss Susan and Linda as irrational, emotional, and wrong. But that would ignore the psychological research, and overwhelming evidence from the daily headlines, that risks that cause cancer or other harms that are perceived to be particularly painful are simply more frightening than risks that may be more likely but involve less Pain and Suffering.

Why do shark attack stories make headlines in landlocked Nebraska? Pain and Suffering.

Why does the United States spend billions more on cancer research than on researching heart disease, a bigger threat? To some degree, because of Pain and Suffering.

Why do so many people so deeply fear nuclear waste when it can be safely transported and stored; it can't harm you unless you're right next to it or you ingest or inhale it; and we know from studies of survivors of exposure to high levels of radiation in Hiroshima and Nagasaki that nuclear radiation is indeed a carcinogen, but it's not a very strong one—of 100,000 survivors, approximately 600 have died of cancer from the radiation from atomic bomb explosions. Those facts don't matter. Radiation causes cancer, and that involves increased Pain and Suffering.

The flip side of the Pain and Suffering Risk Perception Factor is that it leaves us *less* afraid of some really major threats that harm us, but in relatively less painful ways. We've talked about heart disease. How about chronic obstructive pulmonary diseases, like bronchitis and emphysema and asthma, the fourth leading cause of death in the United States per year? Does bronchitis sound like it involves as much Pain and Suffering as cancer? Not to many people.

How about something as mundane-sounding as the risk of death from just plain falling down? Every year, 17,000 people in the United States, 11,000 of whom are elderly, die from falls. Falls are a more common cause of death than murder. But the threat of "falling down to death" doesn't exactly conjure up images of a particularly painful way to go. So we don't hear much about this risk, and we don't take the easy precautions (steadier footwear, firmer flooring, better lighting, more handrails) that could make us safer.

How about the flu? Have you ever had a really bad case of influenza? I hope you never do. Talk about suffering! But influenza does not evoke dreadful images the way cancer or dying in a plane crash do, so the fact that 36,000 people in the United States die from influenza each year—twice as many as are murdered—doesn't evoke as much concern.

The numbers say that it should. The numbers say that we should worry more about accidents and chronic obstructive pulmonary diseases and heart disease. But numbers talk to the rational cortex. The degree of Pain and Suffering talks to the overall Affective nature of our Risk Response and contributes significantly to the Perception Gap, which is a risk in and of itself.

RISK PERCEPTION FACTOR 7: UNCERTAINTY

On March 30, 1979, Walter Cronkite, anchor of the *CBS Evening News,* opened the evening newscast this way: "Good evening. The world has never known a day quite like today. It faced the considerable uncertainties, and dangers, of the worst nuclear power plant accident of the atomic age."

He was reporting on the accident at the Three Mile Island nuclear plant. A combination of equipment failure, poor design, and human error damaged the nuclear reactor at the plant, threatening to release dangerous amounts of radiation into the environment.

The interesting thing about Cronkite's lead is that the first worry he mentions is "considerable uncertainties." Only after that does he mention "dangers."

The more uncertain we are, the more afraid we are likely to be. The two go hand in glove at the most basic biological level of the Risk Response. fMRI tests have shown that when we are exposed to something that might be a threat, the less certain we are, the more active our amygdala becomes, apparently getting busier as it tries to make sense of whether we are in danger.[12] The amygdalas of the people near Three Mile Island must have been going nuts. Public statements from the operators of Three Mile Island, the Pennsylvania state governor, and federal nuclear oversight authorities were confusing and contradictory, and made it pretty obvious that these officials didn't know what was going on. At first they said an evacuation would be necessary. Then they said it wouldn't. Then state officials suggested evacuation just as a precaution for a few thousand pregnant women and families with infants living within five miles of the plant. Ultimately, 140,000 people fled.

There was confusion between various official statements about whether radiation had been released and confusion about what might happen next. There was even confusion about who was in charge. And how did all that confusion and uncertainty make people feel? A local priest offered blanket absolution to people living in the area, something done for people facing death. As a senior Nuclear Regulatory Commission official put it later, "What we had done to these people was just outrageous. We had frightened them so bad, they thought they were going to die."

You don't have to have experienced Three Mile Island to understand the power of Uncertainty as a Risk Perception Factor. Imagine that you're driving on a highway. The day is dry and sunny. Traffic is light. Now imagine closing your eyes. Keep them closed as you drive ahead at 65 miles an hour. Keep driving, farther, farther, eyes closed. How does that feel? Frightening, of course. (Your amygdala may be lighting up just imagining this!)

Why does it feel frightening to drive with your eyes closed? Because you don't have the information you need in order to protect yourself. Your hands are still on the steering wheel, but your *brain* doesn't have as much control because it doesn't know what it needs to know to keep you safe. Closing your eyes increases uncertainty, and your Risk Response shifts from the rational fact-based part of the system to the part that relies more on emotion and instinct to keep you safe.

Uncertainty contributed significantly to people's fears of the metropolitan Washington, D.C., sniper. I have a relative who lives in the area where many of the shootings occurred. He described his feelings this way: "It's scary because there are no clues. It could be one guy. It could be more than one. It could be terrorists. It could be a psycho. There are composite descriptions of two trucks, not just one. Talk about uncertainty. It could be a former military guy. White, black, young, old, male, female. This could be anybody, anywhere, at any time. We just don't know what's going to happen next." It was like driving with your eyes closed.

Uncertainty is a big part of why many women worried for years about hormone replacement therapy for treatment of menopausal symptoms. One study said one thing. Another study said something else, sometimes in conflict with what previous studies had said. For women who were trying to thoughtfully decide what to do, it was like driving blind.

Uncertainty plays a big role in fears of many modern risks. What do the following hazards have in common?

- Bovine growth hormone in cows to increase milk production
- Radiation from cell phone towers
- Pesticides on food

These hazards share several characteristics. First, for some people, the fear is higher than the actual danger, according to current scientific research. Why? In part because all three are human-made, not natural, and that makes them scarier. They are all risks that are imposed on us, and that makes them scarier. And all three involve uncertainty, which takes a few different forms.

First, there is the form of Uncertainty that I'll call "I can't detect it." Look at the three risks just listed. We can't see, smell, taste, hear, or feel any of them. We can't detect them with our own senses. If you have some reason to believe that there is a hazard around, but you can't detect it (you can't know what you need to know to protect yourself), you're driving blind.

Another form of Uncertainty is "I don't understand it." Scientists have studied those three risks extensively. We know a lot about them. But mostly, "we," you and me, are not scientists. For most of us, it's hard to understand the recombinant DNA gene-splicing techniques for increasing the level of natural bovine growth hormone in cows. It's difficult to grasp the physics of electromagnetic radiation waves, of amplitude and frequency and volts and watts and amperes and whatever it is that comes from cell phone towers. The chemistry and biology and toxicology of pesticides are also complex stuff, hard to understand.

It doesn't matter whether science has the answers if we don't understand them. It's like not having the answers in the first place—driving blind. The less we understand the scientific explanations of risks, the less our cognitive, fact-based, analytical brain system can help, and the more we rely on instinctive Risk Perception Factors to help keep ourselves safe.

The third form of Uncertainty common to many modern risks is "nobody knows." Not you. Not me. Not the scientists. We just don't have the answers yet. Radiation from power lines offers a good example. We know plenty *now* about whether the electric and magnetic fields (EMFs) from power lines cause cancer, a suspicion that arose from a few studies in the 1980s and that exploded when those studies were featured in a series of alarming articles in *The New Yorker* magazine. We know *now,* based on hundreds of studies from around the world, that there is no consistent link between EMFs and cancer. But when the news media sounded the alarm, nobody knew whether those first few studies would be confirmed or contradicted by further investigation. Back then, *we didn't know.* We were *uncertain.* So, like a lot of other people, I got rid of my electric blanket. Now I know that I unnecessarily endured cold toes in bed at night. Now our Uncertainty has been reduced, and so have our fears.

Uncertainty and Precaution

Uncertainty is a huge Risk Perception Factor behind the call for a Precautionary Principle, an institutional, legally binding form of "Better Safe Than Sorry". It's an approach to dealing with modern technological and environmental risks that *might* be dangerous when science doesn't have all the answers yet. Right now, existing products and processes that might be dangerous can only be ordered off the market when there is *conclusive* proof that they're dangerous, a pretty high standard. While we're still not sure, those products stay on the market. The Precautionary Principle would turn that around and say that products and processes that *may* be dangerous have to be proved safe *before* being approved. It's all about how to handle risks when we're not sure.

Consider the language in the various definitions of the Precautionary Principle. (Italics are mine.)

- "When an activity raises threats of harm to human health or the environment, precautionary measures should be taken *even if some cause and effect relationships are not fully established scientifically.*" (Wingspread Conference, 1998.)

- "The precautionary principle applies *where scientific evidence is insufficient, inconclusive or uncertain.*" (European Commission, 2000.)
- "Where there are threats of serious or irreversible damage, *lack of full scientific certainty* shall not be used as a reason for postponing cost-effective measures to prevent environmental degradation." (Rio Conference "Earth Summit," 1992.)

The Precautionary Principle is appealing, but opponents say that, taken to its extreme, we'd have to ban everything until we were absolutely sure it was safe. Progress would come to a halt. Advocates of the Precautionary Principle say that of course it would have to be flexible, and would only be applied when there was plausible evidence that a new product might be dangerous. But how much evidence is enough? When is the evidence plausible? How certain would we have to be about some new substance or process before saying, "Yes, it's safe," or "No, we're not sure enough yet, so we should ban it until we are." The whole debate really pivots around the troublingly affective and not purely scientific/factual nature of uncertainty.

The Precautionary Principle is one way of dealing with the fears, held by many, that these are the most dangerous times humans have ever faced. The Uncertainty factor helps explain why so many people feel that way. Yes, life spans in the developed world have more than doubled in the past 100 years. Yes, we have more abundant food, better medical care, longer life spans, and unprecedented scientific and technological power to meet the major challenges we face. But the benefits of modern life also present a host of risks, many of which are not thoroughly understood. Uncertainty is inherent in progress. It is also inherently a factor that feeds our fears.

RISK PERCEPTION FACTOR 8: CATASTROPHIC OR CHRONIC

Roughly 1,800 people in the United States will die of heart disease today. About 800 will die of heart disease in Argentina, 480 in Germany, 440 in Japan, 300 in England, and approximately 100 in South Africa. Today. And tomorrow. And the day after that, every day, all year.

On March 27, 1977, the deadliest plane crash in history took 583 lives in Tenerife, in the Canary Islands, when two jumbo jets collided on the runway. The death toll from heart disease in the United States reaches that number *every eight hours!*

You don't hear much about the catastrophic worldwide death toll from heart disease, yet you hear all about catastrophes like plane crashes. Why is that? Why is a plane crash, with fewer victims, considered a catastrophe, but the huge death toll from heart disease every day is not? As with everything having to do with risk perception, the numbers are not the whole story. Our Risk Response depends upon the Affective nature of the threat, not just the number of victims. "Catastrophic" has three important qualities that cause us to worry more. The *American Heritage Dictionary* defines *catastrophe* as "A *great,* often *sudden calamity.*" (Emphasis is mine.) A catastrophe has to be big, it has to happen all at once, and something about it has to be calamitous—disastrous—really bad.

A plane crash certainly qualifies. It kills a lot of people all at once, in one place, and in a really horrific way. But heart disease, like most of the major causes of death, meets only one of those criteria. As awful as heart disease and stroke and diabetes are, they don't kill people in such vividly awful ways as plane crashes or mass murders or industrial accidents or tornadoes. And they don't kill a lot of people all at once in one place. They are chronic killers. Their victims are spread out over space and time. Those 1,800 daily heart disease victims in the United States die here and there across the country, not in one specific location, like the foggy runway in Tenerife where 583 people died all at once in a horrible crash and fire.

Chernobyl certainly qualifies as a catastrophe. As mentioned earlier, 56 people died from acute radiation exposure in the immediate weeks after the explosion and fire at Chernobyl, and hundreds of thousands of people were exposed to harmful levels of radiation. World Health Organization officials estimate that the lifetime cancer death toll from that radiation could be as many as 4,000. Compare that to the risk of skin cancer caused by radiation from the sun. Approximately 8,000 people in the United States die *each year* from skin cancer—usually melanoma—caused by exposure to solar radiation. The sun is a *much* bigger risk than radiation from the worst nuclear power plant accident. But deaths from solar radiation will be spread out over space and time, so they don't fit the meaning of catastrophe. (And they're natural, and they result from a risk that we take voluntarily, which also makes solar radiation less scary.)

Here is another example. Consider the difference between murder, mass murder, and massacre. All three are violent deaths caused by others, but we hear much more about the second two, the ones with *mass* in their name, even though of the three, murder results in by far the most deaths. A World Health Organization study reported that in 2000, about 500,000 people were murdered worldwide. Each day, 90 people are murdered in Colombia, 40 in the United States, 6 just in the city of Cape Town, South Africa, and 2 in Moscow.

But the *American Heritage Dictionary*'s definition of *murder,* "The unlawful killing of *one* human by another," is missing two of the three characteristics of catastrophe: large scale and something that makes the death particularly awful. The risk of murder is chronic, not catastrophic.

Mass murder, on the other hand—"The act of murdering a *large number* of people, typically *at the same time* or over a relatively short period of time" (Wikipedia)—has two of the three characteristics of catastrophe: large scale and short time frame in a single location. So when Tomohiro Kato stabbed seven people to death in Tokyo in June 2008, or when freshman Seung-Hui Cho slaughtered 32 Virginia Tech students in April 2007, or when Bruce Pardo dressed as Santa Claus at a Christmas party in Los Angeles in 2008 and shot seven family members to death, then set their house on fire, the world heard about it instantly, via nearly every news media outlet.

Or consider massacres, the definition of which—"The act or an *instance* of killing a *large number* of humans indiscriminately and *cruelly*"—contains all three elements of catastrophe: large scale, short time frame and single location, and the murder of people who can't defend themselves, which makes such killings particularly cruel and awful. These events upset us so much that they become infamous. Srebrenica, 1995—8,000 defenseless Bosnian males slaughtered by the Serbian military. Sabra and Shatilla—3,500 Palestinian refugees slaughtered in 1982 by Lebanese militias after the Israeli army surrounded the refugee camps, let the militias in, and allowed them to do their killing. My Lai—U.S. military forces slaughtered 504 Vietnamese civilians from 1 to 81 years old.

And yet the daily civilian death toll from combat in Vietnam during the war was 218. So more Vietnamese *civilians* were killed in 2½ days than died at My Lai. And on the day before Christmas 2008, when Bruce Pardo killed seven family members in Los Angeles, five times that many people were murdered in the United States.

What is it about large-scale loss of life in one place at one time that makes such risks particularly frightening to people all over the world? The sobering list of mass murders and massacres offers one possible explanation. If you look not at how many victims there were, but at *who* they were, victims of mass murders and massacres are often members of one distinct tribe: a community, a religion, or some distinct social group. Blacks. Jews. Muslims. Irish. Native

Americans. Darfuris. Chinese protesters. Students. Family members. Even organized crime gang members (the St. Valentine's Day *massacre* of seven mobsters in 1929). The victims shared some kind of unique social identity.

So? Well, such a Risk Response makes sense in the context of evolutionary psychology. Humans are social animals. We aren't loners. We have always depended on the societies to which we belong for our very survival. When the lion attacks, if everyone is working together, we can fight it off. Alone, we'd each be lion chow. So the better our tribe is doing and the more secure we are as a member of our tribe, the better our personal chances. In that context, it's not hard to understand why, when several members of our tribe are killed all at once, each individual member of the tribe feels threatened.

So when the floodwaters of the Pacific tsunami in 2004 killed more than 500 Swedes, the Swedish media (indeed, the media throughout Caucasian Western Europe) understandably paid much more attention than when 146,000 Asians died in Myanmar from flooding caused by Cyclone Nargis in 2008. That was a different tribe. Americans were probably more worried about the risk of earthquake after the 1989 Loma Prieta quake in San Francisco killed 63 Americans than they were a year later after the earthquake in Iran that killed 45,000 Iranians. And the Iranians were no doubt more worried about earthquakes after the one in Manjil-Rudbar than they were after the one that killed 87,000 Pakistanis in Kashmir in 2005, or the one that killed 69,000 Chinese in Sichuan Province in 2008. Those were different tribes. We worry more about catastrophic threats to the communities to which we belong.

But we also worry more about catastrophic loss of life anywhere, even when the catastrophe doesn't seem to affect any of the tribes to which we belong. Why should a plane crash in Brazil frighten a Briton in Brighton? Why should a fire that kills a family of 15 in Philadelphia fuel fear in Florida? Why do catastrophic risks feel more threatening than chronic ones even if they happen to people in *other* tribes? Well, even if you are not a member of the race, or nationality, or religion, or other unique group that suffered, you still share one tribal membership with the victims. You are a member of the human tribe, and evolutionary psychology would suggest that what threatens the species threatens you too.

That may explain why so many people in so many countries said, "We are all Americans today" (or words to that effect) on September 11, 2001. It may explain why a train crash on the Trans Siberian Railroad that kills 550 people, or a ferry that takes 850 lives when it sinks in the Baltic, or a fire in a nightclub in Rhode Island that kills 100 grabs attention worldwide, while the 550 Russians who die of alcoholism every 10 days, or the 850 Europeans who die in motor vehicle crashes every 2 1/2 days, or the 100 New Englanders who die of cancer every *27 hours* don't. It is possible that the concentrated loss of life in a catastrophe, a concentrated loss of members of the tribe, may trigger instinctive fears in all of us.

RISK PERCEPTION FACTOR 9: CAN IT HAPPEN TO *ME*?

 What's Your Risk Response?

Imagine you are in New York City at the annual meeting of the *Mad Magazine* fan club, and there is a bowl of candy at your table. Each piece is in a little wrapper with a picture of the magazine's figurehead, gap-toothed Alfred E. Neuman, with his silly grin and trademark saying, "What, Me Worry?" You've been snacking away out of the candy bowl all morning. During the coffee break out in the lobby, a newspaper story catches your eye:

Candy Poisoning Threat
A major international candy manufacturer is recalling one million pieces of candy produced last month because a former employee told the company he poisoned one piece as revenge after he was laid off.

How does that feel to you? Are you worried? Probably not. After all, there are a lot of candy manufacturers out there, and one in a million is a pretty low risk. But you keep reading . . .

The company says the candy being recalled was delivered within the past few days to New York City conference venues, and included a specially wrapped candy featuring a picture of *Mad Magazine*'s Alfred E. Neuman saying "What, Me Worry?"

Are you worried now?

Based on the facts, you shouldn't be. The risk is still one in a million. If you took a cab to your conference, you were certainly at greater risk than you are from the candy you ate. If you had breakfast this morning, you are at much greater risk of food poisoning than you are of being killed by that next piece of candy.

But you go back in and take your seat as the conference resumes, and there is the candy bowl with Alfred E. Neuman grinning up at you from those candy wrappers asking, "What, Me Worry?" and despite the one-in-a-million odds, you silently answer to yourself, "Yes, *Me* Worry!"

Any risk feels bigger if you think it could happen to you. If you think that *you* could be the one swimmer out of 4 million in the United States killed by a shark each year, if you think that *you* could be the one person out of every 12 million who gets in a commercial airplane on a nonstop trip and dies in a crash, if you think that *you* could be the one American out of 50 million killed in an elevator accident each year, you could end up avoiding swimming in the ocean, flying, or you might decide to walk up a lot of stairs. The odds are only one part of how we measure risk.

In one way, this makes sense. Your amygdala does not care about the next guy's amygdala. Your job is to worry about *your* survival. If a risk is one in a million, you are less concerned about the survival of the other 999,999 than you are about your own. So if you could be the one, the rest of the ratio doesn't matter as much.

You can see this in the way people respond to risk all the time. Consider SARS (severe acute respiratory syndrome). The first cases were reported in Guangdong, China, in early 2002. Naturally, that's where the fear was most concentrated. The Chinese Army had to help keep civil order in some places. But there was little worry anywhere else.

Then a case showed up in Vietnam and another in Hong Kong and another in Singapore, and the fear spread along with the germ because now people in those places said to themselves, "It can happen to *me!*" Food and animal markets closed. Public events were canceled. International travel to Hong Kong fell to near zero. (I attended a conference there nine months later at which the gift bag to attendees included a thermometer and a personal bottle of antiseptic hand lotion. Most of us used the lotion. Fortunately, nobody needed the thermometer.)

At this point, SARS was getting a lot of alarmist news coverage internationally, but outside Asia, serious concern was radically changing people's behavior only in Asian neighborhoods and shops. Until cases showed up in Toronto in March 2002. Concern there erupted. Stores ran out of medical face masks. International conferences scheduled for Toronto were canceled. The government banned all elective surgery in the entire province of Ontario. A follow-up report found, "Many people with other serious conditions had surgeries cancelled because some hospitals were considered contaminated areas, and some of these people died."[13]

The point is not that SARS was not a serious risk. It was. Quarantines of infected individuals and bans on elective surgery and nonessential travel to affected countries were a response not to fear but to the disease itself. But the fear part of the response was also high. The point is that you can map the Affective Risk Response by mapping the progress of the germ, because only where victims actually showed up did people say to themselves, "It could happen to *me!*"

The same thing happened in the United States with the arrival of a few mosquitoes that hitched an airplane ride from the Middle East, probably Israel, carrying West Nile virus. Indigenous in certain parts of the world, this disease was new in the United States, and that alone made it frightening. (More on the Risk Perception Factor of New versus Familiar coming up.) But the fear was limited to where the cases were: New York City at first, then Connecticut, then New England and the Middle Atlantic states, then the South and Midwest, carried by birds. And in each new community, whenever the first dead bird was found, the headlines blared, "West Nile Virus Is Here!" and people in that community who had heard of the disease in the national news but hadn't worried all that much grew concerned because now they could say, "It could happen to *me.*"

Again, this makes sense. There is no need to worry about a risk when it only threatens somebody else, and real reason to worry when it imperils you. But the fear of West Nile virus was far greater than the actual risk. Most people living in areas where birds are carrying West Nile virus are never infected (by a mosquito that feeds off the bird and then feeds on you), and 80 percent of the people who are infected never show any signs of disease. Their immune system keeps it in check. And of those who do get sick, few get really sick, or die. The likelihood of serious danger from West Nile virus is really low.

But that takes us back to the point that the numbers and probabilities are only part of how we gauge the threats we face. The risk may be one in a million, but if you think you could be the one . . .

The Can It Happen to Me? Risk Perception Factor changed global history on September 11, 2001. Before that, Americans had occasionally been the target of terrorists, and some of these attacks had even occurred on American soil, including the 1993 bombing of the World Trade Center itself. But for the most part, terrorist attacks on Americans had been overseas, in embassies or in nightclubs or on airplanes. Suddenly, on that clear September morning, for 300 million Americans, the risk of terrorism became personal. Now the attacks were taking place here, in the *homeland*, a word that sounds more appropriate to World War II Germany than to any national self-identification ever used in the United States. As President Bush said in his special address to Congress and the country after the attacks, "Our nation has been put on notice: We're not immune from attack." It *can* happen to *us*.

In fact, take the word *homeland* and remove the "ho." You are left with *me*-land. Now the terrorists were *here,* and millions of people thought for the first time, "It could happen to *me!*" And then came the anthrax attacks in October, and everybody with a mailbox suddenly was saying to himself or herself, "It could happen to *me!*"

This was unquestionably the context that allowed the Bush administration to mislead a frightened country about the threat to the United States posed by Saddam Hussein. The administration didn't create the fear; they just used it for their policy ends. We were ready to believe that weapons of mass destruction thousands of miles away might threaten us. We were ready to believe that Saddam Hussein and Al Qaeda were connected. We were ready to believe that starting a war, and relinquishing some civil liberties, and undergoing a massive reorganization of the federal government were justified. Now we thought, "It could happen to *me*," and in large part because of that Risk Perception Factor, at huge cost, America's future, and its relationship with the rest of the world, changed.

RISK PERCEPTION FACTOR 10: IS THE RISK NEW OR FAMILIAR?

Let's talk a little more about the example of West Nile virus. Sometime in 1999, a person or a mosquito or maybe even a smuggled bird got off a plane in New York City that had just flown in from Israel, carrying a microscopic organism that would soon enter the vernacular of fear in North America: West Nile virus.[14] The story of how that fear spread, and then faded, perfectly illustrates how when a risk is new, it's scarier than after we've lived with it for a while.

West Nile virus wasn't entirely new. It had been identified back in the 1930s, and was well known in the Middle East and parts of Europe, where it had affected people for decades. (There is even some suspicion that it killed Alexander the Great.) But nobody in the United States had heard of it, save for a few scientists, because there had never been a case in the United States.

It's important to know a few things about West Nile virus. It is similar to other flulike mosquito-borne diseases like eastern equine encephalitis (Triple E) and St. Louis encephalitis. There are a few cases every year, but not many. Of the people who are exposed to these viruses, most never develop symptoms. Of the few that do, most get flulike symptoms of fever, aches, and respiratory problems similar to a common cold. Only a very few of these people get really sick, and of those, only a small number die. The people who are most susceptible are the very young, the very old, and anyone else with a weakened immune system, as is the case for most infectious diseases. These *Flavaviruses* are essentially the same. And people in the United States had lived with all sorts of them for quite a while.

So there was really only one thing new to North America about West Nile virus—its name. But that was more than enough to trigger a huge Perception Gap between people's concerns and the actual risk, at least at first, when West Nile virus was new. Within a few years, however, when the novelty had faded, so had the excessive concern.

A great way to track this phenomenon is by the attention that West Nile virus got in the media. (I'll be quoting a bunch of headlines and newspaper articles, but the "quotes" are my paraphrases, to preserve the meaning but shorten things a bit.) On September 4, the Saturday of a three-day holiday weekend, a front-page headline in a New York newspaper announced, "Encephalitis Hits 3, 1 Fatally, in Queens." And on September 25, a front-page headline said, "African Virus May Be Cause of Mosquito-Borne Illnesses." The story said, "The mosquito-borne illness . . . may not be St. Louis encephalitis, but a similar disease that has never been diagnosed in the Western Hemisphere."

That story was quite measured about the risk, noting several times that this "new" mosquito-borne virus was similar to more familiar ones. But *"never been diagnosed in the Western Hemisphere"*? Uh-oh!

Two days later, a New York City newspaper front-page headline called the cause of death an "Exotic Virus." Again, the story was measured about the risk, but *"Exotic"*? Uh-oh!

Three days later there was this headline: "Answers about Virus Elusive," and another headline said, "Fears Rise." One story said the disease was similar to other known *Flavaviruses,* but added, "The threat cannot be evaluated because of the *exotic* and *inscrutable* nature of West Nile virus—*never before seen in the Western Hemisphere.*" (Italics are mine.)

There is nothing wrong with these stories journalistically. They only do what the news media do: report what's new. But the stories played up the new, the unfamiliar, the "exotic," "inscrutable," and "never before seen" aspects, and that unquestionably fed people's concerns. Witness this comment by a reader in a New York newspaper: "The West Nile virus outbreak has shocked New Yorkers with the realization that a single mosquito bite can be fatal." Well, no, not really. New Yorkers had lived for a long time in the presence of Triple E and other *Flavaviruses,* potentially fatal diseases spread by mosquitoes. What made this one "shocking" was that it was new.

In a way it makes sense to worry when a risk is new and unfamiliar. Until you've lived with it for a while, when a new risk comes along, the fraction defining the risk looks like this:

$$\frac{1}{?}$$

You are the 1, but you don't know the denominator, so you don't know how big or small the risk may be. That leads to Uncertainty, the factor we talked about a few pages ago. So it's understandable that there was alarming coverage in the news, and lots of fear. Which soon became part of the story. A headline a few weeks into the "panic" declared, "Infectious: Disproportionate Fear." The story talked about pediatricians' offices being swamped by calls from worried parents, local health departments flooded by reports of dead birds, parents in areas where there had not been a single infected mosquito keeping their children indoors, and TV reporters talking dramatically about "the plague among us." The story observed, "This seems understandable. West Nile is *exotic,* so it stirs *fear of the unknown*." The story quoted a senior official at the CDC, who said, "People get frightened by things that are *new and different*."

It didn't take long for a few birds carrying West Nile virus to make their way up the East Coast to Boston, just 189 miles as the crow flies (it probably was a crow that carried the disease). So in 2000, the year after the outbreak in New York, when the first infected birds showed up in Boston, the *Boston Globe* ran 63 stories about West Nile virus, including 4 on July 27, when the first sick bird was found. A front-page story about a dead *bird*, not a person, ran under the headline: "West Nile in Boston. Public Urged to Take Precautions." *Uh-oh!* The *Globe* ran 9 more stories over the next five days. Then a headline read, "State Officials: Stay Calm." Public health officials were being swamped by scared citizens. In just three days, the state Department of Public Health had logged 200 calls about everything from dead herring gulls to cat-mauled finches. It had to hire a courier service to drive around the state collecting dead birds.

More front-page headlines continued to update *Globe* readers on discoveries of dead birds. One day there was even a headline about *no* dead birds: "No New Bird Cases of Virus." After the 63 stories on West Nile virus in 2000, the *Globe* ran 82 in 2001, on dead birds and controversies over government programs to spray pesticides to control mosquito larvae. It was still a high concern. News stories, opinion pieces, and comments from readers all talked about "the fear factor."

There was even more coverage in 2002, but it looked as if the story might be fading. It wasn't new anymore, and, after all, nobody had gotten sick. People didn't seem as concerned. Neither were public health officials. A lot of the West Nile stories were relegated to the back pages of the paper, or included in news summaries under headlines like "Bear Roams Suburban Neighborhood," "Garden Tours," or "Drivers Needed for Elderly Services." On

August 22, the *Globe* ran a story announcing, "Officials Reduce Retrieval of Dead Birds."

But on September 4, the front page of the *Globe*'s second section announced, "Local Woman Has West Nile Virus," and 10 days later, the front page carried the headline "Nile Virus Claims 2 Local Lives." Both victims were in their eighties. This was about dead *people,* not birds. You'd think coverage would erupt again.

But the new had become familiar, and coverage actually subsided. The next year, when the first human case was announced, the *Globe* reported it on page B4, buried inside the second section of the paper. And later that year it ran a story under this headline: "Officials Say West Nile Virus 'Just a Regular Seasonal Risk,'" quoting a local health official as saying, "It's all over the area. It's something we are going to have to live with." West Nile virus was no longer exotic, no longer inscrutable. And we had learned that the risk was low. Now the fraction that had that question mark for the denominator looked more like this:

$$\frac{1}{\text{Millions}}$$

which is a lot less scary. (The actual odds of getting or dying of West Nile virus in Massachusetts as of the end of 2003 were 1 in 113,000 of getting the disease, and 1 in 1.3 million that it would kill you.)

The following table shows the number of stories about West Nile virus in the *New York Times* and the *Boston Globe,* by year, compared with the number of human cases and deaths in New York and Massachusetts, according to the CDC. Note how the number of cases stays reasonably constant and low, as health officials predicted all along, but the story count peaks when the risk is new and then drops off.

	NEW YORK TIMES STORIES ON "WEST NILE"	HUMAN CASES/DEATHS IN NEW YORK	BOSTON GLOBE STORIES ON "WEST NILE"	HUMAN CASES/DEATHS IN MASSACHUSETTS
1999	92 stories	62 cases, 7 deaths	16 stories	No cases or deaths
2000	247 stories	14 cases, 1 death	63 stories	No cases or deaths
2001	134 stories	15 cases, 3 deaths	82 stories	3 cases, no deaths
2002	184 stories	82 cases, 5 deaths	122 stories	24 cases, 3 deaths
2003	138 stories	71 cases, 11 deaths	94 stories	19 cases, 1 death
2004	82 stories	10 cases, no deaths	47 stories	No cases or deaths
2005	52 stories	38 cases, 4 deaths	36 stories	6 cases, 1 death

The same pattern played out in other parts of the country and in Canada as West Nile spread. What had grown familiar in Boston and New York was new in Dallas or Denver or Detroit, and West Nile evoked the same high initial concern and heavy coverage in those places when it first showed up. And just as in New York and Boston, after the first couple years, as West Nile virus became familiar, the concern and the coverage went down. Statistically, the risk was the same, but Affectively, it was no longer as worrisome because it was no longer new.

West Nile virus is just one example of what has happened with many risks in the past, and will almost certainly be a part of how we all respond to most new risks when they arise in the future. A threat that is new and unfamiliar will make us more afraid than we will probably be after we've lived with it for a while.

RISK PERCEPTION FACTOR 11: RISKS TO CHILDREN

The woman caller was frantic, crying, practically screaming into the phone. Her ten-year-old daughter was missing. She had called our newsroom, desperate. We *had* to come do a story *right away*!

Heartbreaking as her fear was, I had to tell her that we got calls like this all the time, and that she should contact the local police. She said she had, and that they were searching, so, as any reporter would, I promised her that I would follow up.

But this was years after the case of Sarah Pryor, the nine-year-old who had disappeared while taking a walk in her quiet suburban Boston neighborhood in 1985. Sarah's disappearance had been the lead story in Boston for days, and reporters always want to work on the biggest story of the day, but I remember that when I was first assigned to it, I asked my bosses not to send me. I had two young kids at the time, and I didn't want to face other parents who were dealing with such trauma. I was sent anyway. It was heart-wrenching to interview Sarah's mother as she begged the public for help in finding her little girl.

But years later, as I talked to this frantic mother on the phone, I was more blasé. There had been dozens of high-profile cases, of which Sarah Pryor was only one, like six-year-old Etan Patz, who disappeared in Manhattan in 1979, or six-year-old Adam Walsh, who vanished from a mall in Florida in 1981. Their abductions had sparked a huge national movement in the United States to protect children from "the epidemic" of abduction. Laws had been passed. A special unit was set up at the FBI. Communities across the country conducted special education programs for parents on how to keep their kids safe. Milk companies put the faces of missing children on their cartons. New Jersey fingerprinted schoolchildren. A "National Missing Children's Day" was created. Some dentists offered parents the twisted reassurance of having identifying numbers etched into their children's teeth—so that their remains could be identified. (How exactly do you explain that to your seven-year-old without terrifying her?)

Across the country, family behaviors changed dramatically. Kids were never left on their own. They were walked or driven to school; their free time was dramatically curtailed; their every movement outside their homes was supervised and chaperoned. Parents said things like, "The world is more unsafe now," or "I watch my two-year-old more closely," or "I won't allow a stranger near my kids."

I had reported on several child abductions since the case of Sarah Pryor. But I also knew how drastically people were overreacting to the risk of child abduction. I had investigated the actual risk and reported on the statistics, which showed—and still do—that while hundreds of thousands of children go missing in the United States each year, after you take out the cases of family abduction and runaways, and even kids who are snatched by strangers but who get home okay, the number of kids who are kidnapped and killed (the kind of case that makes the news and that fed the fear of this new epidemic) had held steady for decades at only about 200 to 300 per year. Held steady! There was no new epidemic, and the risk was tiny compared to the fear, fear that made parents worry that the world was a much more threatening place than it actually was, fear that was unquestionably affecting children's sense of their own safety. The harm from the Perception Gap between people's fears of strangers abducting and harming their children and the actual risk was huge.

I knew that, so my reaction to this mother's fears was, while empathetic, less emotionally powerful than it had been back when I covered the Sarah Pryor case. I waited a couple of hours before checking out the mother's story with the police.

This is one of the most obvious Risk Perception Factors in this book. Any risk to kids evokes more fear than the same risk if it affects only adults. This makes sense at the most basic biological level. We have a genetic drive to survive, and we have a genetic drive to reproduce, to help the species survive. Anything that threatens future generations, our kids, threatens the species. The instinct to protect our children is so intense, and so universal, that this Risk Perception Factor is almost certainly embedded somewhere deep in our biology.

And so we make sure that our kids wear their bicycle helmets even when we don't. Or we tell them not to smoke, when we do.

Or we slather them in sunscreen, but not ourselves. Or we make sure they buckle their seat belts, but sometimes they have to scold us to do the same. News stories about fatal traffic accidents or plane crashes, or earthquakes or floods, always make special note of the child victims. Or a battery company commercial features a frantic mother in a park looking for her missing son and pressing the button on a device that her son is wearing that will beep so she can find him, and it beeps as he runs back to her, smiling, so we should buy those batteries. The marketplace feeds on our fears for our children.

Kids are also the poster children for many campaigns to ban risky substances, like the campaign to ban the chemical Alar (one of the trade names of daminozide), which was used on apples, cherries, peaches, tomatoes, and other fruits to help them ripen and enhance their color. There was evidence that daminozide *might* be a human carcinogen, but the evidence was still soft, so the chemical had not been banned. Lots of people eat the various foods treated with daminozide, not just kids. People of all ages were subject to the potential cancer risk. But the Natural Resources Defense Council and its public relations advisor Fenton Communications highlighted the threat to children, which helped pressure the EPA to ban the substance.

Or take the "Tick" TV commercial of 2008 from the Ad Council, Environmental Defense, and the PR company Ogilvy & Mather. To raise concern about climate change, it starts with the face of a young girl, maybe eight or nine years old, who simply says, "Tick." The shot changes to another kid, who says "Tick," then another, then another, each of them saying "Tick" as a clock ticks in the background along with ominous music. "Tick," "Tick," "Tick," the kids say, as a few of them interject warnings about "massive heat waves," "severe droughts," and "devastating hurricanes"; then, all together, the children conclude with, "Our future is up to you." Our fear for kids is heavily exploited by advocates for all sorts of causes.

Back to the risk of child abduction, the harm from the Perception Gap continues. In reaction to ongoing cases, around the turn of the century the United States established the AMBER Alert notification system, by which law enforcement works with media organizations and other sources of public information to notify the public immediately when kids go missing, since when children are kidnapped and killed, in most cases the child dies within the first few hours after the abduction. (AMBER is an acronym for America's Missing: Broadcast Emergency Response, but it's really named for Amber Hagerman, a nine-year-old child who was abducted and murdered in Arlington, Texas, in 1995.)

Yet an investigation by the Scripps Howard News Service in 2005 found dozens of cases in which AMBER Alerts were put out for kids who police *knew* were just lost in the woods, or who had run away or left their backpack at school, or alerts were issued for vague circumstances that appeared to bystanders to possibly be abductions, but nobody had reported any missing kids. Half the alerts in the United States in the Scripps Howard investigation were for children who had been taken by relatives, which is not the kind of abduction for which the AMBER Alert was set up. Several people in the report worried that the false alarms were weakening the effectiveness of the system, that the public would not take seriously calls for help from a system that is so frequently crying "Wolf!"

Now a new "epidemic" of risk to children is being declared, the risk from sexual predators using the Internet. The National Center for Missing & Exploited Children declares that in the United States, one child in seven between the ages of 10 and 17 reports having received an unwanted sexual solicitation online. Laws have been passed. Protection programs have been put in place. A CyberTipline phone number and Web site have been set up so that people can report unwanted sexual solicitation of minors or other sexually related harms that kids could face from the Internet (e.g., exposure to sexually explicit material, child pornography). As of

February 2009, 43,156 tips had come in about unwanted sexual solicitation of kids.[15] A network news organization created an on-going "investigative" series that baits sexual predators with phony online information made to read as though it was posted by children describing themselves, in order to get the "predators" to show up at a rendezvous point so they can be caught on camera. News organizations play to our fears for children just as business, advocates, and politicians do.

But is this new risk to kids as high as many people fear? Researchers from the University of New Hampshire's Crimes Against Children Research Center (CCRC) found that in 2006, 3,100 Internet users solicited sex from "children" online who were actually law enforcement investigators. There are 49 million children in the United States between the ages of 6 and 17, and about 9 in 10 use the Internet. If you do the math, the odds of a kid being sexually solicited online are pretty low, about 1 in 15,000.

The University of New Hampshire report said, "The facts do not suggest that the Internet is facilitating an epidemic of sex crimes against youth. Rather, increasing arrests for online predation probably reflect increasing rates of youth Internet use, a migration of crime from offline to online venues and the growth of law enforcement activity against online crimes." The report found that arrests for online predation of kids were less than 1 percent of all crimes committed against kids.[16] A report from the Berkman Center for Internet and Society at Harvard University said, "The risks minors face online are complex and multifaceted and are in most cases not significantly different than those they face offline."

As is the case with every risk described in these pages, this is not a judgment about whether the risk of sexual predators using the Internet to harm children is high or low. That is a judgment for each parent to make. The point here is that we are instinctively sensitive about risks to kids, and that this instinct has a big impact on the way we respond to those risks.

There is one other important point here. Knowing that we some-times overreact to risks because they have certain characteristics that trigger instinctive fears, and even knowing what those characteristics are, is not necessarily enough to counteract those instincts so we can more rationally judge the risk based only on the statistics.

I finally called the police to ask whether they were searching for the girl whose mom had called, pleading for our TV station's help. But because I knew from my reporting that society was overreacting to the fear of child abduction, I was casual about it, and it was two hours before I made that call. Yes, the police said, they were taking the case seriously. I told my assignment editor and was sent to the scene, a complex of apartment buildings in the city of Lowell. By the time I got there, the search of the apartment grounds was over. The mother of the missing child was too distraught to speak, so I got a photograph of the girl from police and interviewed a few kids who were running around, who didn't seem particularly worried, and one frightened parent. I learned about the groundskeeper who had been extra friendly with kids, and who reportedly had lots of photographs of young kids on his apartment walls. I did the report, live from the scene, and went home, not nearly as affected as I had been the day I covered Sarah Pryor's disappearance.

The girl's body was found a few days later in nearby woods, and a few weeks after that, the apartment complex groundskeeper com-mitted suicide. I know full well that we are overly sensitive about risks to kids, and that the risk of this sort of thing is very low, so my response to that mother's call had been fact-based and reason-able. But to this day I think back to what might have been had I reacted more instinctively and less "rationally" to that woman on the phone and moved faster, or tried to find out where the grounds-keeper lived and gone there to interview him, or done something else. Just maybe the end would have been different.

My second-guessing makes no sense. The statistics say that she was dead hours before I got there. I know that. But then, risk perception isn't just a matter of what we know. Our special fear about risks to kids runs deep. It's been more than 20 years, and I still can't drive by the spot where they found her body, or Sarah Pryor's old house, without remembering.

RISK PERCEPTION FACTOR 12: PERSONIFICATION

 What's Your Risk Response?

Here are two ways to describe the risk of child abduction in the United States. Let's see which one evokes a more powerful reaction in you.

Version 1. In 2007, there were roughly 74 million people in the United States age 17 and under. About 800,000 of these children go missing each year, so the odds that "the average" child in America will go missing are a little less than 1 in 100. That's pretty high. But a lot of those kids are runaways, or just lost for a short time. Only about 260,000 children are abducted each year in the United States, so the odds that "the average" child in America will be abducted are about 1 in 300. Still pretty high. But most of those abductions are by family members. The odds that "the average" child in America will be abducted by a stranger are 1 in 1,300. And the odds that a child will be abducted by a stranger and harmed or held for ransom—the stereotypical kidnapping that makes the news—are 1 in 650,000.

Now here is the same risk, presented a different way.

Girl's Killer Will Strike Again, Police Believe.
San Lacita, Calif.—Five-year-old Lucia Ramirez was kidnapped, sexually assaulted, and suffocated before her body was dumped near a rural road in what investigators said Wednesday was a "calling card" from the killer warning that he intends to strike again. Sheriff Jerry Gomez said Ramirez was asphyxiated sometime Tuesday. Autopsy results showed she was alive for hours after her abduction Monday.

Which account hits you harder?

If you're like nearly everyone in the places I speak and teach, the second one. The information presented in Version 1 puts the risk in perspective, but Version 2 puts it *in person*. Most people find that when a risk is personified, when the victim or potential victim is represented as a real person, the risk evokes more concern. The same risk represented merely as an idea, or in terms of impersonal statistics, or on a population-wide or global basis, evokes less concern.

When you look in a mirror you don't see an idea; you don't see millions of people; you don't see a fraction that looks like 1/1,000,000. You see a face, a person. A risk that is represented in human form, even if it's a risk to somebody else, is more real than when it is represented in the abstract. If something bad happens to a person, well, that could be you. If it happens to a number, so what? This explains what brought mass murderer Josef Stalin to observe, "One death is a tragedy. One million deaths is a statistic." This factor also helps explain why, in several experiments by Paul Slovic, a pioneer in the research on risk perception psychology, when people were asked to donate money to save one child and separately were asked to donate to save a group of children, they were willing to pay more to save the single child. They could envision a single child as a person. The group was just a number.

I once had the privilege of explaining risk perception psychology to Lester Brown, founder of the Worldwatch Institute, currently head of the Earthwatch Institute, and someone whom the *Washington Post* called "one of the world's most influential thinkers." He is a thoughtful, intellectual person and, in a low-key way, very warm. Brown writes and lectures about huge environmental challenges that threaten millions of people, like shortages of food or clean drinking water. I had explained several of the factors you just read about, but when I explained the Personification factor to him, Brown started to weep. I asked him why, and he explained that the discussion brought images to his mind of three starving children he had once seen. Three individual faces. This generally low-key and reserved man, who speaks of threats to millions, wept when he envisioned those threats personified by those kids.

So when the risk of global warming is represented by images of the Earth from outer space, or by videos of melting ice or parched soil or hurricanes or polar bears or bleached coral, it probably won't evoke as much worry as if it is represented by real people in real places who are affected by the kinds of severe weather that scientists say is likely to grow more common as the climate of the planet rapidly changes. (See Figures 3.1 and 3.2.)

Or if you read about war and the statistics on how many soldiers were killed, it may not have the same impact that pictures of coffins and body bags do. This explains why governments that are trying to maintain public support for a war ban the press from taking pictures of deceased soldiers on the battlefield or even in coffins when their bodies are returned home. (U.S. President Franklin Roosevelt banned photos of American war dead for the first three years of World War II.)

The most powerful type of personification, of course, is the first-person kind, when you know someone who suffered or died from, or who survived, a given hazard. If a friend or relative has had a specific disease, or a neighbor or colleague was on a plane

3.1: RADAR IMAGE OF A HURRICANE

3.2: WOMAN SITTING IN THE RUINS OF HER STORM-RAVAGED HOME

that crashed, or a member of your church group has a child who went to a developing country and was paralyzed by a water-borne parasite, all those risks will seem more real, and more frightening, than if you read or hear about victims you did not know, and they will certainly seem more real and frightening than if you only read about the prevalence of that disease, or the relative statistical rarity of plane crashes, or even the extreme rarity of that paralyzing parasite.

The more closely we identify with the victim(s), the more worrisome a risk will be. But even if we don't know the victims personally, we naturally identify more closely with victims when they are real people with faces and names than when they are numbers and abstract ideas.

RISK PERCEPTION FACTOR 13: FAIRNESS

 What's Your Risk Response?

What feels worse, a healthy nine-year-old boy who chases a ball out into the street and is hit and killed by a car, or a nine-year-old boy *who is blind* who chases a ball out into the street and is hit and killed by a car?

Most people say that the death of the blind child feels worse. They're both awful, of course, but the risk to the kid who couldn't protect himself somehow feels *more* awful. Risks that affect the poor or the weak or the disadvantaged, people who can't stick up for themselves, or risks where all the danger is faced by one group while another group gets all the benefits, tend to seem worse because they aren't fair. This often shows up when developers propose to build a potentially dangerous facility in a poor neighborhood. When the National Institutes of Health held that special hearing on the Boston University proposal to build a high-security biolab on its medical campus, which borders a poorer section of Boston, several witnesses who first said that they were worried about safety issues then spent most of their time saying things like, "People in that neighborhood are constantly being disenfranchised and stepped on" and "Maybe [Boston University] gets benefits. We don't. We don't suffer from plague. We don't suffer from Ebola, the things they'll be studying. Maybe BU gets the jobs. We don't."

Fairness is important to all of us, in many ways. By way of a possible explanation, here's a question: Did you ever give any money to a homeless person? Many of us have. Did you ever expect a panhandling homeless person to give anything to you? Probably not. So why do you give up resources for no return? It is not to your survival advantage to behave that way, at least not according to cold-blooded economics. But such behavior, called *reciprocal altruism* (giving up resources with no immediate expectation of a return), does have survival advantages in larger terms, and this is where Fairness as a Risk Perception Factor probably has its roots.

In the recently depressed economic environment, some people who had enjoyed comfortable lifestyles lost their jobs and needed donations from food banks and other charities, charities to which those people had actually given when they were employed. We want, we *need*, society's rules to offer basic fairness, so if *we* are ever in material need or can't protect ourselves from some risk, we'll be looked after. That sort of general social cooperation *is* worth investing in, even if we may never directly benefit. This may explain why when some risky product or event or process threatens someone else unfairly, someone else whom we may not know but who is a member of the tribe of humans to which we all belong, the unfairness of that feels a little unsettling, and the nature of the unfairness makes the risk seem worse.

RISK PERCEPTION FACTORS REDUX

This is a good example with which to wrap things up, because the Fairness factor was just one of the Risk Perception Factors contributing to the fears those people testified about at the special NIH hearing on the Boston University biolab. They were also afraid because of Uncertainty, and a lack of Control, and a deep lack of Trust in BU and the Boston city officials and NIH officials who were supporting the project. Several residents also described their fear of "Catastrophe." Supporters of the lab, nurses, and construction union members, on the other hand, thought the Benefits the facility would provide outweighed the Risks. As mentioned at the beginning of the chapter, in any given risk situation, several of these qualitative characteristics are usually involved. Some may be more influential than others. Each factor can make us either more or less afraid, depending on the situation and on our personal experiences and life circumstances and culture and all the things that make each of us unique as an individual.

And the BU biolab is a good reminder that the Risk Perception Factors are just one part of the overall Affective Risk Response system. There are all those mental shortcuts described in Chapter 2 that we use to make sense of partial information quickly. In addition to the Risk Perception Factors of Fairness and Uncertainty and lack of Trust and lack of Control, consider, for example, how the Categorization Effect played a role in fear about the lab. Opponents associated work on germs like anthrax with the general threat of bioterrorism and worried that the lab would be used to make biological weapons and would be a target for terrorists. Consider how the Awareness/Ready Recall Effect played a role. Many opponents vividly remembered how scared they were during the anthrax attacks in the United States in 2001, and said they didn't want that kind of risk anywhere near them.

But there are still other forces at work influencing people's fears in this example. Social forces played a role too. Media attention spread the concerns of the neighbors of the proposed site. At the NIH hearing, people from several towns came to testify that they had heard about the issue in the news and they, too, were afraid. Environmental and business advocates got involved to advance their perspective. Politicians stirred the pot. And there was a clear underlying cultural divide between the opponents and those who saw the project more favorably.

So we now turn to those social and cultural inputs into the Risk Response. It's not just something that comes from your own amygdala or your own personal perceptions. External forces play important roles in shaping our perceptions of and responses to risk. The media, politicians, the marketplace, advocates, the creed of your religious community, your family's history and beliefs, even the general attitudes of your friends also influence what you are afraid of and just how afraid you are, or aren't. The stew of factors that go into the Affective Risk Response is a complex mix of internal and external ingredients. Let's examine some of what society and culture put into the pot.

CHAPTER 4

THE WISDOM OR THE MADNESS OF THE CROWD?

Man seeketh in society comfort, use and protection.

—SIR FRANCIS BACON, *THE ADVANCEMENT OF LEARNING*

Call it a clan, call it a network, call it a tribe, call it a family. Whatever you call it, whoever you are, you need one.

—JANE HOWARD, *FAMILIES*

A CONVERSATION ABOUT CLIMATE CHANGE

You get up early, go for a walk along the beach, and head for your local breakfast restaurant. You get a table with a great view of the ocean, and as you settle into your seat, you overhear a group of friends at the next table discussing a story about climate change in the morning paper. Scientists say that the ice covering Greenland is melting faster than was previously thought, so ocean levels may rise higher, sooner, than experts were predicting just last month. The study says sea level has already risen eight inches this century, and that the accelerated melting of the ice in Greenland could raise sea levels three times that much in the next 100 years. The study also says that the geological record shows no evidence that this kind of rapid melting has ever happened before, which means, the study's authors say, that this is probably being caused, at least in part, by human activity. The study was published in a highly respected scientific journal.

You look out at the waves gently lapping up the beach across the street and think about what this might mean for your ocean-front retirement home half a mile away, then you listen in on your friends' conversation. You've just read the first sections of this book, and you can hear the factors that shape risk perception come up as your neighbors talk.

"This puts things in a whole new light," April says. That's the Framing Effect at work. The issue has been framed in a new way for April, more urgent and more immediate.

"Yeah, a wet one, right where we live!" says Beth. She is clearly more concerned about climate change because she thinks, "It Can Happen to *Me*!"

"Wait a minute," argues Stan. He points to the article in the newspaper at their table. "Three inches, six inches, nine inches—*inches*! Doesn't seem like that much to me, even if they're right." Stan looks out at the ocean. "*My* house is up high enough to deal with a few inches." He is less worried about climate change because of Optimism Bias.

"But it could be *12* inches, or *15*," Beth shoots back. "Or more! They said they're not sure, and it could be more! At some point it's gonna be up on your porch and mine!" Beth's concern is fueled by a healthy dose of fear-inducing Uncertainty.

April adds in a quiet voice, "You know what depresses me about this? We can't do a darn thing about it. You can put in all the compact fluorescent lightbulbs you want, and drive all the Priuses you want, and it won't stop it, won't undo what we've already done. That's frustrating. That makes me angry." April is concerned because of a lack of Control.

Phil, the other man in the group, rolls his eyes. "That's if you believe all this garbage in the first place," he says dismissively. "Take a look at who these so-called experts are. Every one of them is making money off saying this stuff. The worse they make it sound, the more money they get for their research. We're just being taken for a ride by a bunch of self-appointed experts feeding at the trough." Phil mistrusts the experts who say that climate change is real, so for him, lack of Trust equates to less concern about the risk.

"Phil," answers April, "you're telling me you don't believe that all the things we do, all the pollution we create and the waste and everything, isn't having some kind of impact on the climate?" April is like most of us, more worried about risks that are Human-Made. "And by the way, Macho Man Stan," she teases gently, "just how *is* driving that Hummer?"

"The climate of the whole earth? Yeah, I'm skeptical that we're changing something that big," Stan answers with a disdainful snort, disregarding the dig at his gas guzzler. "We've added a few parts per million of CO_2 to the parts that have been there for hundreds of thousands of years. It's a huge natural system. If anything is changing, it's not us who are changing it. It's nature. Besides, CO_2 is part of nature. Hell, it's what we breathe out!" Stan is arguing that disruptive changes to the climate and the local weather are less of a concern because they're natural.

"Besides," he adds, frustration clear in his voice, "They can't predict the damn *local* weather *tomorrow*! How the hell do they claim that they can predict what's gonna happen to the whole *globe* in a *hundred years*?" Again, you hear the Trust factor in Stan's response. Because he doesn't trust those who are claiming the risk is high, Stan sees it just the other way.

"But what if they're *right*?" asks Beth, agitated. The word *if* is a huge clue to what Beth is thinking. It means that she's uncertain, and Uncertainty = fear.

You think to yourself, "Listen to these people. None of them are experts. They're not having a rational argument about the facts. They're just using the few facts they have and combining them with all these other psychological factors to make up their minds about climate change."

But you keep listening, and there seems to be something else going on, something that doesn't really seem to be about the risk of climate change at all. The conversation sounds as if it's more about ideology than about scientific facts. It's almost as if each person is just parroting the party line learned from Al Gore or Rush Limbaugh. It sounds as if these people's minds are already made up. And there is something else. The volume of their voices is rising. What started as a conversation is turning into a confrontation.

That's no surprise, you think, given what you know about the participants, your neighbors. Stan is a retired Army colonel. He is a devout Catholic, supported the U.S. invasion of Iraq, votes Republican, coaches Pop Warner football (the kids love him), and refuses to give up those way-too-loud plaid pants and cigars you're always teasing him about when you play golf together. He buys a big new car every three years. Only American cars.

Phil is a rabid New England Patriots fan who doesn't socialize much besides the weekly walks he takes with the group along the beach. He is an independent voter, a humanist who is proud of his atheism, and it seems as if every time you pass his house, he's on his porch reading.

Beth is a regular at her Unitarian Universalist church, where she serves on the social action committee. She teaches history at the local high school, where she is the faculty advisor of the student Gay and Lesbian Support Group. She votes Democratic but isn't active politically. She grows great fresh tomatoes every summer and loves sharing her crop with the neighbors.

April moved to Cape Cod from Vermont after she sold her crafts store, which she started after she realized that her graduate degree in philosophy wasn't going to pay the bills. She has a wide circle of friends and acquaintances: two book groups and membership on three town committees. She seems to know everybody in the neighborhood.

They make an odd foursome, but they get together every Saturday morning, have their breakfast, and walk the beach, and despite their differences, they're neighborly friends.

You've heard them arguing about politics enough to know where this conversation is going. Phil says, "Remember how much snow we had this winter? What was it, like five feet of snow or something? Global *warming*? C'mon! I don't need anybody to tell me about what I can see with my own eyes. If things are supposed to be getting hotter, why did I have to buy a new snow blower in December?"

"That's just one year, Phil," April answers impatiently. "The hottest years ever recorded since they started keeping records were in just the last 10 or 15 years or whatever."

Beth jumps in. "And they don't say that *everywhere's* going to be hotter every day than it was on the same day last year. They say that the weather's going to change. It *is* changing. There'll be more severe weather, like heavy rain or snow or storms. Or hurricanes. How would that be for us here on the Cape? Especially if the sea level is higher already!"

"Yeah? Well when was the last hurricane *here*?" Phil asks. He pauses, sits back in his chair, and folds his arms across his chest, smug. Nobody answers, because nobody remembers. Phil senses that the Awareness/Ready Recall Effect makes the risk of hurricanes fueled by climate change seem smaller because nobody can readily recall the last hurricane to hit Cape Cod. He's not simply describing his perspective on climate change, though. He is arguing, trying to convince the others that he's right. And he is instinctively applying the risk perception factors that diminish the threat as he presses his case. It's as if he's using them as tools to make his case, rather than truly why he believes what he believes.

"It was Hurricane Bob in 1991, and we all made out just fine in that one," Phil says, answering his own question. "Look, we knew there was a risk of hurricanes when we moved here. It's the chance we take for living in such a pretty place." Now Phil is playing down the risk by framing it through the lens of Risk versus Benefit.

Stan jumps in. "And living in this pretty place is what we worked so hard to get. So now they're telling me I have to pay more for gas and electricity, and turn off my air conditioner, and drive less, and stop buying things I want, because of some things that *may* be happening that they want to blame me for when they're probably not happening, and if they are, they're probably natural anyway. I've got a real problem with that. I've got a real problem with people who blame this good life I've got for problems that are problems for polar bears and Eskimos and poor people in Africa, if they're problems at all. For them I'm supposed to give up what I have? Yeah, I've got a real problem with that!" Stan is talking loudly now, his body leaning forward across the table toward Beth and April.

The conversation stops. You can feel the tension. You peek over and notice that Beth is staring at Stan, and getting a little red in the face. Stan is glaring back. April is looking down at her salad, poking it aimlessly with her fork. Phil takes a sip of coffee, and breaks the mood. Or tries to.

"Look, I don't want to see anything happen to polar bears. Nobody wants anything to happen to polar bears. Or poor people in Africa or here or anywhere. That's not the issue, I don't think. And it's not really about the weather or hurricanes or sea level or whatever. To me it's a matter of just how far government should be able to butt into our lives. At some point this social engineering just goes too far. I don't think any government should have the right to tell me how I'm supposed to live my life because some people think everything's supposed to be fair for everybody. There are always winners and losers. I know that stinks, but it's the truth. It always has been, and it always will be. What are they going to regulate next, the weather itself, so that it rains the same and shines the same on everybody?"

"Phil, I don't *believe* you!" Beth snaps. "How selfish can you be? We *all* deserve things like clean air and water, or protection from things like floods or storms or droughts. I don't care if you're rich or poor or black or white or if you live in a mansion in Hyannisport or some refugee camp in Darfur. Just because there's always been winners and losers doesn't mean that we have to accept that that's the way it's supposed to be!"

She hears the edge in her voice, and she catches herself, takes a breath, and sits back in her chair. More calmly, she says, "There are people who can't protect themselves. We need government to protect us all when we can't protect ourselves. We can't protect ourselves if global warming is going to cause stronger hurricanes, or if it's going to flood our homes. We can't protect ourselves from pollution that's going up in China or India. You can't, Phil. You can't, Stan. Government is us. It's us, working for each other. It's you and me, working for you and me."

"Sometimes," Stan snaps back. "And sometimes it's just a way for people to try to get things they can't earn for themselves on their own. Like the Kyoto Treaty. We're supposed to do something that the Chinese won't do, and the Indians? China emits more carbon dioxide than we do now, and we're supposed to cut ours but they don't have to cut theirs!" He's angry. "We're supposed to hurt our economy, and lose jobs, and give up our standard of living, because it's *fair*? And they want us to do stuff they won't do! What's fair about that?"

Phil asks, "At some point, don't people just have to take care of themselves? Like Carol's house, when she rebuilt it up on stilts after the last storm flooded her out so bad. She took out a home loan to pay for that. She didn't go looking for some handout. She didn't go sue the coal industry. She took care of things herself." He pauses to collect his thoughts, and adds, "I mean, I know we're our brother's keeper, and we're all in it together, and all that—sure. But at some point we have to just take care of things ourselves. This Big Brother government idea has just gone way too far, is all I'm saying."

April answers quietly, "In some ways it has, Phil; you're right. But sometimes we have to do things together that we just can't do for ourselves. Like global warming. They call it 'global' for a reason. We all live on the same globe, and what we do affects people somewhere else, and what they do affects us. If these scientists are right, we could be in big trouble. Too much trouble for us to do anything about as individuals. Stilts won't hold up Carol's house if a big hurricane hits."

Stan begins to bark back. "That's *if* there is a problem in the first place. Smart people like Senator Inhofe say this whole global warming thing is just a hoax, and . . ."

Phil interrupts. "Stan, shut up and eat your eggs. We're all done, and we want to go for our walk."

"And I want to go for a ride in your Hummer," Beth teases. "Actually, I really do," she admits. "It looks kinda nice. What's it like?"

⚡

What was *that* about, you wonder. What started as a conversation about perceptions of climate change sounded at the end more like a battle over cultural values. How did that happen? What do cultural values have to do with the way we respond to risk?

Actually, quite a bit. Risk perception is not just a matter of what your amygdala says. It's not just a matter of what mental shortcuts you use to help you make decisions. And it's not just a matter of those psychological Risk Perception Factors. The perception of risk, it turns out, is also a matter of the fundamental ways we see ourselves as social creatures in a social world.

CULTURAL COGNITION

As noted earlier, humans are social animals. And that's not just because it's fun to go to the movies with friends or have some pals over to watch the Super Bowl. Society, in a very real way, is survival. We have belonged to tribes for as long as modern humans have been around, and we have depended on our tribes for our very existence—for food and for protection. We have evolved to be keenly attuned to how our tribes are doing, because the better the tribe is doing, the better our chances are, and vice versa. So we tend to adopt behaviors and attitudes and perceptions of risk that reinforce the beliefs of the tribe, that reinforce cohesion in the tribe, and that also strengthen our acceptance *by* other members of the tribe.

To some, the word *tribe* prompts thoughts of Choctaw or Sioux, Hutu or Tutsi, Maori or Yanomani. But tribes are merely societies of people with shared ancestry, cultural beliefs, territory, or other commonalities that bind the members together. Think of the tribes to which you belong. One tribe is your family. You also may be among the billions who identify with a particular religious tribe. Another important tribal association for most of us is our local community. (Most sports fans root for their local teams, even if they stink.) You are a member of a national tribe, a gender tribe, a racial tribe, possibly a political tribe, and a professional tribe.

And, although you may not be consciously aware of it, as your tribes' fortunes go, so go yours. When your local team wins, you feel better. Think about those huge tribal celebration rallies in communities where the local team has won the championship! Tribal warriors, wearing the tribal colors (okay, we call them uniforms), having represented the tribe and won in battle! Everybody at the rally singing tribal chants and wearing tribal clothing and waving tribal banners! Conversely, if your team loses, you feel worse. (The phenomenon was first observed on a college campus in the late '70s. If the home team won, the next day many more people were wearing the school's colors than the day after the team lost. Researchers call it BIRG-ing, Basking in Reflected Glory, or CORF-ing, Cutting Off Reflected Failure.[1])

When the head of government is from your political tribe, you feel better. If your nation is attacked, even if the attack occurs thousands of miles away from you personally, you feel attacked. When a member of your tribe is injured, even if she is thousands of miles away, you feel connected. (News stories often make special note of the passengers in a plane crash who were citizens of the country in which the paper or TV newscast is based.) When members of various religions shun a member who wants to marry outside the faith, they are resisting in the name of tribal unity. There are many more examples. We have evolved as social animals, dependent on our social communities for survival. It is adaptive and deep within us to behave in ways that strengthen the tribes to which we belong, and in ways that strengthen our acceptance as members of those tribes.

This is what anthropologists Mary Douglas and Aaron Wildavsky called the Cultural Theory of Risk in *Risk and Culture: An Essay on the Selection of Technological and Environmental Dangers* (Berkeley: University of California Press, 1983). Current scholars like Dan Kahan and others call it Cultural Cognition. "Cultural cognition," Kahan writes, "refers to the tendency of individuals to form beliefs about societal dangers that reflect and reinforce their commitments to particular visions of the ideal society."[2] It's what you heard in the conversation about climate change. At the beginning, it was about the facts. But as the conversation turned into an argument, it was more about underlying worldviews on how society is supposed to be organized. And it wasn't about political ideology or religion or any of the other factors that we normally use to identify the sides in the Culture Wars. It was a response to risk that was being framed by something much more fundamental: each person's underlying views of the way society should be structured, the way he feels his tribe should work.

Let's start with Stan, our politically conservative American-car-buying churchgoing retired colonel. Stan pretty clearly thinks that leveling the playing field is not his job. Remember what he said? "I've got a real problem with people who blame this good life I've got for problems that are problems for polar bears and Eskimos and poor people in Africa, if they're problems at all. For them I'm supposed to give up what I have?" Stan is the kind of person who believes in the class system and in hierarchies of power. His view of the basic structure of society is that certain people of certain races or certain religions or with certain backgrounds get the power and the perks: the better-paying jobs, the bigger houses in the more affluent communities, the luxury cars. Stan believes in the social rules that determine who gets the country club memberships, who gets invited to which party, and who gets included in which social circle. It's not that Stan wants all these things for himself (although he pines for a country club membership every time he has to play a public golf course). That's just the world he believes in and feels safe in, a structured world of order and hierarchy in which positions and power and social stratification are based on fixed and unchanging characteristics like race, gender, ancestry, and wealth. When things work that way, he feels better, so according to Cultural Cognition, Stan's beliefs will conform to, and reinforce, those norms.

Phil, political independent, atheist, and Patriots fan, is part of Stan's tribe. "There are always winners and losers. I know that stinks, but it's the truth. It always has been, and it always will be," he said. But Phil also said something that reflects another part of his underlying worldview, something that also seems important to him. "At some point we have to just take care of things ourselves. This Big Brother government idea has just gone way too far, is all I'm saying." Phil is a fundamental libertarian, in way more than the political meaning of the word. He supports a social structure that favors individual rights more than the rights of the state and of government. He believes in a tribe that comes together when it's time for everybody to fight to defend the group, and a tribe that shares some basic resources, but other than that, Phil's ideal is a village that mostly leaves the individual villagers alone. Phil is less of a joiner and has a smaller circle of friends and social contacts. The opinions of others matter less to him. His opinions are formed in support of a social structure that emphasizes the independence of the individual.

Then there is April, the ex-hippie feminist liberal group joiner from Vermont. Remember that she said, "But sometimes we have to do things together that we just can't do for ourselves." April feels safest in a social order in which we all act together, and that means that we empower the tribe to actively protect us and provide for us. For somebody like April, a large-scale threat to the whole group, like climate change (or any environmental threat), is the kind of cause that she will engage in quickly, because it's a threat that should bring the whole group together. In Cultural Cognition terms, environmental issues are good news to April, because investing in them helps her reinforce the norms of a society that is constantly looking out for the greater common good.

Finally, meet Beth, the churchgoing social activist Democratic neighborhood tomato grower. Beth doesn't seem to buy Stan and Phil's views on social hierarchy. Anybody should be able to get into any country club or college or job based on merit. To Beth, society's opportunities should be open to anyone, regardless of ancestry or race or wealth or gender. "I don't care if you're rich or poor or black or white or if you live in a mansion in Hyannisport or some refugee camp in Darfur," she said. "Just because there's always been winners and losers doesn't mean that we have to accept that that's the way it's supposed to be!" Beth seems to think that the hierarchy in the tribe shouldn't be fixed, and that anybody should be able to climb up the ladder. Beth is most supportive of, and feels safest in and most supported by, a society in which anyone can achieve anything.

Now how do you think a guy like Stan is going to see the problem of climate change, if the solutions to climate change are going to require him to sacrifice in the name of the greater good? The position consistent with the way in which he thinks society is supposed to operate is that climate change is not a problem. So he'll mistrust the scientists who say it is, cite the skeptics, selectively note the facts that raise doubts, and argue the issue using Optimism Bias or Risk Perception Factors like Risks versus Benefits that let him play down the risk.

What do you think independent Phil thinks about something like the Kyoto Treaty or other government agreements that impose limits on emissions of greenhouse gases? Given his underlying libertarian view of the basic way the tribe is supposed to run, it's no surprise that he would play down a risk when its solution seems to call for a collectivist government-regulated response, as many environmental threats do.

How do you think "equal-opportunity-for-all" Beth feels about climate change, a threat that billions of poor people around the world will suffer from the most? How is April, who seems to belong to every social group, likely to feel about a risk that threatens every one of them? Beth and April are likely to adopt positions that are consistent with their fundamental views that society should be fair for everybody, and that government should have the power to act in pursuit of the common good. For people like them, acknowledging the threat of climate change and embracing social solutions is right up their tribal alleys. So they will cite sources like Al Gore and the Intergovernmental Panel on Climate Change, deride the skeptics, pick the facts that support their side of the issue, and argue their case emphasizing Risk Perception Factors like Human-Made, It Can Happen to *Me*, and Uncertainty, factors that make the risk seem greater.

None of this is conscious, of course. At the conscious level, the discussion is about climate change. What these people *say* is that either they believe global warming is real or they don't, that either they trust the science or they don't, that they believe in this or that approach to the problem. But this is about so much more than the facts, so much more than the issue of climate change. This is the Affective Risk Response playing out, and a great deal of it is subconscious. Fundamentally, what is driving the perceptions of these social animals is their underlying view of how society is supposed to work and what the rules of the tribe are supposed to be. They have adopted positions that confirm and reinforce the position of their groups, and that reinforce their membership in those groups.

This is why the discussion of climate change was really an argument, not a discussion. Winning the argument on climate change has nothing to do with the weather or sea level or alternative energy, and everything to do with how powerfully invested people are in the dominance of their tribes, on whose success *their* success in part depends.

Kahan and colleagues demonstrated this effect at work in public opinion on climate change.[3] They surveyed 5,000 Americans between December 2006 and September 2007. The respondents were asked to identify themselves by standard demographics like age, race, gender, political identity, income, and education. They were also asked a series of questions that allowed the researchers to place each respondent on the Stan–Beth scale and the Phil–April scale. They called the Stan side Hierarchists, the people who "believe that rights, duties, goods, and offices should be distributed *differentially* and on the basis of clearly defined and stable social characteristics." The Beth types were called Egalitarians, those who believe that "rights, duties, goods, and offices should be distributed *equally* and without regard to such characteristics." The Phil folks, the less-government/libertarian types, were called Individualists, and the April people were labeled Communitarians, who "believe that societal interests should take precedence over individual ones and that society should bear the responsibility for securing the conditions of individual flourishing."

The grid for these four types is shown in Figure 4.1.

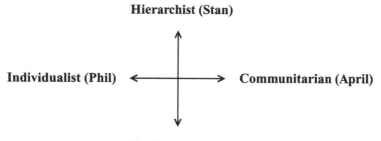

The researchers then asked the respondents, "How much risk does global warming pose for people in our society?" And the way the respondents identified themselves on the Stan–Beth and Phil–April scales (Hierarchical ↔ Egalitarian, Individualist ↔ Communitarian) was strongly associated with their views on climate change. The more Stan/Hierarchist they were, the less they thought climate change was a risk. The more Beth/Egalitarian, the greater they perceived the risk. The more Phil/Individualist, the lower the risk. The more April/Communitarian, the greater the risk.

Remarkably, these underlying worldviews were more accurate predictors of people's perception of the risk of climate change than any of the other more commonly cited demographics, including political affiliation, gender, or income level. They were 70 percent more accurate at predicting attitudes on climate change than people's political affiliations, and 90 percent more accurate than their gender!

Kahan and colleagues tested the group on another risk as well: nuclear power. They showed some respondents one of two versions of a newspaper article about a scientific analysis supporting more nuclear energy as a way to reduce CO_2 emissions to reduce climate change. Both articles said that the biosphere is warming, that human activity is the cause, and that the changing climate could have disastrous environmental and economic consequences. In both, the scientists said that nuclear power should be part of the solution. But in one article, the scientists said that nuclear power should be promoted through "increased anti-pollution regulation." Government intervention through regulation that evens the playing field! That's good news for we're-all-in-this-together April and egalitarian Beth, and bad news for hierarchical free marketers Stan and Phil, right? In the other article, the scientists didn't mention anything about government intervention, but noted that their proposal would foster "revitalization of the nation's nuclear power industry." Helping an established powerful industry, part of the existing hierarchy in the economy! That's great for Stan and Phil, but bad news for Beth and April, right?

Right! Respondents were asked what they thought about climate change after reading each story. (Remember, the climate change facts were identical in each version.) Some read the first version, which mentioned the idea of regulation. Some read the second, which talked about support for industry. The Stan/Hierarchists and Phil/Individualists who read the version about revitalizing industry were more inclined to agree with the facts about climate change: that it's real, caused by human activity, and could lead to catastrophic consequences. The Stans and Phils who read the same facts framed by the anti-pollution *regulation* language disagreed with what the article said about climate change! They read the *same facts,* but just the mention of either regulation or revitalizing industry triggered underlying worldviews that colored their perceptions of the risk of global warming.

You should be able to predict how the Beth/Egalitarians and the April/Communitarians felt about the two articles. Egalitarians and Communitarians who read the article supporting the idea of a revitalized nuclear industry, part of an economy stratified by wealth and that creates class divisions and haves and have-nots, were more inclined to reject the facts. Those who read the article framing the same facts in terms of regulation of pollution, leveling the playing field by government fiat, were more inclined to agree with those same facts.

What's Your Risk Response?

Now let's try this on you. There are two steps to this one. First, I'll give you some basic information on a few risk issues and ask a question about each one.

1. **Bovine growth hormone.** Scientists have identified the gene in cows that makes a protein that controls milk production. By splicing the gene into bacteria, they can get the bacteria to produce large amounts of that protein, which they then collect and inject back into cows so that the cows produce more milk. This does have negative health effects on many cows, but the milk itself is unaffected, since the gene is the same one the cows make naturally. Scientists believe there is no risk from drinking milk or eating dairy products produced this way. The milk is identical. There is just more of it. Critics of genetic engineering disagree and say that the process does pose risks to consumers. They have called for regulations to ban this process. The U.S. FDA says that there is no risk, and therefore it has not banned the practice.

   How much of a risk do you think the process of using bovine growth hormone to increase milk production poses for people in our society? Rate the risk on a 1 to 10 scale, with 1 being "not at all" and 10 being "a great deal." Write down your answer.

2. **"Cosmetic" pesticides.** Homeowners and property owners use large amounts of pesticides for aesthetic reasons, like having greener lawns, fewer weeds, and prettier flowers. Toxicological testing on these products has shown that the health risk to people from these pesticides is very small because the levels of the active ingredient in the product are kept low by regulations. Risk to certain other species, like bees and birds, is higher. Some scientists and health groups, however, believe that the risk to people is high enough that these products should be banned.

   How much of a risk do you think pesticides used for cosmetic purposes pose for people in our society? Rate the risk on a 1 to 10 scale, with 1 being "not at all" and 10 being "a great deal." Write down your answer.

3. **Irradiation of food.** It is legal in many nations for food processors to use radiation to disinfect food in order to kill germs that spread disease and accelerate spoilage. The process doesn't cook the food or change it in any way that would affect its safety or taste. It does not make the food radioactive. Governments around the world have approved this process as safe.

   The process is widely used on some products, like spices, but not for meats and poultry or fruits and vegetables, which often carry living bacteria that cause millions of cases of food-borne illness each year around the world. Food companies are reluctant to use food irradiation because they're worried that consumers might not buy food that was disinfected in this way. They want to sell such food without a label indicating that it has been irradiated, but most governments require such labels.

How much of a risk do you think food that has been disinfected using radiation poses for people in our society? Rate the risk on a 1 to 10 scale, with 1 being "not at all" and 10 being "a great deal." Write down answer.

Okay, now for Step 2. Let's see where you stand on the Cultural Cognition scales. Step 2 has two sets of questions. The first will help you rank yourself on the Phil–April scale. The second will help you rank yourself on the Stan–Beth scale. (This is a revised version of the Stan–Beth and Phil–April questions that Kahan and colleagues asked in their survey.)

Question Set 1. Rank yourself from 1 to 10 on each of the following statements, where 1 means that you absolutely disagree and 10 means that you absolutely agree. Write your answers down somewhere. You'll need to add them up in a minute.

1. The government interferes too much in our everyday lives.
2. Government needs to make laws that keep people from hurting themselves.
3. The government should stop telling people how to live their lives.
4. The government should do more to advance society's goals, even if that means limiting the freedom and choices of individuals.
5. Too many people today expect society to do things for them that they should have to do for themselves.
6. People should be able to rely on the government for help when they need it.

7. Society works best when it lets individuals take responsibility for their own lives without telling them what to do.
8. It's society's responsibility to make sure that everyone's basic needs are met.
9. People who are successful in business have a right to enjoy their wealth as they see fit.
10. Taxes should be higher on the wealthy as a fair way of getting them to share the benefits that society gives them.

Now add up your answers to the odd-numbered questions, then add up your answers to the even-numbered questions. If the total for the odd-numbered questions is bigger than the total for the even-numbered ones, you tend toward an Individualist/Phil worldview. If the even-numbered total is bigger, you are more like April, and you tend to think that society should be more Communitarian. The greater the gap, the stronger your beliefs.

On to Question Set 2.

1. Our society would be better off if the distribution of wealth were more equal.
2. Nowadays it seems as if there is just as much discrimination against whites as there is against blacks.
3. We need to dramatically reduce inequalities between the rich and the poor, whites and people of color, and men and women.
4. It seems as if blacks, women, homosexuals, and other groups don't want equal rights, they want special rights just for them.
5. It's old-fashioned and wrong to think that one culture's set of values is better than any other culture's way of seeing the world.

6. The women's rights movement has gone too far.
7. We live in a sexist society that is fundamentally set up to discriminate against women.
8. A lot of problems in our society today come from the decline in the traditional family, where the man works and the woman stays home.
9. Parents should encourage young boys to be more sensitive and less rough and tough.
10. Society as a whole has become too soft.

Repeat the same process. Add up the odd-numbered answers, and separately tally the even-numbered ones. If the total for the odd-numbered questions is bigger, you tend toward an Egalitarian view, like Beth. If the total for the even-numbered questions is bigger, you tend more toward a Hierarchical/Stan-like worldview. The greater the gap, the stronger your beliefs.

Now, having rated yourself as either more Egalitarian/ Beth or more Hierarchical/Stan, and as either more Individualist/Phil or more Communitarian/April, go back to those three risk issues that I asked you about before you rated yourself on the Cultural Cognition scales— bovine growth hormone, cosmetic pesticides, and food irradiation—and consider whether your underlying cultural worldview seems to be playing a role in your perception of those risk issues. It probably does.

A Few Criticisms of Cultural Cognition

The Cultural Theory of Risk started by Douglas and Wildavsky has been attacked for a number of reasons. One good argument is that the definitions of the basic ways in which people think that society is supposed to operate—Hierarchical or Egalitarian,

Individualist or Communitarian—seem limited and simplistic. Also, Douglas and Wildavsky's Cultural Theory of Risk is really just about how people perceive environmental and technological risks, although Kahan and his colleagues have found that these definitions are also strongly correlated with people's views on other issues in the culture wars, like gun control and abortion.

But that's the thing with efforts to describe the Risk Response. The Affective Risk Response process is like a bubbling stew. It has a lot of ingredients, all of which contribute to the overall product. There is cognitive analysis of the facts. There are the mental shortcuts that we apply to make use of incomplete information, the psychological Risk Perception Factors, and the cultural norms of the tribes with which we identify, and under all that, there is the amygdala and its hair trigger set to sound the alarm at the slightest sign of danger. They all play a role.

But because we are social animals, evolved to enhance our own survival by behaving in ways that strengthen the tribe and the tribe's acceptance of us as members, the influence of cultural and social forces is strong. On we go, then, to the social influences on our perception of risk.

CHICKEN LITTLE, POLLYANNA, AND OTHER SOCIAL FORCES

Picture a small French village nestled in a gentle valley in eastern France, a quiet, safe little village of 2,000 people. One quiet Saturday afternoon in November, a small house fire breaks out on rue des Cares, a street near the police station that's just a few blocks long. The volunteer fire department puts it out easily. No one is hurt. The next day, two doors up the street, another fire starts. Again, it's small and easily extinguished. No one is hurt.

The next weekend, there are two more small fires, one on rue des Cares, the other a few blocks away. Again, there are no injuries and little damage. But firefighters are puzzled. There are none of the usual signs of arson. The fires seem to have started spontaneously, mysteriously. It's a small town. The volunteer firefighters tell their friends about the strange fires, and those friends tell *their* friends, and soon nearly everyone in town knows about them and starts to worry.

One Saturday afternoon, there is a fire on rue des Cares in the home of Jean-Pierre Raffin. An unusually large crowd of citizens gathers at the scene to watch. The fire is easily and thoroughly extinguished, but as the firemen are packing up to leave, flames break out again in a clothes closet upstairs, erupting so quickly and fiercely that damage is heavy before they can put this one out. When they do, they find that the fire appeared to start with the inexplicable spontaneous combustion of a metal rod in the closet. Within hours, word of the strange cause of the fire shoots from people at the scene to their friends, and throughout the town. Now people are really starting to get scared.

The fire department makes regular patrols past the house for the rest of the evening. Just after 8 p.m., minutes after the last patrol goes by, fire breaks out in the house for the third time *that day*! Firemen are there within two minutes, but flames are already raging in the upper story of the house. The owner, Jean-Pierre Raffin, escapes, but his wife, Annie, is trapped. She screams for help. Against the smoke and flames, firefighter Gerard Davin rushes in to save her. Annie and Gerard are both killed.

The small village, where many people knew both victims, is devastated. And afraid. Firefighters report seeing strange flames, with odd colors, jumping strangely from walls to ceiling. Water did not seem to affect them. And there were no obvious signs of arson: no ignition source and no accelerants.

Fear continues to spread, fueled by rumors that the cause might be swamp gas, field mice gnawing through cables, even the ghostly revenge of World War II firing squad victims. The normally volunteer fire department is put on 24-hour watch, with a crew always in the fire station. To calm growing public concern, firefighters stop turning on their sirens when they respond to a call.

The story is picked up by the French national news media. Mystics and psychics volunteer their services. The press calls the fires *mysterious* and *unexplained*. Parapsychologists from France and Switzerland come to the town to study the phenomenon. To quell rumors that an exorcist has been brought in, a local priest declares his faith that a scientific explanation can be found.

Two weeks later, after several more weekend fires, police arrest Pascal Raffin, who admits that he set several of the fires. Pascal is a 36-year-old relative of Jean-Pierre, and a loner and a drinker. Investigators have seen him in the crowds watching all the blazes. He tells police that he used a cigarette lighter to ignite readily available materials. Investigators report that a unique combination of materials in the Raffin home caused the odd behavior of the flames. It was arson, plain and simple.

Many people in France will remember the mysterious fires of Moirans-en-Montagne in 1995 and 1996.[4] They will remember how the fears of the public grew far beyond the actual risk, and how weeks of worry and rumor in a small town fed a perception of the risk that was far greater than the actual peril, causing stress and changing people's behaviors.

Several Risk Perception Factors were at work. We fear what we don't understand. We fear what we can't control. We fear a risk that is personified, as the fires became when Annie Raffin and Gerard Davin died. But our perceptions of danger are also driven by the perceptions of those around us and by the mechanisms and institutions of society. The Risk Response is not solely an individual act. We are social animals, evolved to be aware of cues from other members of our tribe on whom we depend, in part, for our welfare and survival. Remember from Chapter 1 that just seeing a fearful or angry face can trigger a Triple F response in our amygdala. We are hard-wired to read in those around us any sign that could be relevant to our survival. Social forces can amplify our worries or dampen them.[5]

In Moirans-en Montagne, the perception of the risk was amplified by several social factors. Everyone was talking about the fires for weeks. Society itself acted as an agent to keep awareness high, contributing to the Awareness/Ready Recall Effect. Society also helped magnify the influence of the Uncertainty factor. Was the cause swamp gas? Ghostly victims of the Nazis in World War II? These speculations spread quickly from person to person throughout the town and fed the feeling that nobody really knew what was going on.

Other social forces fed the fear. A priest spoke out. The mayor convened a crisis committee that called in outside experts on electricity and radiation and seismology. The fire department turned off its sirens, not wanting to alarm people by the sound, but alarming people by the very action of not using the sirens the way it normally would. These actions by some of the institutions and leaders of society certainly influenced the perceptions of the residents.

Social psychologists know that we are more likely to pay attention to things if a lot of other people are already paying attention to them. That would certainly have contributed to fear of the fires. Social psychologists also know that we have a tendency to adopt the beliefs of those around us, and that this tendency increases as the number of people holding those beliefs grows. So as more and more people in Moirans-en-Montagne focused on the possibility that some unexplained phenomenon was causing the fires, the social momentum of that idea almost certainly drew others to the same belief. At the same time, the peer pressure to believe what everyone else believes helps explain why most people, other than police and fire investigators, dismissed the possibility that the fires were simply the work of an arsonist.

Moirans-en-Montagne is a good example of the general point: that risk perception is both a personal and a social process, a combination of individual psychological influences interacting with social, institutional, and cultural forces that all contribute to our perceptions. Here is another example—the story of Goiania, Brazil—that illustrates one powerful type of social influence on risk perception: the effect of Stigma.

The Pariahs of Goiania

In 1987, two men scavenging in a garbage dump in Goiania, a city of one million people in the middle of Brazil, found a piece of discarded medical equipment. They tore it open, revealing a strange and beautiful blue glow—strange and beautiful, and deadly. It was radioactive cesium, in a machine that treated cancer. The device was left behind when a clinic closed and was eventually tossed in the trash. The two scavengers, who would eventually suffer severe burns from the radiation, sold the device to a junkyard, where the owner saw the beautiful blue glow inside and had the cylinder containing the cesium smashed open by his workers so that he could use the glowing pellets to make a ring for his wife. His brother brought home some of the pretty blue pellets, which were the size of rice grains, and his daughter ate some. She was vomiting violently within 10 minutes.

Fortunately for the junkyard owner's wife, she never got her ring, but she got sick anyway. Her mother came to nurse her, and the mother got sick. Lots of relatives and friends who visited were getting sick. So the owner's wife put the strange blue pellets in a plastic bag and took them to a hospital.

Sounds pretty bad, right? High-level radiation spreading all over the place. It was tragic, certainly, for the junkyard owner's family and workers. In all, four people died, including the owner's niece who ate the radioactive cesium and the two workers who hacked the cesium out of the machine. But considering how widely the radiation spread, the health damage was remarkably limited. In total, 46 people needed medical attention for acute radiation burns, 250 people got significant doses of radiation in or on their bodies, and roughly 1,000 people were exposed to enough radiation to increase their chances of developing cancer by as much as 1 in 100.

But the *perception* of peril from Goiania was *far* greater than the actual physical risk, and that perception was magnified dramatically by social forces. The area of the junkyard was cordoned off, which sent a strong institutional message about people living in that neighborhood, and for months those people were ostracized. One woman from the area who went to a hospital to be decontaminated found her house burned down when she returned. Residents of the neighborhood were denied seats on local buses, or kicked off buses when it was discovered where they were from. People from the entire city of Goiania were denied hotel rooms when they traveled elsewhere in Brazil. Buses coming from the city were stopped. Two pilots were fired after they refused to let people from Goiania board a commercial flight. People flocked to a local medical facility for weeks to be checked for radiation, roughly 100,000 in all, and many of them came simply for the certificate they could get that declared them radiation-free and safe to be near. Some people in the affected neighborhood brought their pets to be certified as safe after someone started shooting stray animals, afraid that the *animals* were radioactive and dangerous.

Remember Hester Prynne in *The Scarlet Letter*, forced to wear the bright red A, for adulteress, and socially shunned? The people in the affected area of Goiania might just as well have been forced to wear a bright blue R, for radiated, or G, for Goiania, given how they were shunned out of fear. Goiania was an example of a powerful social force that amplifies our perceptions of risk: stigmatization. The people from Goiania were treated like plague-infested rats. In fact, the very word *stigma* speaks to the way in which social pressures play a role in our Risk Response. People who are stigmatized, branded with a mark or a reputation, are social outcasts, to be shunned by the tribe. There may be some underlying reason to fear them, as was the case with lepers long ago. But the stigma—the mark itself—adds to our fears. And stigma doesn't happen only to people.

Technologies can become stigmatized, like genetically modified food in Europe. Substances can become stigmatized, like mercury. Whole classes of substances can become stigmatized. Remember the earlier example of the class of substances generally referred to as "chemicals"? A survey asked people what came to mind when they heard that word. The leading category of answers included words like *toxic, hazardous, deadly, destruction, accidents, kill, harmful, bad,* and *cancer.*[6] In the 1970s, the Monsanto Chemical Company had an advertising slogan, "Without Chemicals, Life Itself Would Be Impossible," specifically designed to counteract the stigmatization of chemicals.

Even ideas about how to manage risks can become stigmatized. A survey in 1986 asked residents of Phoenix, Arizona, to say whatever came to mind when they heard the phrase "underground nuclear waste storage." This was at a time when the most likely site for such a facility was Yucca Mountain in neighboring Nevada. The top five categories of responses were "dangerous" (including words like *danger, hazardous, toxic, harmful,* and *disaster*), "death" (*sickness, death, dying,* and *destruction*), "negative" (*wrong, bad, terrible,* and *horrible*), "pollution" (*contamination, spills,* and *leakage*), and "war" (*bombs, nuclear war,* and *holocaust*).[7] Certainly there are sound reasons to be cautious about such a facility. But the stigma attached to it is a social construct that adds to our fears. In many parts of the world, the idea of an underground nuclear waste storage facility has been stigmatized as something to be shunned every bit as much as those people from Goiania were.

Other Social Influences

Other behavioral phenomenon can be important social contributors to perceptions of risk. One is called Groupthink. Under threat, people tend to make quick and Affective decisions about risk based more on everybody agreeing (the tribe can protect itself better if everyone in the tribe sees the threat the same way) than on carefully analyzing the facts, testing them against reality, and applying the morals of the group to the potential options. (You don't want to have a long-drawn-out, democratic discussion of what everybody thinks about the risk of a lion attack when the lion is actually attacking!) Groupthink is a sort of fear first, think second, and fear more, think less response, just the way the individual human brain does it, only on a social scale.

A fair argument can be made that Groupthink contributed to the support that most Americans gave to the invasion of Iraq following the terrorist attacks of September 11, 2001. Americans were afraid, so they did not carefully analyze whether Iraq was in fact a direct threat to the safety of America, either via weapons of mass destruction or because of a working relationship with Al Qaeda (both of which turned out not to be the case). In retrospect, Americans, both those outside the White House and apparently those inside as well, didn't think carefully about the consequences of breaking up a government in a country with seething historical religious divisions. We certainly didn't give much thought to the consequences of the moral leap of neoconservatism, the belief that the United States has the right to use its power, including military power, to impose its way of life on others. We simply fell in line with the group, which felt safe but created a huge Perception Gap that caused immense damage to the United States and the world, given the results of that invasion. But that's fact-based hindsight. At the time of the invasion, the influence of Groupthink on America's risk perception was strong. A Gallup poll found that 80 percent of Americans supported the war.

The fear of terrorism in the United States after the September 11 attacks, and the anthrax attacks that followed just weeks later, demonstrates another important social influence on our perceptions of risk. Advocates, politicians, businesses, opinion leaders, and just about anybody with access to the Internet and some kind of opinion they want to share are constantly trying to get us to see risk issues their way. For years after those attacks, to pursue what it thought was the best way to fight terror, the Bush administration dramatized the risks, contributing to the public's fear. (Republican presidential primary candidate Rudolph Giuliani was still trying to exploit that fear six years later in his 2008 presidential campaign.) But they were hardly the first politicians to use fear to advance a political agenda. A quick scan of world history would have no trouble finding some version of "Vote for Me. I'll Keep You Safe" in many political campaigns.

But politicians aren't the only ones deliberately playing with our perceptions of risk. Environmental advocates dramatize the risks of bovine growth hormone, offshore drilling, Alar, hazardous waste sites, and mercury (all of which are risks, but not nearly as dramatic as some make them out to be). Businesses that sell potentially risky products or services, such as pesticides, nuclear power, and hormone replacement therapy medications (all of which are relatively low risks, but riskier than the industries manufacturing them would have you believe), play down those risks. Businesses that sell things to keep us safe play *up* the dangers from which their products or services will protect us: crime (buy a gun), sudden infant death syndrome (buy our monitor to hear if your sleeping infant is still breathing in the other room), or child abduction (buy our fingerprint and DNA swab kit—honest, that's a real product). Consumer advocates dramatize the risks from food, toys, or drugs, while the food, toy, or drug industry, and sometimes the government agencies that regulate those products, try to play them down. Critics of government magnify fears about food safety, drug safety, highway safety, or environmental dangers in order to dramatize their calls for the reform of agencies that oversee various aspects of public health. In some cases, advocates, regulators, and businesses all play *up* risks to achieve their own goals on a given issue (government antismoking campaigns and companies selling products to help people stop smoking, government highway safety campaigns and car manufacturers both talking about safety features on certain vehicles, public health advocates who want us to lose weight and companies promoting the healthy benefits of their oatmeal or exercise machine or diet book). Lawyers jump in when a risk issue arises and play up our fears in search of class action riches (brain cancer from cell phone radiation, silicone breast implants, drug side effects). Pundits and professional "opiners" advocate their views on risk issues, playing the danger up or down depending on which position supports their underlying worldview. And the global spread of the Internet and social media have created millions of new advocates adding their voice to society's 24/7 Tower of Babel about risk issues, all trying to shape what you and I think.

If you pay a little attention to the way these social intermediaries play risk up or down, you'll find that they are tapping into the risk perception psychology that we've been talking about. The environmental campaign against Alar played on our fear for children. The Monsanto campaign "Without Chemicals, Life Itself Would Be Impossible" tried to frame things from the perspective of Risk versus Benefit. Politicians who promise safety from terrorists play on your fear of Uncertainty. Companies that sell products with which you can protect yourself emphasize that their products give you Control. These social intermediaries are really only taking advantage of (and further confirming the reality of) what we've been talking about all along, the Affective roots of how you and I and all of us respond to risk.

But there is one social institution that we haven't talked about yet that profoundly shapes what we think about risks: the news media. Their impact is so important that they deserve a special section all their own.

AND THAT'S THE WAY IT IS

Blaming the news media is a favorite way to explain why many people are convinced that these are the riskiest times humans have ever faced, despite the fact that we live in a safer world than humans have ever lived in. That blame is well deserved—and it isn't. It's correct. But it's naive and simplistic.

People may be living longer, healthier lives than ever (not in some places, of course), but new risks—profound risks like climate change and terrorism and all sorts of pollution and overconsumption of resources—have replaced bygone threats like dying in childbirth or lack of clean drinking water or smallpox or polio. It's too simplistic to say that the media are making us afraid. There are plenty of real reasons to worry. But the media are certainly making things worse by contributing to a general sense that the world is a scarier place than it actually is.

First let's define our terms. The information continuum from which we find out about the world "out there," beyond our own personal experience, is vast: movies, music, books, magazines, television programs, theater, advertising, the online blogosphere, information Web sites, social networking sites, and instant messaging. They all play a role in shaping what we know. However, the focus here is on the part of the continuum thought of as "news": newspapers, TV, radio, and news magazines, in both their old media and new media forms, along with online news sources that purport to report more than they opine (although the line here is frustratingly fuzzy).

I focus on the news media not because they are the principal way by which people find out about what's going on. They aren't.

According to the Pew Research Center for the People and the Press, only half of Americans say that they check out the news in one form or another on a daily basis.[8] They are the focus here because, uniquely among all the ways in which we get information, the news media are *supposed* to just report the facts. They are *supposed* to tell the truth. They are *supposed* to be balanced and neutral. We depend on the news media for accurate information that we can trust, information on which we can base intelligent choices.

Walter Cronkite used to sign off the *CBS Evening News* saying, "And that's the way it is." It was just an innocuous way to say goodbye. But Cronkite's trademark close perfectly captures a more profound truth about the news media. For better or worse, pretty much all we know about "the way it is" is what the news media tell us. How do we know what's happening to the climate of the earth? All we know about on our own is the local weather. How do we know what's happening to the economy? All we know about on our own is whether we still have jobs and what things cost. How do we know about the risk of nuclear energy or mercury or terrorism or vaccines? For most things, "the way it is" is the way the news media tell us it is.

So the news media play a crucial role in the way we see the world. In general, the news media tend to play up the scary, the negative, the dramatic, and the controversial aspects of things, so "the way it is" often seems darker and more threatening than things really are.

Before I go on, *mea culpa.* I was a daily television reporter for 25 years, and most of the things that journalists do that make the world sound like a riskier place than it is, I did. I won the DuPont Columbia Award twice, one of the top awards for quality broadcast journalism. But I regularly played up the dramatic aspects of my stories, emphasizing the negative or the frightening or the controversial, and deemphasizing (or omitting altogether) the aspects that would balance things out or put them in perspective. To the best of my knowledge, I never lied, and I tried not to twist the facts to reflect any personal beliefs. But I did what most journalists do: I made choices that would make my stories more newsworthy, more dramatic, and more likely to attract attention. And that left my viewers with a distorted and more alarming view of the world than was actually the case.

Some call this sensationalism. That's too strong. Sensationalism to me is the lurid gossip—"Actress in Sex Romp!"—and wild lies— "Baby Born with Antlers" (you should have seen the picture)— featured in tabloids and celebrity outlets. Fortunately, the public apparently can recognize blatant sensationalism and gossip. According to the Pew Research Center, in the United States, of those who read *People* magazine in 2008, only 8 percent found it credible. Only 5 percent of readers of the *National Enquirer* thought they could believe what it said. There are similar data showing that the British public doubts the credibility of tabloids like the *Sun* and the *Daily Mirror* compared with the credibility of the *Telegraph* and the *Times* and the *Guardian*.

Sensationalism is easy to spot, and to doubt. We can avoid being too heavily influenced by overtly sensational news coverage because it's obvious. But the more mainline news media dramatize their information in subtle ways that are harder to spot and defend against, and are therefore more insidious in how they affect us. In daily run-of-the-mill news coverage, the alarmist tendencies of the news media are manifested more in the smaller editorial decisions about which stories to include and which ones to omit, which ones to put on the front page or to lead the broadcast, which facts or quotes or pictures to use, and which facts to play up or play down or simply omit. These choices don't make the news "sensationalist," but they certainly make "the way it is" sound more alarming.

Consider the following two hypothetical stories, based on precisely the same facts. Note the headlines, the page in the paper on which the story ran, and the choice and placement of facts and quotes.

CHEMICAL SPILL CAUSES CONCERN

Section A, p. 2

Will Scarem, News Staff

State environmental officials say they are testing a suspicious bright blue chemical, believed to be a cyanide compound similar to the material used in rat poison, found yesterday on the banks of the Housatonic River just upstream from the drinking water intakes of the cities of Lowell and Lawrence.

They say the material appears to be a form of cyanide called 1-2-3-4, which is not harmful. But they say they will be doing further tests to be sure. The material was removed from the site by workers in special protective isolation suits. As much as 30 grams of the material had to be removed.

The spill was found adjacent to the controversial Peterson Johnson chemical plant, which was the site last month of a leak of hydrogen chloride gas that caused the evacuation of 30,000 people for more than 16 hours. Authorities say they believe the spill did not emanate from the plant. They think it came from a passing B and M freight train that, according to a spokesperson, "had a valve that wasn't completely closed." State investigators say they intend to interview officials of the railroad. They could face fines or other legal action for possible violation of environmental laws.

The Housatonic River supplies drinking water to the downstream cities of Lowell and Lawrence. Environmental officials said they never notified operators of the water systems in those cities about the spill.

CHEMICAL SPILL REMOVED

B Section, p 13

Will Scarem, News Staff

State environmental officials say a small amount of a cyanide compound found on railroad tracks in Nashua yesterday was safely removed and posed no threat to public or environmental health.

They identified the compound as cyanide 1-2-3-4, an inert, harmless material used by industry in making soap. A chemistry professor at a major local university confirms that cyanide 1-2-3-4 does no harm to people or the environment. Approximately one teaspoon of material was found, and it was removed without the need for special equipment.

Officials say they believe the material came from a small leak in a freight car from the B and M railroad, which runs freight trains carrying chemicals on those tracks. Officials say they will question railroad operators, but added, "They have a clean record. We've never had a problem with them before."

The spill was found near the Peterson Johnson chemical plant, where a release of a dangerous gas last month forced the temporary evacuation of 30,000 people. Officials say the plant had nothing to do with this spill.

Neither story lies. Both use the same information. But the first one clearly makes things more dramatic, from the bigger headline, to its placement on a more prominent page in the paper, to the story itself. The first version calls the spilled substance "suspicious" and likens it to rat poison. The second version says the material is not dangerous. The first version highlights that the spill occurred near the drinking water intakes of two large cities, and says officials from those cities were not notified. This is true, and worrisome, but the second story reports that information in a more neutral way, noting that there was no threat to those drinking water supplies.

The first version magnifies how much material was spilled ("*As much as* 30 grams"), while the second story describes the amount as "a teaspoon." The first version dwells on the proximity of the spill to a chemical company that has had problems in the past.

The second story notes this fact, but adds that the company wasn't involved this time. The first version notes that the railroad that is possibly responsible for the spill might face fines. It does not include the moderating quote that shows up in the second story from an official, who says, "They have a clean record. We've never had a problem with them before."

Version 1, "Chemical Spill Causes Concern," exemplifies how the news media handle risk stories. They don't make things up, and they don't wildly sensationalize. But they magnify. They dramatize. They emphasize the parts of the story that make it more attention-getting. Why? The usual answer is, "to sell papers." But that's only half true. Yes, the editors and news directors and show producers in TV and radio do this to sell tomorrow's product. Their journalism is profoundly driven by profit.

But reporters and photographers dramatize for a different reason. They want their work to get attention. They want to be on the front page, or to be the lead story in the newscast, or to run at the top of the home page. Yes, they want to please their bosses, and they know their bosses want product that will draw a reader or viewer or listener's attention in order to enhance corporate profits. But mostly the reporters who gather the facts, who decide whom to interview and what to ask and how to interpret what they find out, who decide which facts to include or omit and which facts to emphasize or play down, and the photographers who decide what information should be included and highlighted in their pictures or video—they really don't care about selling tomorrow's paper or boosting tomorrow's ratings or Web site hit count. They just want their work to get attention.

The end result of those different motivations, though, is the same. People in the news media make choices that help make their story a "better" story, a more attention-getting story. The net effect, when it comes to stories about risk, is that the more dramatic, alarming aspects of the news get played up. And aspects that would ameliorate the alarm or moderate the drama get played down, or left out. And because most editors and writers and producers and reporters and photographers are making decisions like this all the time, the news generally depicts a world more filled with controversy and risk and drama and danger than is actually the case.

Consider those two stories on mad cow disease featured back in Chapter 2 in the section on Framing. They're worth a closer look because they perfectly illustrate the subtle ways in which the news media tend to play up the scary, controversial, negative aspects of things. The *Wall Street Journal* story, "Scientific Data Offer No Proof of Beef Safety," was about whether eating the muscle meat from a mad cow can make people sick. Based on more than a decade of experience in Britain, where the disease began, the overwhelming consensus among the top scientists in this field was that meat from cows did not spread the disease. Only brain and spinal cord tissue did. But the *Wall Street Journal* story emphasized that doubts remained about meat. In the fourth paragraph, the report said that beef hasn't been shown to be dangerous, but then cited "leading experts" who said that the risk from meat is "unknown." (*Uh-oh! Uncertainty!*) The story then devoted several paragraphs to just one lone dissenting expert and his doubts about the safety of cow meat.

It wasn't until the eighteenth paragraph that the reporter told his readers about the overwhelming evidence from extensive research that meat from mad cows is not what makes people sick. Not until deep into his story did he finally offer the reassuring evidence that out of tens of millions of Britons exposed to beef for years in a country that was known to have lots of sick cows, only 143 got sick. And it wasn't until the nineteenth paragraph that the reporter finally cited another scientist, who described extensive research done specifically to see if meat can carry the disease from cow to human, that found that, no, it can't.

This is an example of the "Chemical Spill Causes Concern" sort of coverage that risk stories usually get. The coverage doesn't lie, but the alarming parts are played up, and the facts and quotes and experts that might moderate that alarm are played down. By the time a meat-eating *Wall Street Journal* reader got to the reassuring eighteenth and nineteenth paragraphs (*if* the reader got that far), that reader would have been good and worried about his next steak or burger.

The clarity of this example was highlighted by the *Washington Post* story on the same issue, which is more like the "Chemical Spill Removed" kind of coverage. The headline (paraphrased) said, "Most Scientists Agree; Muscle Meat Is Unlikely to Transmit Mad Cow Disease," a much more balanced and less alarming choice of words than the headline in the *Wall Street Journal*. The *first* paragraph cited "carefully acquired evidence . . . showing that muscle from sick cows does not transmit the disease." The *third* paragraph acknowledged the remaining doubts, but put them in perspective, telling the reader, "The evidence for [the safety of meat] is strong and convincing. But as with all assessments of biological risk, it is not absolute and unqualified." The *fourth* paragraph cited the expert whose views represent the overwhelming scientific consensus, the one that wasn't quoted until paragraph 19 in the *Journal*. The *Washington Post* article also cited the critic whose perspective was the thrust of the article in the *Journal*, but in the *Post*, the lone critic came later, in paragraph 25.

Here are two stories, in two reputable newspapers, by award-winning reporters, on precisely the same subject at the same time, using the same facts and citing the same experts. In one, the reporter clearly emphasized the scarier facts and made the risk sound more alarming. This approach dominates the way the news media report on risk. Whether it's because the reporter wants her story on page one or because her editor wants to sell tomorrow's paper doesn't matter. The effect is the same. The public's perception of "the way it is" is influenced like Henny Penny and Turkey Lurkey and all the other animals that started worrying when Chicken

Little yelled, "The sky is falling," and we suffer a Perception Gap between our fears and the facts, a gap that can be harmful in and of itself.

If It Scares, It Airs

How do people in the news media figure out what will get our attention? Well, reporters and editors are people too, people with amygdalas, people whose judgments are affected by Representativeness and the Framing Effect and the other mental shortcuts that we all use to process partial information, people whose Risk Response is influenced by perception factors like Trust and Control and Natural versus Human-Made and all the others. Only what makes you or me more afraid makes a journalist more *excited*. If a journalist senses something threatening about a set of facts, he senses that those facts will make for a "better" story, i.e., a story that will get more attention. And those aspects will get played up.

Consider news about the Guidant Corporation, the story described in the section on the Trust factor in Chapter 3. To refresh your memory, Guidant got reports that one of its popular products, a defibrillator, was failing, but the failures were rare, so the company chose not to announce the problem publicly.

But the doctors of a 21-year-old patient who died after his device failed demanded that Guidant report the defect. When the company refused, the doctors took their story to the *New York Times*. The newspaper reported that Guidant had withheld information from the public about a risk associated with one of its products. The company had violated the trust of patients and their doctors by denying them information that they needed if they were to make informed health-care choices. The Risk Perception Factor of Trust (as in betrayal of) made this an attention-getting story.

Trust was central to the first *New York Times* stories, which suggested that the company kept the secret to protect its profits at the expense of its patients' well-being. Meanwhile, the reporter barely mentioned how low the risk of failure of the device actually was, and didn't report for weeks on the far greater risk that people would face if they chose operations to remove or replace their defibrillators. That's the Risk Perception Factor of Risk versus Benefit, a critical aspect for readers trying to decide what to do. But noting the trade-offs would have diminished the alarming, attention-getting nature of the risk side of the story. So the Risk Perception Factor that might have diminished the fear got played down.

The *Times*'s reporting, which led to national coverage of the story, produced a media-fueled Perception Gap that created real risk for the public. As a direct result of that coverage, thousands of people with defibrillators made by Guidant or other companies had them removed or replaced, creating far more risk than existed because of the one Guidant product that had the defect.

You can see this risk perception psychology in a lot of news coverage about risk, which will generally play down the benefits and play up the dangers. Stories about the danger of airbags spiked in the United States in the mid-1990s after deploying airbags killed several children. (That Personified the story, another Risk Perception Factor that always piques journalists' interest, and, all the better/more dramatic for the news, it was about a risk to Children.) The reports cited the number of kids killed, but practically none of the coverage (including mine, *mea culpa*) offered statistics on how many lives, of children and adults, had been *saved* by these devices.

Coverage of the issue of mercury is another example of how the risk gets played up and the benefit either gets played down or is left out. Almost invariably, the risk from the mercury contained in seafood is mentioned earlier and more frequently than the trade-off benefit of the nutrients in seafood. In fact, sometimes the benefit side of the mercury story is omitted, or stories about the benefits never appear. Remember that study in the *Lancet* that reported that the benefits for the cognitive health of their newborns of pregnant women consuming seafood outweighed the risks to the cognitive health of their newborns from pregnant women consuming seafood?[9] That's a pretty apples-to-apples risk/benefit trade-off. That study was not reported in the *New York Times, USA Today,* or the *Wall Street Journal,* according to a check of their archives, which turn up plenty of stories on the risks of mercury.

Risks that are Catastrophic (plane crashes) get covered more than risks that are Chronic (heart disease). Risks that involve greater Pain and Suffering (shark attacks) get covered more than much more likely threats that involve less suffering. (Food poisoning strikes 76 million Americans a year, 5,000 of whom *die.* But only occasional high-profile outbreaks are reported.) Risks to Children get covered more than the same hazards if they imperil adults. News stories highlight Uncertainty and lack of Control, and they are built around Personification. In almost any news story on risk, you will find at least a couple of Risk Perception Factors highlighted that make the story more dramatic. Those will be the elements that get played up, while information that evokes psychological factors that would cause less fear will be played down.

News Consumer Beware: Tools to Protect Yourself from Overly Scary News Coverage

You can defend yourself against some of this sort of dramatized risk reporting. There are several specific ways in which the news media play up the alarming aspects of stories about risk that you can watch out for. One is the selective emphasis on either the relative or the absolute risk numbers. Relative risk is when the statistical danger is *compared to* something else. The relative increase of a risk going from 1 in a million to 2 in a million is 100 percent. *Whoa!* The absolute risk is simply the number of victims, 2 people out of a million. Not so *Whoa!* News stories frequently emphasize whichever number, the relative or the absolute risk, sounds more dramatic. In 2006, the Associated Press reported on a study that found that women using a patch to deliver estrogen for birth control had double the risk of blood clots compared with women who take birth control medication in pill form. The relatively greater risk from the patch was 100 percent. Buried down in paragraph nine, the reader finally got the absolute risk numbers: 3 to 5 women out of 10,000 on the pill ran the risk of the clots, so a 100 percent increase only meant that about 6 to 10 women out of 10,000 using the patch were at risk. That was hardly as alarming, so this information was buried in the story. *You should look for both numbers, the relative and the absolute risk.*

Journalists personalize their stories around actual victims. This is a fair device for compelling storytelling. Frequently, however, to make things more dramatic, they choose victims who are more compelling, like a young mother with breast cancer, rather than victims who actually represent most of the people at risk (3 out of 4 cases of breast cancer affect women past the age of 55). If a family is at risk, the news story will often focus on the children simply because any risk to kids is scarier than the same risk if it threatens only adults. *So ask yourself if the victim in the story fairly represents the population most at risk.*

Lots of stories dramatize risks by failing to even include the two elements required for something to be risky, Exposure and Hazard. For something to be a risk to you, it has to be potentially harmful *and* you have to be exposed to it. Think of a poisonous snake. A snake in a cage might be scary, but you're not at risk because you are not directly exposed to it. Now think of a *non*poisonous snake that is *not* in a cage, but slithering right at your feet. Again, it might be scary, and you are exposed to it. But in this case it's not a risk because it's not hazardous. Consider, then, stories about methyl tertiary butyl ether (MTBE), a gasoline additive that leaked out of storage tanks and polluted local drinking water. Pretty scary, right?

We are being *involuntarily* exposed to a *human-made* chemical, two big Risk Perception Factors (along with the Stigma of anything to do with chemicals triggering the Representativeness Effect). But is MTBE hazardous? Few of the initial stories on MTBE included any specific information on whether or how MTBE was harmful, because there was no sound evidence yet that it was. Stories that acknowledged the lack of any hard evidence of hazard did so only at the end, burying the facts that would downplay the drama and the alarm. Are the MTBE leaks newsworthy? Absolutely. But emphasizing exposure while omitting or downplaying the lack of hard evidence of hazard is an example of how the media play up the scarier aspect of things. (Since those early stories, the evidence has built that MTBE may be hazardous.)

The opposite happens too. Many stories report on the hazard without including information on the exposure. Stories about hazardous waste sites do this all the time. Piles of rusting drums leaking strangely colored gunk, or stories about various harmful things with long chemical names dumped on the ground, make for attention-getting news. But in almost all cases, the only risk is to people exposed by direct contact with the hazardous material, and usually, fortunately, the number of people who are directly exposed to hazardous waste sites is pretty small. But mentioning how few people are actually in peril from hazardous waste makes the story *less* dramatic, so the exposure side of stories on hazardous waste often gets played down or left out. (*Mea culpa* time: I did many stories like this, pointing an accusatory finger at pollution emitted from smokestacks or drainage pipes without offering my viewers any information on whether the tiny amounts they were being exposed to were hazardous.)

So look for information on whether you are exposed, and whether the substance you're exposed to is actually hazardous.

And one more note on exposure: *how much* matters. In many cases, the amount of the hazard to which we're exposed is below the level that is thought to do harm. Not surprisingly, in those cases, information on dose rarely appears in the story, or it shows up only at the end. (Sometimes tiny doses do feature prominently in stories, usually in stories that warn ominously that science doesn't yet know whether those doses might be hazardous. *Uh-oh!* Uncertainty!) When the information about dose amplifies concern, it is played up. When it moderates the concern, it is played down. So *look for information about dose in the risk stories you read.* (In the next chapter, there are more details on the facts you need to know in order to make a more informed judgment about any risk.)

In the News Media's Defense

Let's be careful here. News is what's new, what stands out, what is different or interesting or noteworthy. News is not what we already know, the status quo. It is not news when planes *don't* crash. Stories about dramatic events (plane crashes) will be reported more than stories about the mundane (the daily death toll from heart disease). Stories about a new risk, like West Nile virus, will get more coverage than other larger risks simply because the risk is new, not necessarily because of the scale of the threat. Information about what might harm you is more noteworthy than information about what is safe. The business of news—and let's not naively forget that it *is* a business—is to provide information that is noteworthy, relevant, or valuable. Information *we want.* So the very definition of news preselects for stories that are more dramatic and alarming.

It is also simplistic to charge that the media are unduly negative. It turns out that they play up the hopeful, too, for the same reasons. Anything that threatens your health will get your attention, and anything that promises to protect it will too. Both sorts of stories are about survival. The hopeful aspects of certain stories are played up too, like the initial study that finds a possible cure for some disease, which only mentions much later in the story that the possible cure is at best several years away.

It is also simplistic to complain that smaller risks are overreported and the big ones go underreported. While the charge is certainly true, the basis of this argument is the assumption that it is journalism's job to educate us, to teach us about what is really important, to decide for us what we need to know. That is not only wrong, it's dangerous. Think about it. Suppose you think the news content in the *Wall Street Journal* is too conservative. (It isn't, but some people who don't like the conservatism of the paper's editorial pages think it is.) Do you want those gun-toting right-wing free-market editors and reporters deciding for you what you should know about which risks are the most important? Or suppose you think the *New York Times* news content is too liberal. (It isn't, but again, news content and editorial opinion get confused, especially by anyone looking at those editorials from the other side of the political spectrum.) Do you want those Prius-driving chardonnay drinkers deciding what you should know about what *they* think are the most important risks?

There is another danger here. Can we trust the human beings who bring us the news to perceive risks any more "rationally" than we do? Journalists are people too, subject to the same Affective influences on *their* risk responses that we are. If something is Uncertain or fraught with Pain and Suffering, or if it triggers some instinctive fear in the amygdala, or if it is Framed in a certain way by advocates, or if it triggers loud alarms because of the Ready Recall/Awareness Effect, those factors will influence a journalist's judgment the same way they will influence yours or mine. The result will be an Affective Risk Response, not the kind of more purely fact-based response that we suppose journalists should make in the public's best interest. The same things that shape our perceptions of risk, a mix of facts *and* feelings, shape the judgments of the human beings who make decisions about what we know about "the way it is." We can't entrust editors and reporters and photographers with the responsibility of telling us what we really need to know, because they're no better at separating their feelings from the facts than we can ever be.

Journalists also bring their personal experiences and life circumstances to their decision making. There is a joke among reporters in the news business that "news is what happened to your boss this morning." It's funny to people in the news business, because it's true. I remember one boss who assigned me to do a story on the risk to motorists driving past private country club golf courses of having their cars dinged by errant golf balls, because that's what had happened to his new luxury car that morning on his way to work. Another boss once decided against a story on the dangers to kids at day-care centers, which she didn't think would interest most people, because, she later admitted, she didn't have kids.

Biases show up in other ways too. The very definition of what is a news provider is changing, as more and more people get their news and information online. Overt biases reflecting all sorts of political and cultural and religious and economic points of view riddle online information sites, many of which are actually the sites of advocates *posing* as providers of unbiased information. For example, you can get your environmental "news" from ACSH.org (American Council on Science and Health), whose mission statement says that it tries to "add reason and balance to debates about public health issues and bring common sense views to the public." In other words, *we want to counteract those overemotional environmental doomsayers.* Or you can get your environmental news from ENN.com (the Environmental News Network), whose mission statement says, "We help nonprofits, governments and businesses from around the world get their information published and read by the people who want to help make this planet a better place." In other words, *we make money by presenting as "information" the views of environmental advocacy groups.* Do you think either site is going to provide the kind of neutral, unbiased information that you need in order to make informed choices about environmental risk issues?

Welcome to the democratization of information, where the prospect of news distorting and polarizing our views on risk (and anything else) grows worse and worse as pretty much anyone can become an information provider, where bias and opinion mix so heavily with information content that standards of accuracy and neutrality and balance and fairness fly out the virtual window. The growth of online news media that blur fact and opinion will surely exacerbate the role that the media play in feeding the Perception Gap between our fears and the facts.

Somewhat reassuringly, a survey of American online news consumers finds that they trust the credibility of what they read online even less than they trust the news they get from TV, radio, or newspapers. Fewer than half of the respondents to the 2008 survey by the Pew Center for the Press and Society said that they trusted the credibility of four high-profile "news" sites: the Drudge Report, Slate, the Huffington Post, and Salon. Even aggregators like Google and Yahoo!, who merely bring together news from existing journalism organizations, are thought credible by only 50 to 60 percent of their visitors. The bad news here is that more and more people are getting their news online, although they have doubts about the trustworthiness of what they're getting.

Not so reassuringly, psychologists have well established the theory of cognitive dissonance: we tend to believe what we already believe, and to dispute anything that conflicts with it. As a result, we seek out information that agrees with what we already believe and simply don't go looking for anything else. The online world makes that dangerously easier. It provides information that has been filtered through all sorts of biases, and we can simply choose the sites that agree with our perspectives and not pursue other views on those same facts. The Internet's wide-open flow of information is appealing for many reasons, but there is a very real prospect that it will make our views on risk issues (and all the culture war issues) more polarized and more destructive, because now we can seek out only the information with which we agree, and we just plain won't know anything else.

The argument that the news media should pay more attention to the big risks because it is their responsibility to decide for us what we ought to know is not just risky for all those reasons. It's also naive. Yes, journalism serves a vital civic role by keeping people informed, but editors and reporters and photographers are not public servants. Critics of the news media fail to understand, or accept, that the information gatekeepers who decide what we know (and also therefore what we don't know) are not making their decisions in the public's best interest. News is a business. It sells us a product we want: information we might find interesting or valuable or relevant, information that will get our attention. And we will pay attention to information about risk in direct relation to how that information *feels,* not just to the facts. It is *our* psychology, the *customers'* psychology, to which the media are responding. The gatekeepers try to figure out what we *want* to know, not what we *need* to know. As critical as the news media are to society, profoundly shaping "the way it is," expecting them to report on risk in direct proportion to the scale of the risk in the name of public health is like asking shoe companies to sell only shoes that are good for our feet.

A few other points in the news media's defense. The news is simplistic because it has to be. Space and time limitations don't allow for inclusion of all the details, and the attention span of most news consumers wants information to be short and simple anyway. The first draft of history, as some have called daily news, is written as a summary.

The 24/7 competition among the media makes this worse. Deadlines are minute by minute. Even at large newspapers, which offer more depth, the average reporter is filing copy for the paper, up-dates for the Web site, and sometimes blogs or even audio or video for the podcast every day. In the new media age, reporters have little time to dig into stories and learn everything they need to know before they have to file their work. So if a study shows up that says that MTBE is leaking into groundwater supplies, report-ers often don't have time to find out whether MTBE is hazardous, in what ways, or at what dose, even if they wanted to.

Journalism also gets more of a bad rap than it deserves because the news media don't create the risks, they just report them. Yes, they selectively choose stories that are more dramatic, and yes, they play up the dramatic and the negative, and sometimes the overly hopeful aspects of things. But journalists didn't put mercury in seafood. Journalists didn't cause the Chernobyl accident. Journal-ists didn't cause MTBE to leak into drinking water.

And finally, for all the harm they do by magnifying the scary aspect of things, the news media play a vitally important role in providing us with information that we need in order to keep our-selves healthy and safe. They may dramatize, but the news media tell us about things we need to know that we would not otherwise know. The *Washington Post* made the public in the metropolitan D.C. area aware of the high level of lead in its drinking water. BBC news anchor (presenter, in U.K.-speak) Ann Diamond focused at-tention on sudden infant death syndrome, when babies suffocate because they've been left face down in their cots to nap, saving hundreds of lives. We need the news media to find out when poli-ticians or government officials or companies are keeping secrets about things that bear on our safety. It was the Japanese news me-dia that found out that the government was lying about its claim that the public was safe because there was a ban on feeding cattle in ways that might cause mad cow disease to spread. There are plenty of examples in which the news media sounded an alarm we needed to hear.

So What Does It All Mean?

It has been well observed that the media do *not* tell us what to think. We decide for ourselves what to think, based on a dynamic mix of biology, psychology, experience, and social and personal life circumstances. What *is* true is that the media tell us what to think *about.* They decide which stories are reported and which ones aren't, which facts to include in each story and which ones to omit, which facts to emphasize and which ones to play down, which pictures or sound bites or graphics to use, which stories go on page one or the top of the broadcast or in the online wrap-up of "latest headlines" and which stories get less prominent placement. These "gatekeeper" choices determine what we know *and what we don't know* about "the way it is." And in covering risk, the news media generally emphasize the things that lead us to think that we live in a world where the sky is falling, more than is actually the case.

It's no great leap to see how this might affect us. People who are more afraid of defibrillators failing may increase their risk by having their device removed or replaced. People who are more afraid of terrorism may be more willing to drive rather than fly, or to change how they vote, or to support restrictions on civil liberties. And by playing *down* big risks that don't happen to make us as afraid, the media can also contribute to a Perception Gap that has serious consequences. Remember, it can be harmful to be *too* afraid, but it can also be risky when we are not afraid *enough.* Less news about heart disease than about cancer contributes to less concern about the relatively greater risk of heart disease. If there is less in the news about "regular" flu, fewer of us will get flu shots.

It may surprise you, but many news organizations have specific policies against doing news coverage that will cause people harm. That's why you don't see many stories about bomb scares or suicides, coverage that might prompt copycat behavior. Sometimes newsrooms actually hold on to scoops and revelations, at least for a little while, when publishing the information would clearly be harmful to public safety. May I make the humble suggestion that responsible people in the news media need to consider much more carefully the direct harm they cause to people by some of the professional practices mentioned earlier, which make people more worried than they need to be or leave us far less worried than we ought to be, leading to choices and behaviors and general levels of stress that do widespread *actual harm*.

There really can't be much argument that news coverage of risk contributes to what media theorist George Gerbner called "The Mean World Syndrome."[10] That's the idea that the more news people see about how dangerous things are, the more worried they are, which influences their behavior. It's the Chicken Little effect. If all we hear all the time is that the sky is falling because that's what the news media constantly tell us, and that's all we know of "the way it is," we start to walk around carrying umbrellas or ducking or looking worriedly over our shoulder. Gerbner put it this way: "Whoever tells the stories of a culture really governs human behavior." That may be excessive, but it captures the idea. As discussed throughout this chapter, there are a lot of social forces that shape our perceptions of risk, and there is no doubt that one of the most influential is what we see and hear on the news.

CHAPTER 5

CLOSING THE PERCEPTION GAP

Fear grows in darkness; if you think there's a bogeyman around, turn on the light.
—DOROTHY THOMPSON

THE RISK OF GETTING RISK "WRONG" AS INDIVIDUALS

Remember Sarah, whom we met earlier, the woman who, in the days after the September 11 terrorist attacks, chose to drive rather than fly to her mother's birthday party, and never made it? Sarah was more afraid of flying than the statistics indicated she needed to be. She was worried less about driving than the statistics suggested that she ought to. Because of the Perception Gap between her fears and the facts, Sarah made an entirely understandable choice that lead to her death. The same choice contributed to many of the additional motor vehicle deaths in the three months after the September 11 attacks, between 317 and 1,018 (depending on which of three studies you choose to cite) beyond what would have been expected for October through December. The terrorist attacks themselves killed 2,998 people, so here's the grim math: the death toll from the September 11 attacks was between 11 percent and 34 percent higher than just those killed in the attacks themselves, because people did something that felt right but that raised their risk.

Was Sarah wrong to ignore the facts or right to go with her gut? It doesn't matter. The most realistic way to think about the Perception Gap is not to judge whether it's right or wrong. It just *is*, the product of a complex Affective system composed of powerful biological roots, basic patterns of information processing, psychology, personal experiences, social and cultural influences and instincts, as well as careful conscious reasoning. While the process certainly can lead to a Perception Gap, judging such thinking as "wrong" is the same as thinking about how "wrong" it is that your heart races when you're watching a scary movie.

"...Kinda makes you not think."

But let's not kid ourselves. When we get risk wrong, when we are more afraid or less afraid than the facts suggest we need to be, the Perception Gap becomes a risk in and of itself. Just ask Sarah's kids. So we have to be honest and observe the danger of fear itself, too much *or* too little. For our own good, we must recognize that getting risk wrong, based on the statistics and other scientific facts as best science can say, can be harmful. Then we can start to ask ourselves *why* the Gap exists—what parts of the Affective system are producing fears that don't match the facts—and *that* should help us make smarter, healthier choices.

Let's consider a few examples of personal choices that lead to a potentially harmful Perception Gap. (We'll deal with the dangers of a *societal* Perception Gap next.) Many of the biggest threats to our health and safety are risks that we don't seem to worry about enough, so we'll start with a few of those.

How do you feel when bathing suit season comes around? Is that scale in your bathroom friend or foe? If you weigh more than you should, you're not alone. The World Health Organization estimates that 400 million people worldwide are obese and 1.6 billion adults are over-weight. (There would be only 1,599,999,999 if I lost about 10 pounds.) There are a lot of explanations for this. Affective risk perception is certainly one of them. Lifestyle, and the risks that come with it, are to a great degree a matter of Choice. We choose to eat those fried foods or drink those sugary soft drinks or wolf down those mega portions. We choose to lie around watching TV or movies or surfing the Net or reading or doing any number of other activities for which the root of that word, *active,* does not seem appropriate. But those are matters of choice, and when risks are voluntary, they don't worry us as much.

There is also the factor of Control. How many times have you said to yourself, or heard from a friend, "Hey, I can go on a diet," or "I'm going to start exercising." That's the same as saying, "I can do something about this." If we think we can do something about the risk, the feeling of Control can cause us to worry less. So those lifestyle changes that we need to make don't get made. ("I can go on a diet" = "One more piece of pie.")

Here's another risk where the Perception Gap creates its own danger because we aren't worried enough. Do you use a mobile phone when you drive? Millions of people do. But many of them (myself included from time to time) say to themselves, "Yeah, but I'll be careful. I'm a good driver." That's a combination of a feeling of Control and Optimism Bias. There is also some Risk versus Benefit thinking going on, since you get some benefit out of using the phone while you're driving. Influenced by all these factors, you end up raising your risk by convincing yourself that the risk isn't as high as it actually is.

Or maybe you're one of the many who have chosen to reduce the risk of DWP (driving while phoning) by operating with a hands-free device or a voice-activated system in your car. That's taking Control, isn't it? You're reducing the risk, right? Wrong! It *feels* like you're taking control, but all you're doing is freeing up your hand, which isn't the problem in the first place. The real distraction from using a phone while driving is cognitive. A brain paying attention to a phone conversation is a brain paying way less attention to operating the motor vehicle. However, since you've gone "hands-free," you may *feel* that you're safer because, after all, you've taken Control. What does that do to your sense of caution as you are DWP? It might reduce it. Which could actually raise your risk.

Have you ever spent some time in the sun trying to get that "nice healthy tan"? Or gone out for a round of golf or game of tennis or a walk with your dogs or any other sort of outdoor activity on a sunny day without putting on a hat or wearing any sunscreen? Risks that are Natural cause less concern than risks that are Human-Made, so even if you are aware of the statistics (1.3 million cases of sun-caused skin cancer in the United States each year, and approximately 8,000 deaths from melanoma), you tell yourself, "A little sun is good for me." Which is true. Only "a little" means just a few minutes, after which your reduced concern about a natural risk is actually increasing the danger you face.

But what about those millions of people who pay to get that "nice healthy tan" in salons? That risk isn't natural. It's Human-Made. Why aren't people *more* afraid of *that*? Well, first of all, it's a Choice. We do it voluntarily. And there is the Risk versus Benefit factor; "It's bathing suit season" means that you don't want to look all wan and pasty the first time you wear shorts or go to the beach. That "nice healthy tan" is perceived to be attractive. So the benefit of looking the way you want to look outweighs the risk of lying in a machine and baking your skin in carcinogenic ultraviolet radiation (and don't forget that the radiation will speed up the aging of your skin and deepen the wrinkles you will probably think are *un*attractive a few years down the road).

Drinking and driving? We think we're in Control. We Optimistically believe that it won't happen to us. The Benefit of the extra drink outweighs the Risk of driving into a tree.

More worried about outdoor air pollution than indoor air? Nine breaths out of ten are taken indoors, where pollutants include not only what came in from outside, but mold and germs and dust and chemicals given off by paint and furniture and carpet, and sometimes the levels of all these potential hazards to which we're exposed get pretty high because we don't ventilate our homes and offices and schools very well. But outdoor air pollution feels imposed. Indoor air pollution feels more voluntary. So it concerns us less, although it may well threaten us more.

Unprotected sex? Risk versus Benefit. Not wearing your seat belt? Choice, Control, and Optimism. Drinking unpasteurized milk (while protesting against milk produced with bovine growth hormone)? It's Natural. The list of risks we take when the initial risks don't evoke much of a Risk Response is long.

Now let's switch gears and consider examples of things that many of us are *more* afraid of than the evidence suggests we need to be, which also causes a dangerous Perception Gap.

As mentioned earlier, following the September 11 attacks, there was a surge in the number of Americans buying guns. FBI background checks for handgun sales jumped 39 percent in October 2001 compared with October 2000. What perception factors were at work?

Awareness of the terror threat was high, contributing to our fears. Uncertainty was high, and that usually makes people more afraid. People wanted to do something, anything, that would give them a sense of Control. So some of them bought lethal weapons, even though it was highly unlikely they would need a gun to protect themselves from terrorists, and despite the fact that guns purchased for self-protection far more often end up being used in a suicide or a crime or harming someone in an accident than actually being used for self-defense. People were subjecting themselves to higher risk, driven by fear.

When U.S. authorities announced in September 2001, just weeks after the airplane attacks, that someone was mailing "weaponized" anthrax spores in the United States, officials reassured the public that the antibiotic ciprofloxacin could treat people who had been exposed. Within hours, public demand for the drug shot up, and it stayed high for weeks. No one can quantify just how much cipro was sold or taken, but it was far more than people needed in order to stay safe. The demand was a predictable response to several Risk Perception Factors. Awareness of the threat of anthrax was sky high, Uncertainty was fierce, and, once again, people wanted something that would give them a sense of Control. An Internet medical supply company in Canada reported filling hundreds of online orders per hour. A spokesman said, "We didn't want to play into this hysteria, but popular opinion is what it is."

That fear raised people's risk by accelerating the decline in effectiveness of one of the most important broad-spectrum antibiotics we have. Bacteria are mutating all the time, and if one of them happens to mutate in a way that helps it resist cipro, then taking the drug kills off the still-susceptible germs and clears the playing field for the new, more resistant ones, which then thrive. That's bad not only for the person in which this first happens, but for all of us, because the cipro-resistant germ will almost certainly spread from person to person.

Early in 2002, a scientific paper came out showing that the effectiveness of ciprofloxacin had dropped from 86 percent to

76 percent between 1994 and 2000. So the huge increase in its use in 2001 and 2002 surely made the problem worse. In effect, our fear of anthrax, which killed 5 people and sickened 22, contributed to a Perception Gap that created a much bigger risk, since cipro is one of the last drugs we have to treat not just anthrax but a wide range of more common bacterial infections.

Here is one last quick example of a dangerous Perception Gap because of more fear than the evidence suggests is necessary. A reporter for the *Los Angeles Times* wanted help in understanding some strange behavior. She told me that a friend of hers was worried after reading several recent news stories about construction cranes collapsing and killing passing motorists. So despite the freakishly low odds of this sort of being in the wrong place at the wrong time, the friend was driving several miles out of her way on her daily commute to avoid sites with construction cranes—raising her risk of being hurt or killed in a motor vehicle crash far more than she was lowering the likelihood of being crushed by falling crane parts. I suggested that the friend might be worried because of those news stories about falling crane parts, so her Awareness was up, and the friend was trying to make herself safer, or at least make herself *feel* safer, by taking some Control.

But I also suggested that while the friend was raising one risk, she was actually reducing another danger that can arise from the Perception Gap, a far more insidious risk that most of us probably suffer from at one time or another: the risk of all sorts of damage to our health that comes from worrying too much.

The Perception Gap and Stress

Time for a brief refresher on the neuroanatomy of fear. Remember the instinctive, subconscious, instantaneous response to danger described in Chapter 1 that happens when you see a line on the ground that could be a snake or a stick? The same thing happened in that LA woman's mind whenever she saw—that's right—a construction crane. The visual information went to her thalamus, was partially processed, and was quickly relayed to the amygdala, the part of the brain where fear begins. Because the woman had associated falling crane parts with danger, her amygdala had encoded an implicit memory that made her alert for information about such a risk in the future. So now, as her amygdala got information about the presence of a construction crane, it said, "I remember that. That's dangerous," and initiated a Fight or Flight or Freeze (Triple F) response. Yes, at the biological level, the sight of a construction crane set off the same protective system that goes off when we see a snake or a spider or detect in any way, even with a thought, anything that might be dangerous.

In biological terms, perceiving a risk = stress. You may also remember that part of the Triple F response is the release of stress hormones, epinephrine and norepinephrine, and a group of hormones known as glucocorticoids, messengers that help turn up the systems that the body needs in order to deal with the threat and turn down the systems that are not immediately required. There are a host of these changes, and they all matter to your health, so I'll describe them in a bit more detail in a minute. But the first and most important thing you have to remember is that these changes aren't supposed to continue for too long. When we're confronted by a threat, we are designed to Fight, Flee, or Freeze, and then go back to normal. In the short term these changes are protective. But if they persist—that is, if you stay stressed for too long—these changes are damaging in a number of serious ways. This is all wonderfully described in Robert Sapolsky's entertaining book *Why Zebras Don't Get Ulcers*. They don't because the zebra either runs away from the attacking lion and calms down or it turns into lion food. In either case, it's all over quickly. Zebras don't stay stressed. We do, but our bodies aren't designed to handle the changes if the stress lasts more than a few days.

The specific mechanisms involved in the body's response to stress vary depending on the nature of the threat. But in general, in the short term, when you face a threat, you need energy, so the Triple F response makes your heart beat faster and does several things to raise your blood pressure, which helps speed the flow of fuel throughout the body. That's great in the short term, but chronic high blood pressure is a huge risk factor for atherosclerosis, the buildup of plaque on the lining of our blood vessels, which increases the risk of heart disease and stroke, the number one and number three causes of death in the United States.

To increase the supply of available energy, the Triple F response also changes your blood chemistry so that instead of converting whatever you may have recently eaten into energy and storing it away in your cells, energy already stored in your cells is released. A big part of this change involves a severe drop in insulin levels, since insulin helps with energy storage. Changes to natural insulin levels can, if they persist, raise your risk of diabetes, the fifth leading cause of death in the United States.

A major part of the stress response is to concentrate available resources on the systems that will help protect you by diverting those resources away from those that won't, like digestion. Processing lunch is not a priority if you're under attack. Shutdown of digestion interferes with the natural formation of stomach acid and the thick, gooey cells that line the stomach walls to protect them from that corrosive acid. That imbalance, if it persists, can contribute to ulcers and colitis and other problems with your gastrointestinal system. (Lucky zebras.)

Another system that gets turned down under conditions of chronic stress is the immune system. Actually, in the first minutes of a response to stress, the immune system gets turned up. But if the stress persists, or if it is severe, the net effect is to suppress immune function. A weakened immune system has obvious implications for your health. In fact, it's probably safe to say that the more worried you are about getting sick from something like swine flu, and the longer you stay worried, the more likely it is that you will actually get sick (although probably from something else), become sicker than you otherwise might have, stay sicker longer, or, in the worst case, die from an infection that you might otherwise have been able to fight off. The immune system is also an important part of what keeps us from developing all sorts of diseases, including cancer. There is a growing body of research that links higher levels of chronic stress with increased likelihood of developing some forms of cancer and increased difficulty in fighting those cancers once they've developed.

You don't need to devote energy to forming new bone cells when you are fighting off an attacking lion, so stress contributes to the risk of osteoporosis, a softening and weakening of the bones.

You don't need to grow while you are under attack, so stress reduces the body's normal levels of growth hormone. Chronic stress is associated with impaired growth rates in children. Acute chronic stress shuts down fast-growing hair cells and contributes to hair loss.

You don't need to procreate while you are under attack, so the fertility system is suppressed. Chronic stress is associated with fertility problems.

Do you remember from Chapter 1 that the stress response helps an area in the brain called the hippocampus to form and recall explicit memory, the kind I am currently asking you to consciously summon up? Good. That means you're not too stressed. Because if you were, your memory wouldn't be working as well. Memory formation and recall are energy-hungry processes. Stress initially prompts increases in glucose levels, which help the hippocampus with those jobs. But keeping the body under chronic or high levels of stress is like driving a car with the gas pedal mashed to the floor. You're using up fuel faster. And neither your car nor your hippocampus works very well when the fuel runs out. When glucose runs low because chronic stress has burned it up at an accelerated rate, the ability of the hippocampus to form and recall memories is impaired.

The biochemistry of stress contributes to the greater likelihood and severity of clinical depression by interfering with the neurotransmitters that help regulate mood. Each year, 19 million Americas are diagnosed with clinical depression, which contributes to half the suicides in the United States, more than 16,000 deaths.

Finally, stress impairs your ability to think, remember, and make thoughtful judgments. The more stressed you are, the harder it is for you to pay attention, to shift your attention from one thing to another, or to make decisions. (I once was told that I had a medical condition that was imminently life-threatening. I distinctly remember the sensation that some people describe as, "It was suddenly like I wasn't there, like I was numb." My hearing and vision declined. When I spoke, it was as if I was listening to myself in a movie. My ability to pay attention to the doctor went down, even as he continued to describe what I had and what I had to do.) Short-term memory is impaired (an hour later I didn't remember a lot of what the doctor had said), and because of the impacts on the hippocampus described previously, you can't remember things you learned further back either. So stress can reduce your ability to think carefully, about anything.

The evidence for these effects of stress comes largely from the lab, but many studies of real people in the real world support it. A study of Americans three years after the September 11 attacks found that those who reported ongoing worry about terrorism were three to four times more likely to report a doctor-diagnosed heart problem. Most of those people had only been exposed to terrorism by seeing it on television.[1] Studies of people who are under chronic stress show that they are more likely to come down with common colds. Many studies of cancer patients show that stress can affect the growth or spread or recurrence of tumors. Workers who report job stress are much more likely to suffer clinical depression.

So the Perception Gap can be a dangerous thing simply because of the biological effects of stress if you worry more than the evidence suggests you need to, and if that worry persists for more than a few days. (No one is sure, but experts in chronic stress believe that it needs to persist for weeks or longer before it causes some of its most insidious damage.) And the Perception Gap leads to dangerous personal choices when you are too afraid or when you are not afraid enough. It's bad for us, as individuals. But when you and I are afraid, or not afraid, of the same things for the same reasons, our concerns, or lack thereof, can lead to social policies that feel good but might not be doing us the most good. That is a societal Perception Gap, and that creates all sorts of risks too.

THE RISK OF GETTING RISK "WRONG" AS A SOCIETY

In 1987, senior managers at the EPA were trying to get a handle on a huge problem they'd been struggling with for years. They felt that the agency was spending too much to reduce some relatively smaller risks, and not enough on some bigger ones. A task force of top agency officials, in a report titled "Unfinished Business: A Comparative Assessment of Environmental Problems," found that the greatest risks were radon, global warming (this was back in 1987!), and chemicals being dumped into rivers and coastal waters. But they found that the agency was spending far more time and money on hazardous waste sites, underground fuel tanks, and garbage dumps, all of which were hot topics in the news back then, but none of which was nearly as big a risk as those other threats. The report said it directly: "'EPA's priorities appear more closely aligned with public opinion than with our estimated risks.'"

This is the Perception Gap writ large, when we as a society are more afraid of some things than we need to be, and less afraid of some other things than the evidence suggests we need to be. Just as the Perception Gap can be a risk in and of itself at the individual level, the Gap can create danger at the social level too, because when many of us as individuals are worried about similar things for similar reasons, the policies we press for as a group may not protect us from the things that actually threaten us the most. Conversely, when we aren't afraid *enough* of some relatively greater risks because they don't happen to ring our Affective alarm bells, we *don't* press for protection from *them*, and that's bad for our health too. We are Affective as people and Affective in how we respond to risk as a group. Here are some examples.

Cancer and Heart Disease

By most measures, the United States invests more in researching and fighting cancer than in researching and fighting heart disease. But statistically, heart disease is a *much* bigger risk. It has been the leading cause of death in the United States (and the world) for a long time. In the United States, heart disease killed 652,091 people in 2005. Cancer killed 559,312. Heart disease kills more men 50 and older (who have never smoked) than the three leading cancer causes of death in men combined (lung, colon, and prostate). In 2005, the greatest cancer killers in women were lung (69,000), breast (41,000), and colon cancer (26,000), a total of 136,000 women. Heart disease alone killed 329,000 women that year—140 percent more than the top three lethal forms of cancer for women, *combined.* But it's not just deaths. Millions more people have some form of heart disease than have some type of cancer. The Centers for Disease Control estimates that heart disease costs the U.S. economy $304 billion per year in health care and lost productivity. The American Cancer Society estimates that cancer costs the U.S. economy $219 billion annually.

Now let's take a look at the government's response to these two threats. In 1971, Congress passed and President Richard Nixon signed the National Cancer Act. The introductory language in that legislation makes it clear that the War on Cancer was being declared in response to public concern, noting that "cancer is the disease which is the major health concern of Americans today." Ever hear of a War on Heart Disease?

No one reliable number is available for total U.S. government spending on either cancer or heart disease. The government spends money fighting these diseases in many ways. But the figures from one agency are telling. The bulk of the U.S. government's investment in disease *research* is done through the National Institutes of Health (NIH). The NIH says that spending on cancer across its various agencies came to $5.6 billion in 2008. Spending on heart disease was $1.6 billion. (It's not as though heart disease is better understood and therefore needs less investigation. In fact, we may know less about the actual biological mechanisms of various forms of heart disease than we do about cancer, and we understand roughly the same amount about the behavioral risk factors for each.)

The table below shows the top four causes of death in the United States, how many people die from each cause per year, what the NIH spends on research on each disease, and what that comes to in research dollars per death. Note the disproportionately large investment in research on cancer.

COMPARING SPENDING ON THE FOUR LEADING CAUSES OF DEATH

CAUSE OF DEATH (U.S.)	DEATHS PER YEAR (2005, FROM CDC)	NIH SPENDING PER YEAR (2008)	RESEARCH SPENDING PER DEATH
1. Heart Disease	652,091	$1,584,000,000	$2,429
2. Cancer	559,312	$5,570,000,000	$9,958
3. Stroke	143,579	$296,000,000	$2,061
4. Chronic Lower Respiratory Disease	130,933	$75,000,000	$572

SOURCE: National Institutes of Health.

Heart disease and cancer make for a fair comparison by many factual criteria. They both disproportionately affect older people and, roughly speaking, affect people in similar demographic groups. But in terms of perception, the two diseases differ dramatically in several important Affective ways, and therein lies a big part of the explanation for this Perception Gap.

Remember those questions I asked you in the section on Pain and Suffering in Chapter 3, about whether you'd rather die being eaten alive by a shark, by fire, or by cancer, compared with heart disease? Most people choose heart disease over any of the other ways to die because the other three, including cancer, involve more pain and suffering. The greater the perceived pain and suffering, the greater the fear.

There are other Risk Perception Factors that make cancer and heart disease *feel* different too. Most people know that they can reduce their risk of heart disease with better diet and more exercise, so to some extent the elevated risk of heart disease from eating all those temptingly rich foods and being lazy feels like a matter of Choice. And the knowledge that we can always change what and how much we eat, or exercise, gives us a feeling of Control. When it comes to cancer, many people feel that the risk is imposed by genetics or environmental insults or other external factors that are *not* a matter of Choice. Compared with heart disease, cancer feels more like something that is done *to* us by someone or something else, a risk that is involuntary, and that changes how it feels. And few people realize that we can significantly reduce our risk of cancer with the same lifestyle choices that reduce our risk of heart disease, so cancer feels more like something that we can't do much about—which gives us less of a sense of Control. For protection from risks that are imposed, risks we don't feel we can do anything about once they *are* imposed, we turn to the government.

Awareness of cancer is also higher, since cancer gets a lot more attention in the news media than heart disease, and, as we learned in Chapter 2, greater awareness fuels greater concern. (A quick search of Google News for all dates turned up 3,930,000 hits for "cancer" and 910,000 hits for "heart disease.")

Social intermediaries and advocacy groups working to raise cancer awareness have been more successful than those working on heart disease. Quick, name me one celebrity wearing a wrist bracelet or a ribbon to help raise heart disease awareness. Struggling? Maybe it's easier to remember that Lance Armstrong survived testicular cancer, or Liz Taylor survived brain cancer, or Sheryl Crow, Edie Falco, Suzanne Somers, Melissa Etheridge, Cynthia Nixon, and many other famous women survived breast cancer, because they all publicly campaigned to raise concern about "their" disease. (And why is there far more advocacy about breast cancer than lung cancer for women, when lung cancer kills 60 percent more females per year in the United States? Could it be in part because lung cancer seems like a risk taken voluntarily, and breast cancer seems imposed? That's just one factor, of course, but it probably plays a role.)

So cancer and heart disease do not compare Affectively. It makes complete sense, then, that we pressure the government to protect us from cancer more than from heart disease, despite the statistics. It scares us more.

But consider what that means for Americans' health. Out of a finite amount of federal research money, more is being spent on a statistically smaller risk, and less is going to the condition that will kill far more people. It would be impossible to quantify by just how much, but this disproportionate spending means that Americans' risk from heart disease is higher than it would otherwise be if our spending matched not our fears, but the statistical realities of where the greater danger lies.

I am not suggesting that statistics alone should determine how we as a society respond to risks. As appealing as a perfectly rational, completely science-based, quantitative approach to government risk-management decision making might be, such an approach is at best naive and at worst intellectually arrogant, because it flies in the face of overwhelming evidence of the Affective way in which we human animals perceive and respond to danger. Things other than statistical probability matter, and those concerns must also be included in how the government—*our* government—responds to risk. But there can be no doubt that affect-driven risk management contributes to societal Perception Gaps, which can create dangers in and of themselves. And it's not just a matter of how we allocate money.

Fluoridation

The right-wing John Birch Society opposed fluoridation of drinking water as a communist plot. Environmental groups oppose it because, they say, fluoride is a neurotoxin and a potential carcinogen. Some people argue against fluoridation simply because too much remains unknown about its health effects. (Uncertainty. *Uh-oh!*) Here is what we *do* know, according to a major review of decades of scientific study of fluoridated drinking water by experts brought together by the U.S. National Research Council. Their 2006 report said that young children exposed to maximum allowable levels of fluoride in drinking water are at greater risk of developing fluorosis, white spots on their teeth. The expert review estimated that about 200,000 children in the United States are exposed to those maximum levels.[2] So the health risks of fluoridating drinking water are that roughly 3 percent of America's children are at risk of developing spots on their teeth. That's a real risk, but it's a long way from communism and cancer and poisoning the brain.

Meanwhile, fluoridation has been called one of the greatest public health advances in the last century because of the vast improvement in dental health that it provides, spots on some kids' teeth notwithstanding. It has reduced cavities by between 20 and

40 percent. That might not sound like much, but consider that, even with fluoridation, dental decay is the most common chronic disease in children in the United States, five times more common than asthma. After Pearl Harbor, the U.S. military had to drop its requirement that enlistees have at least 12 good teeth (normal is at least 24, which is still only three-quarters of a full set, 32) because there weren't enough Americans who qualified, *not enough Americans with half a healthy set of teeth to fight the war!* (That's a big reason why fluoridation started right after World War II.) Tooth decay can contribute to poor nutrition, weight loss, and higher rates of general infections. To put this in monetary terms, a 2001 study found that when a community invests in fluoridating water, it *saves* between $17 and $19 per person per year in reduced medical costs and lost worker productivity.[3]

But again, those are only the numbers. Water fluoridation hits several risk perception buttons. Perhaps the biggest factor is that the risk of fluoride is Imposed. As a city official said while leading a campaign to get rid of fluoride in Bellingham, Washington, in 2005, it is "an issue of . . . individual rights." In terms of Cultural Cognition from Chapter 4, "Individualists," people with an underlying sense that government ought to butt *out of,* not *into,* our lives, sure don't like the idea of society deciding for them what risks they should be protected from. As a state official said in Nevada during a fight over fluoride there, "There's a distrust of anything that the government says is good. Why are you a better guardian of my health than I am? It's reflexive."

Also, fluoride is invisible and odorless and tasteless, the form of Uncertainty called "I can't detect it." Fluoride triggers the Categorization/Representativeness mental shortcut for some people, who oppose it because it fits into a whole class of things (chemicals, environmental toxins) that some people think of as risky in general. The fluoride that people worry about is the kind that is put into the water by people, not by nature, so the risk is Human-Made. And so, despite the overwhelming health benefits of fluoridated water and the relatively minimal risks, 3 people out of 10 in the United States who drink from public water supplies, or 78 million people, drink water that has not been treated with fluoride. Major cities like Fresno and San Jose, California; Colorado Springs; Honolulu; Wichita, Kansas; and Portland, Oregon, do not have fluoridated water. Everywhere that fluoride is not used, dental health declines.

This is not an argument for or against fluoride. I'd choose it for myself, but your choice is up to you. The point here is that our choices about fluoride, and about any risk, are an Affective mix of fact and feeling that sometimes results in a Perception Gap that can have health consequences in and of itself.

Nuclear Energy

I reported extensively on nuclear power issues in New England, and I wish I knew then what I know now about the danger. The risk is real, but it is not nearly the threat I said it was in much of my reporting. So, my apologies for having contributed in my small way to a societal Perception Gap that has significant consequences for public and environmental health.

Here's what I knew back then. Radiation from nuclear power plants causes cancer. High-level radioactive waste from nuclear power plants stays radioactive for hundreds of thousands of years. There were serious questions about the competence of the people running nuclear power plants. There were questions about the independence and integrity of the government agencies that were supposed to protect us from the risks of nuclear power. That's a recipe for a lot of worry (and for a lot of attention for my news stories).

Here is what I didn't know. Ionizing radiation does indeed cause cancer, but it's not very good at it. More than 60 years of studies of nearly 86,000 of the Japanese survivors of the atomic bombs dropped on Hiroshima and Nagasaki, the *hibakusha*, have found that 582 of those survivors died prematurely from cancer as a result of their radiation exposure.[4] *Less than 1 percent* of the population exposed to ferociously high levels of radiation died of cancer. The *hibakusha* got it on their skin, they inhaled it, they ingested it, at levels *far* higher than anything that came from the worst nuclear power plant accident the world has ever known, at Chernobyl. They were guinea pigs in a horrific experiment that tells us that nuclear radiation *is* a carcinogen, but a weak one. That is pretty central to the degree of risk from nuclear power.

Here's another thing I didn't know that bears directly on how big a risk nuclear radiation is. (This is just a wee bit of science, but bear with me. It's the TV news–level version.) Some atoms, like atoms of uranium, are unstable. That just means that the natural forces holding the atom together aren't in balance, so sometimes these atoms break apart, and a bit of them goes flying off. That is radio*activity,* when the atom is *actively* breaking apart. Scientists call this *decay,* and if you happen to be within a few feet of an atom that decays and a flying atomic bit hits you or you inhale or ingest it, it *could* cause damage. But it depends on what kind of bit hits you, because it turns out that there are different types of atomic bits that go flying off when an atom decays, and the most common decay particles can't even get through a sheet of paper or a T-shirt, much less the walls or windows of buildings or cars. So even if you *are* right next to a radioactive atom when it decays, there's a good chance that it will do you no harm. (Some radioactive decay doesn't cause an actual bit of anything to fly off, but produces a wave of energy, which has more penetrating power.) There. That wasn't so complicated, was it?

That means that if the worst-case scenarios about nuclear power plants come true, and there is a huge release of radiation from some sort of accident or attack or there is a leak from a waste disposal site, a significant amount of the radioactivity (the flying bits) can't do anything to you if you are wearing clothes or you're inside. And as we've learned from the *hibakusha,* even the bits that *can* penetrate a wall or that you inhale or ingest, while carcinogenic, are not particularly potent carcinogens. So, based on the science, yes, the risk of nuclear radiation is real. But no, it isn't nearly as big as I made it sound in my reporting. Ah, but that's just the science. How does nuclear radiation feel Affectively? *Red alert!*

Radiation can cause cancer, which evokes the Pain and Suffering factor. Radiation is undetectable to our senses, raising our fear because of Uncertainty. It's also scientifically hard for most of us to understand, *adding* to Uncertainty. The Human-Made nuclear power source of ionizing radiation frightens us more than radon, which, as Linda, the neighbor of Three Mile Island, said back in Chapter 3, "it's not . . . manmade." Nuclear risk is seen as Catastrophic because of dramatic events like Three Mile Island and Chernobyl. Exposure to radiation leaking from a nuclear power plant or nuclear waste would certainly feel Imposed. The long-lasting nature of nuclear waste triggers fears for our Children. Vivid images and dramatic events feed a powerful Ready Recall influence on our ongoing worries about nuclear radiation. (Many people still think that nuclear power plants can blow up like atomic bombs. They can't.) Social forces have Stigmatized nuclear power. And underneath all these other factors, Trust in the nuclear industry has been damaged by the defensive way it has argued that the risks are small, based on the science, but failed to respect deep and very real (and scientifically explainable) public fears about the danger.

That's a long list of factors that add up to profound concern. As a result, the regulatory and financial obstacles to building nuclear power plants in the United States and many other countries around the world have dramatically curtailed the contribution of nuclear power to our energy supply. But we still want the lights to go on, so the gap has been filled by fossil fuel. Burning coal and oil and gas to make electricity evokes far less fear. It doesn't cause cancer, it's low tech and easy to understand, it's familiar, and it's not associated with the dramatic negative images of atomic bombs or catastrophes like Chernobyl. So we are comfortable with this choice. But it has come at a significant health cost that we need to acknowledge.

Fossil fuels produce massive amounts of carbon dioxide, contributing to climate change. Fossil fuel–fired power plants are a major source of particulate pollution, microscopic particles that get deep into our lungs and cause an estimated average of 24,000 premature deaths per year in the United States in people who are susceptible to respiratory and heart problems.[5] On an adjusted basis, that comes to 3,600 deaths per year from power plant emissions.[6] Compare that *annual* death toll with the estimated *lifetime* radiation-induced cancer death toll from the worst nuclear accident in history, Chernobyl—possibly as many as 4,000 deaths, according to the World Health Organization. As of 2008, there have been fewer than 100 radiation-related deaths caused by Chernobyl since the accident in 1986. In that same time span, roughly 79,000 people in the United States have died because of exposure to fine particle pollution from fossil fuel–burning power plants!

So our greater concern about nuclear power and our lesser concern about fossil fuels have created a societal Perception Gap that has profound implications for your health and mine, and for the health of the very climate on which all life depends.

Climate Change

A majority of people in most places agree that global warming is real and that human activity is contributing to rapid changes in the earth's climate, and support the idea that we ought to act now to address the problem. But when you ask people about their personal willingness to actually do something about it, like pay higher gasoline taxes, pay higher electricity costs, or moderate our consumptive lifestyles, the majority that believes the problem is real turns into a minority that is willing to act if it costs them anything. This isn't a case where people are too afraid of some environmental risk. It appears to be a case where many people aren't afraid enough.

The potential harms to human and environmental health from climate change are clear, although they are hard to predict in detail at the local level: massive coastal flooding (3 billion people will be living in coastal areas by the year 2050); more frequent and severe extreme weather (heat, droughts, floods, or hurricanes); the spread of disease-carrying insects into vast new areas; loss of water supplies in many major cities; acidification and warming of the ocean, threatening food supplies; massive species extinctions, threatening who knows which parts of the ecosystem on which human life depends; political and social instability in poorer countries, fueling terrorism and mass migrations of millions of environmental refugees—to name just a frightening few.

Yet people don't seem to be taking the risk as seriously as we should be, given the plausible prospect of such huge dangers. Concern about climate change is wide, but thin. Experts and pundits have offered several explanations. Some complain that environmentalists are too dark and dour, and people tune out the constant negative doom and gloom. Maybe. Some complain that selfish business and political interests have successfully framed climate change as a threat to the economy and cast doubt on the science that explains what's happening to the biosphere of the earth. This is certainly true. (In my opinion, the people who have done this for selfish political or business reasons, to support their ideology or their profits, stand out in the history of the human species as exceptionally selfish, short-sighted, and destructive.) Some simply say that shallow public concern about the threat is a matter of semantics, that global warming and climate change are the wrong words to use. Perhaps.

But any careful reader of the previous chapters can name several more fundamental explanations for the public's response to the risk of climate change. Perhaps the most important of all is the "Can It Happen to *Me*?" factor. If you think that a risk can happen to you, you are more likely to worry than if you think the risk only threatens somebody else.

What's Your Risk Response?

Can you name one specific way in which climate change is going to have a serious negative impact on *you or your family* in the next 20 years?

Most people can't.

Consider the findings of a survey of public perceptions of climate change in the United States by Anthony Leiserowitz.[7] The survey asked, "Who will be most harmed by climate change?" and respondents said that climate change would mostly affect

- Plant and animal species: 45 percent
- Future generations of people: 44 percent
- People in developing countries: 31 percent
- People in other industrialized nations: 22 percent
- People in the United States: 21 percent
- *Your local community: 13 percent*
- *Your family: 11 percent*
- *You personally: 10 percent*

Those categories in italics (my emphasis) reflect the percentage of people who are most concerned that climate change will affect *them*—about one person in ten. Nearly five times as many people in the United States are more worried that climate change will affect polar bears and plants than are worried about themselves.

Small wonder, then, that the study found the following support for various ways to deal with climate change:

- Fund renewable energy research: 53 percent
- Require better fuel efficiency in cars: 41 percent
- Regulate CO_2: 30 percent
- Create a national cap-and-trade carbon market: 11 percent
- Increase the gasoline tax by 25 cents: 9 percent

This isn't just in the United States. A Pew Global Studies survey in 2006 asked, "How much do you personally worry about global warming?" Fewer than half the respondents worried "a great deal" about climate change as a personal threat in France (46 percent), Turkey (41 percent), Germany (30 percent), Indonesia (38 percent, in a nation that includes 6,000 inhabited islands), Great Britain (26 percent), China (20 percent), and, bringing up the rear, the United States (19 percent). In this survey, roughly half of Americans and one-third of Chinese said that they had no personal worry about climate change *at all*.[8] Consider a Globescan survey of 22,000 people in 21 nations released by the BBC in November 2007. An encouraging 83 percent said that personal changes in lifestyle are needed to help combat climate change. But when respondents were asked if they themselves would be willing to make such changes, the number dropped. It was still large, 70 percent, but note that it went down. Fewer still, 61 percent, agreed with the idea of paying higher energy costs. Asked if they'd be willing to pay higher taxes to combat the problem, it effectively became a toss-up, with 50 percent saying yes and 44 percent saying no.[9] Another key factor contributing to the Perception Gap on climate change is Cultural Cognition. Remember, cultural identity in this case means your underlying views on how society should be organized, not your political views or which kind of music you like. But political affiliation is one reflection of how people think society should be organized. In the United States, Democrats are more likely to be Egalitarians and Communitarians, and Republicans are more likely to be Hierarchists and Individualists. A Pew Research Center poll in 2008 found that 84 percent of Democrats believed that global warming is happening. Only 49 percent of Republicans did. Of those who thought that the climate of the earth is in fact undergoing rapid change, 58 percent of Democrats thought that the cause is human activity. Only 27 percent of Republicans did.

The Framing Effect also plays a role in perceptions of climate change. Social intermediaries, from politicians to advocacy groups to industries, are doing all they can to manipulate how you and I see the issue, and they are playing up or down the Risk Perception Factors that frame the issue the way they want you to see it. Advocates who want you to be more worried will point out that climate change threatens your Children (scarier), that it is caused by Human-Made forces (scarier), and that the results could be Catastrophic (scarier). Those who would have you worry less note that a warming world could bring Benefits that might outweigh the Risks (less scary), that if things *are* warming, the causes could be Natural (less scary), or that the changes will occur slowly enough that we can adapt, meaning that climate change is a Chronic, not a Catastrophic, risk (less scary), and that we can do something about it, so we have some Control (less scary). Each side is cherry-picking the aspects of the science that appeal to the innate psychological factors that make things more or less worrisome.

Why does this matter? As long as the societal will to act remains weak, the political risks for government leaders to take strong action remain high. The overwhelming body of evidence on climate change says that it is pretty likely we're in for big trouble. It's not certain just how the trouble will happen, or when, or how bad things will be, or for whom. But trouble is far more likely than not.

Even if you set aside the question about whether climate change is human-made, there can be no doubt that the climate *is* changing in potentially devastating ways. Nonetheless, as a result of a societal Perception Gap, the kinds of major changes that most experts say are needed to protect against the realistic possibility of the damage from climate change are not being made, because the breadth and depth of social pressure isn't there to push politicians to act. That Gap between our fears and the facts is potentially increasing the risk for you and me.

Narrowing the Perception Gap

It is entirely fair to suggest that making policy based more on our fears than on the facts can lead to decisions that feel good but that increase our overall risk. But it is important to say again and again that judging this sort of societal decision making as right or wrong, rational or irrational, smart or stupid, will get us nowhere. The Affective way we perceive risk is, to paraphrase Walter Cronkite, "the way it is," an intrinsic, biologically rooted, inescapable part of how the human animal behaves at this point in our evolution. It is time to stop lamenting such behavior as wrong, criticizing it as irrational, or defending it as right and wise, and instead to use what we have learned about the way humans respond to risk in order to help ourselves make better, healthier choices.

We understand the components of the affective risk response with reasonable precision. We know many of the factors that can sometimes contribute to a Perception Gap between our fears and the facts. We have ample evidence of the harm that such Gaps can cause. We can use these insights as tools for making better, smarter, healthier choices. *That* would be rational. So let's consider some ways of using what we've learned to help narrow the Perception Gap, as individuals and as a community.

TOWARD HEALTHIER INDIVIDUAL CHOICES

So what was Susan Napolitano supposed to do? Her daughter was in danger from human-made chemicals that could cause cancer, going to a school run by a superintendent whom Susan didn't trust to protect her kid. Powerful Affective circumstances made that a very scary situation. How could Susan *not* freak out?

Should she instead have rationally considered the scientific evidence that the cancer risk to her daughter was less than one in a million? Should she have learned more about the toxicology of trichloroethylene? Should she have made some sort of computer spreadsheet to analytically compare the trade-offs between the risks of Stephie's going to the school with the trace amounts of chemicals in the air and having the school shut in the middle of the year, disrupting Stephie's education and putting her at risk by having her bused to another building during the snowy New England winter?

Hopefully, by now you can see how ridiculous it is to expect that kind of purely rational response. The human brain is not a purely cognitive, "thinking" organ, and, despite the rather naive expectations of some economists, the human animal is not a heartless, soulless, valueless computer, and the human Risk Response is not simply a matter of the facts. We are Affectives. No superior amount of cognitive analysis and reasoning can completely overcome the neural architecture and chemistry that ensure that the instinctive/emotional/*sub*conscious processes of risk perception have so much influence on our judgments and behavior.

But as Katherine Patterson wrote in *Jacob I Have Loved,* "To fear is one thing. To let fear grab you by the tail and swing you around is another." We can recognize that our Risk Response system evolved in a less complex environment in which evaluating and reacting to danger was a simpler affair. We can recognize that the Perception Gap can be a risk in and of itself, and that our Affective

Risk Response system isn't always right and can lead us into harm's way when it's wrong.

The very first idea here, then, is that in addition to being on the lookout for "regular" risks, we should get into the habit of second-guessing ourselves a little, assuming that our response to those risks may be causing a Perception Gap between our fears and the facts—and that we may be at risk from getting risk wrong. This won't be easy. Our amygdalas aren't wired to look out for these secondary risks. We'll have to do this work upstairs, in the thinking cognitive cortex, and you'll remember from Chapter 1 what neuroscientist Joseph LeDoux said, that "conscious control over emotions is weak, [but] emotions can flood consciousness." Biologically, our brain is wired such that we fear first and think second, and we fear more and think less.

But that doesn't mean that we don't think *at all*. If we tell ourselves that the Perception Gap is a risk that we have to cognitively watch out for, we can use what we've discovered about the details of the Affective Risk Response, laid out in the previous pages, to understand why the Gap exists and try to narrow it. As Sir Walter Scott said, "A thousand fearful images and dire suggestions glance along the mind when it is moody and discontented with itself. *Command them to stand and show themselves*, and you presently *assert the power of reason over imagination*." We know a lot about the psychology that produces those "fearful images and dire suggestions." That knowledge can help us force those images and suggestions to stand and show themselves, to be understood, so we can be aware of how they are influencing our perceptions. That might give reason more of a say in the way we respond to risk, and that should help us make healthier choices.

Reason can never rule. And, as I hope I have also made clear, just because we are Affectives doesn't mean that we always get risk wrong. But sometimes we do. For times like those, it's reassuring to remember that we are not just an amygdala and a puddle of stress hormones. We do have some pretty powerful abilities to think, to analyze, and to reason. We can consciously apply what we understand about the mental shortcuts we use to make decisions under conditions of Bounded Rationality to keep factors like the Framing Effect, Anchoring and Adjustment, the Awareness/Ready Recall Effect, and Optimism Bias from leading to a potentially dangerous Perception Gap. We can consciously apply what we understand about the emotional/instinctive Risk Perception Factors that make risks more or less worrisome, and simply ask ourselves whether factors like Trust, Control, Pain and Suffering, and Human-Made versus Natural may be contributing to perceptions that *feel* right but that may be raising our risk. We can take what we have learned about social influences such as the way the news media dramatize things, Cultural Cognition, and Groupthink and consciously ask ourselves whether those factors might be leading to a potentially harmful Perception Gap between our fears and the facts. With what we've learned about the inner workings of the Risk Response, we can bring those factors out of the subconscious shadows and use them as practical tools to allow our rational thinking to have more influence in the process.

So Susan Napolitano might have said to herself, "I know we tend to be really afraid of anything that can hurt our kids, and we tend to be really afraid of cancer because it involves so much pain and suffering, and we tend to be really afraid when we don't trust the people who are supposed to protect us or our kids. So am I really being smart about what's in Stephie's best interest, or are all those things freaking me out so much that maybe I'm not making the best choice for my kid?" Simply by making the psychological reasons for her "fearful images and dire suggestions . . . stand and show themselves," Susan might have put herself on the road to *balancing* her very real feelings with a bit more careful reasoning, which is the critical first step toward narrowing a potentially harmful Perception Gap.

Practical Tools for Making Healthier Choices

But it's only the first step. Here are some specific suggestions that might help you make healthier choices about the risks you face. The first are general ideas for making better decisions. Then there are suggestions that are risk-specific. All of these suggestions are offered in the hope that they might help you make choices that both *feel* right in the context of your own life *and* maximize your health and safety.

Keep an Open Mind. The Affective system of Risk Response has worked pretty well so far. Your first instinct is often right. But remember, the Risk Response system we are using now evolved in earlier, simpler times. Figuring out whether that neighboring tribe was going to attack or whether to worry about that pack of wolves running toward you was easy. But the instinctive ingredients of what made something feel risky back then might not be the most precise tools for making sense of more complex technological perils and trade-offs in the modern world. Weighing the risks and benefits and scientific details about mercury in swordfish, or nuclear versus fossil fuel power, are trickier calls. They demand a little more careful thinking. So as English magician Robert Heller said, "Never ignore a gut feeling, but never believe that it's enough." Remember, an Affective response to risk may *feel* right, but it also might get you into trouble. In the name of your own safety, try to keep an open mind, so that your feelings and instincts don't smother what the facts may have to offer.

Give Yourself Time. Remember, your brain is hard-wired to fear first and think second. At first, emotions usually dominate the facts when we assess risk. And remember that the amygdala fires off its warning signal at the first hint of possible danger. And don't forget the influence of the Framing Effect and how your initial perception of a situation shapes how you think about that situation later. So just realize that your first response is going to be power-fully influenced by emotions and instincts, which could lead to a Perception Gap, and if you can, try to give yourself a few minutes (or more) before making a judgment about a risk, to allow the ana-lytical part of the risk perception system to share the stage with the powerful Affective side.

Get More Information. Remember a little while ago, I admitted that there were some important things about nuclear radiation that I didn't know back when I was reporting on those issues? Don't make the same mistake I made. I could have been more informed about the risks of nuclear power, and my viewers would have been better informed, had I challenged myself to learn a little more. In-stead, I went with the information that was easiest to get. I suffered from a worse case of Bounded Rationality because I didn't have some of the key information I needed to make a more informed judgment. In the absence of that information, my instincts and emotions played a bigger role, and there was definitely a Perception Gap between my view of the risk of nuclear power and the facts.

I'm not suggesting any heavy lifting here. Finding out more doesn't mean finding out everything. But more information is better than less if you're trying to make a careful judgment about something, especially something as important as your health. Few of us know as much as we need to know in order to make more fully informed choices about most things. *So just assume that you don't know as much as you need to know to make a good decision.* Fight back against the primal brain systems that let emotion and instinct dominate reason. Learn more = decide better.

Get Your Information from Neutral Sources. Do your best to get your information from neutral and reliable sources, sources that have no obvious bias. Don't just rely on sources with which you agree. Remember, you're trying to learn, not just reinforce what you already know. And remember, many risk issues are controversial and contentious. There are advocates on all sides, twisting and manipulating and framing the facts to support their view, trying to get you to think what they want you to think. *Don't be a victim of spin and bias.* Be mildly skeptical of the motives behind *any* source of information, even (*especially*) when it's information with which you tend to agree. Question the sources' motivation. Check out their funding, or the political views and connections of the people providing the information. *Ask the same hard questions of sources you agree with that you would use to challenge sources on the other side.*

With the explosion of information sources on the Internet, it's getting harder to find information about controversial issues that hasn't been spun, doctored, or manipulated. More and more, the suppliers of information have political, economic, cultural, religious, or other reasons to see things one way or another. So another way to empower yourself with balanced information is to *deliberately seek out what both sides of an issue have to say.* See how "the facts" according to one side compare with "the facts" as presented by the other side. See what Greenpeace says about nuclear power (www.greenpeace.org/international/campaigns/nuclear) *and* what the nuclear industry says (www.nei.org). You may agree with one side more than the other, but seeing the same basic information presented in two different ways is a good way to help you think about the issue more carefully.

Questions to Ask about Any Risk. It's obvious to suggest that you should get more information, and that you should get it from neutral sources. But what information should you get? There are a few basic things to ask about any risk that will always help you make a more informed judgment.

First things first. Just what does *risk* mean? In general terms, risk is simply the chance that something bad might happen. But in practical terms, risk means Hazard X Exposure. You need two things for a physical risk to exist. First, there has to be something potentially hazardous. Second, you need to be exposed to the hazard. (This is the focus of a book I wrote with George Gray, *Risk: A Practical Guide for Deciding What's Really Safe and What's Really Dangerous in the World Around You*, which explains the basic ideas of risk and describes in detail 48 of the risks that people most commonly worry about.) Let's use the snake example again, and Charles Darwin and his self-experiment with the puff adder in the London Zoo. Was Darwin at risk from the snake in the cage? No, and he knew it. It *felt* scary, and it was a poisonous snake, which was definitely a hazard. But it wasn't a risk to Darwin because he was not directly exposed to it. No exposure = no risk. That's why Darwin felt dumb being afraid. (Darwin was actually doing what is proposed here. He recognized that his fear made no rational sense and was trying to figure out why, so he could make a smarter choice of not looking stupid at the zoo.)

But now let's change two things. Let's say the snake gets out of the cage, and it's on the ground at Darwin's feet! *Uh-oh?* Not necessarily. Let's say the snake at his feet is not poisonous, and is not one of those squeeze-you-to-death constrictors. Let's say the snake is a shy little green-and-yellow-striped garter snake, not dangerous at all. Is Darwin at risk now? He *is* exposed. But he is *not* at risk because now *there is no hazard.* For something to be a risk, you have to have both.

Many news stories about risks leave out information on either hazard or exposure. Look at those early stories about MTBE, the chemical additive in gasoline that leaked out of underground tanks and got into public drinking water supplies. They made a big deal about how we are being exposed, which is important for us to know, but they carried little or no information about whether MTBE could be hazardous. So the stories might sound scary, but if you ask yourself about both hazard and exposure in those stories, you realize that you don't know whether MTBE is actually a risk.

Sometimes the information about hazard is there, but the information about exposure is missing. I did plenty of news stories about dangerous substances, like lead paint, but sometimes I failed to include information about whether people were actually being exposed to these substances, which in the case of lead paint doesn't happen unless the paint gets scratched into dust particles and inhaled, or flakes off and kids eat the flakes. (Kids eat lead paint because it tastes sweet. Do *not* use lead paint instead of sugar in your coffee!)

So always ask about both hazard and exposure. But just knowing that you have both still isn't enough. The details matter. Even if something is hazardous, you have to know *how* hazardous. And hazardous *to whom*? And hazardous *at what levels*? And, of course, hazardous *in what ways*?

And there are key questions to ask about exposure. *How much* exposure is hazardous? *Over what period of time? At what age?* By *what routes* might I be exposed? (Do you eat it or drink it, inhale it, or get it on your skin?)

To lay out the details you want to ask about hazard and exposure, let's use mercury as an example.

THE HAZARD

What does it do? When you are directly exposed to huge amounts of mercury, it can literally drive you nuts. It is neurotoxic. Hatters used mercury to make felt and inhaled fumes every day, thus the phrase "mad hatters." At lower levels of exposure, mercury has been found to cause very subtle neurological damage to the cognitive abilities of the developing fetuses of pregnant women. (Given how great the concern about mercury is, it is actually stunning how little damage it does. The major study on which most of our rules about mercury are based found that the children of mothers on the Faroe Islands in the North Atlantic who had diets of fish and whale meat that were high in mercury had less than a

1-point loss of IQ, and similarly tiny deficits on other cognitive tests.[10])

A hazard to whom? Except for acute poisoning from high levels of mercury, scientists are confident saying only that mercury is harmful to the developing fetus and to infants in the first years after birth, whose brains are still developing. There are hints of effects to adults, but the science about those possible hazards is still preliminary. There aren't a lot of bricks in the wall of evidence on those.

What levels are hazardous? The current recommendations for mercury are for pregnant women or women who may become pregnant in the next couple years to avoid certain amounts of certain species of fish that are more likely to have higher levels of mercury, and to reduce—but not eliminate—consumption of other species.[11]

THE EXPOSURE

Am I exposed? Mercury exposure comes mostly from seafood, and even then, only from certain species that are likely to have higher concentrations: shark, swordfish, king mackerel, and tilefish. Shrimp, canned light tuna, salmon, pollock, and catfish have some mercury, but much less. If you don't eat those fish, you're probably not exposed.

To how much? Like anything that might be poisonous, the dose you get matters. A couple of aspirin are good for a headache. Too many will kill you. With mercury, only eating large amounts of those certain species of fish will expose you to a high enough dose that, if you are a pregnant woman or a woman who may become pregnant in the next few years, you need to worry.

Over what period of time? One meal alone almost never carries a dangerous dose. It takes consumption of mercury-bearing fish over several days or weeks before exposure levels become potentially harmful. And while mercury stays in the body for a while, we *do* metabolize it and excrete it. So the exposure has to be continuous. (Many risks are assessed by the government based on an assumed *lifetime* of exposure, getting *daily* doses every day for 72 years. Ask yourself if that applies to you as you consider any specific risk.)

At what age am I (was I) exposed? Mercury is a great example of how important this factor is, more important with many risks than most people realize. As you learned, the normal kind of low dose exposure to mercury is only a risk to a developing fetus or infant. After that, the neurotoxic effects of mercury are caused only by unusually high "mad hatter" exposures.

By what route am I (was I) exposed? You ingest mercury. It doesn't get into your lungs, which would be worse, and although it can be absorbed through your skin, that's not a route of exposure that raises your risk much, either. A better example here is anthrax. Get it on your skin and you may get a rash. Ingest it and you may get sick. Inhale it and you could die.

So you can see that there are some important details about hazard and exposure that can help you make a more informed judgment. There are also some details that you need about risk numbers.

Remember the Challenge of Innumeracy. Number numbness can really interfere with making a healthy choice about some potential hazards. Here are some simple number questions to ask. (They won't make your head hurt, I promise.)

> **TRY TO FIND OUT THE NUMBER FOR YOUR SUBGROUP: YOUR GENDER, AGE, HEALTH STATUS . . . THE NUMBERS FOR YOU.** In 2009, the average risk of cancer for an American male younger than 40 years old was 1 in 70, but for an American male 70 and older it was 1 in 3. Subgroup matters.
>
> **TRY TO FIND OUT BOTH THE RELATIVE RISK AND THE ABSOLUTE RISK.** If you hear that the risk of something "has doubled in

the last year," that's what the risk is now *relative to* what it was. Find out how many more people that means, the *actual* risk. Maybe the risk doubled, but it only went from one person in a million to two in a million!

THE NUMERICAL RISK OF WHAT OUTCOME? Is it a one in a million risk of *getting* a disease (morbidity)? Or of *dying* from that disease (mortality)? Which disease? (There are more than 120 different kinds of cancer. Some are more treatable than others, and they each have very different health impacts.)

IS THE RISK PER YEAR, OR FOR YOUR LIFETIME? The lifetime risk of cancer for the average American female is 1 in 3. Some people might find that a scary number. But the chance that the average American woman will get cancer *per year* is much lower, and is age-dependent.

(These suggestions are simplified from a wonderful book that can help you understand numbers when judging health risks, *Know Your Chances: Understanding Health Statistics* by Steve Woloshin, Lisa Schwartz, and H. Gilbert Welch.) But let's not get stuck on getting more factual information. It can really help, but remember, the Affective Risk Response is not a purely fact-based process. So here are some more practical suggestions for narrowing the Perception Gap.

Think about Trade-Offs. We are generally Loss-Averse and prone to focus on the dangers. But remember that most risk choices involve trade-offs, sometimes with benefits and sometimes with other risks. Again, let's consider mercury. High amounts of mercury in certain species of seafood can cause very subtle cognitive impairments in children who are exposed to it *in utero* or during infancy, while their brains are developing. But remember that the fatty acids in the seafood *improve* cognitive ability in children who are exposed to it *in utero* or during infancy, while their brains are developing. That's a risk/benefit trade-off.

Consider a risk/risk trade-off. Some people who are worried about industrial agricultural practices choose to drink completely natural, unpasteurized milk. They are trading one very low risk, from tiny doses of chemicals and antibiotics used in animal agriculture, for another (much higher) risk, the potentially lethal bacteria in a single serving of unpasteurized milk. So whenever there are trade-offs, and there almost always are, thinking about both sides will help you make a healthier choice.

Think for Yourself. We are often victims of what is called *confirmation bias,* when we seek out or listen to only information that reinforces what we already believe. I can't think of anything more dangerous for careful risk decision making than shutting down your reasoning brain and letting someone else do your thinking for you, regardless of whether you are on the political right or left or what any of your personal views may be. Listeners to talk radio host Rush Limbaugh sometimes call themselves "Ditto Heads," which is often shorthand for "I agree with you, Rush," or "I agree with the last guy." When it comes to careful thinking about risk, *don't be a Ditto Head.* Remember, the objective, in the name of making healthier choices, is to learn something new, not just to reinforce what you already know and believe.

Remember the Influence of Cultural Cognition. This one will be hard. We tend to adopt positions on issues that confirm the thinking of the members of our group, both to strengthen the group and to increase our acceptance within the group. It's comfortable to be a Ditto Head, and we all do it. But it can contribute to a Perception Gap that might not be good for your health. Challenge your own thinking. Second-guess yourself. *Try to look at the issue the way the other side would.* As René Descartes said, "If you would be a real seeker after truth, it is necessary that at least once in your life you doubt, as far as possible, all things."

Be a Smarter News Consumer. First, just keep in mind that the news media tend to make things sound more dramatic than they are, not by lying or by making things up, but in subtle ways, like which parts of the story they emphasize, or where in the newspaper or in the broadcast or on the Web site they place the story, or even which words or pictures or graphics or tone of voice they use. This isn't obvious, so be alert to this tendency.

Also, bear in mind that you are *not* hearing about things that, frankly, aren't news. You don't see many headlines like "Planes Didn't Crash Today" or "Most Kids Don't Have Autism." Don't let the media's choices of what they tell you and what they don't turn you into a Chicken Little. The media may be telling you about all those acorns falling on your head, but look up. It may not make news, but usually the sky *isn't* falling.

Also remember that journalists are people, too, and, like you and me, they intuitively sense the Risk Perception Factors that make something more or less scary. Those are precisely the aspects of the news that get played up. So, for example, in a story about the risk of cancer, the reporter might Personalize the risk (which makes it scarier) by telling about a victim who is a child (*which makes it scarier still*). But remember that three out of four cases of cancer happen to people who are over 55 years old. The use of the child as a victim is attention-getting but not accurate about who is mostly at risk.

Or you may see news stories dramatizing a risk by emphasizing that it is being *imposed*, without paying much attention to how big the risk itself actually is. A Salt Lake City, Utah, newspaper did several stories about how worried people were that radioactive waste was being shipped to a site in Utah from overseas, and because of the way the law was written, there was nothing the people in Utah could do to stop it. That's what the stories focused on. They didn't talk much about the actual risk from the low-level waste, which was tiny.

News coverage of a risk about which a government agency or official or company has lied, or kept information secret, or fouled up will emphasize the lack of Trust involved, but may not pay much attention to the actual risk itself. The news coverage of mad cow disease in Japan and of those defective defibrillators made by the now-defunct Guidant Corporation are examples where the media dramatized the risk not because of the actual danger, but because of the mistrustful way in which the Japanese government and Guidant behaved, feeding a large and dangerous Perception Gap in each case.

So just be aware that the psychological factors that make things scarier to you and me are likely to be emphasized in the media. Try to look past the Risk Perception Factors and find the information about the risk itself. Trying to filter out the psychological Risk Perception Factors that are emphasized in the news will make you a smarter, more careful news consumer.

Next, the antidote to being alarmed by the news media is not to read, watch, or listen less. Instead, read, watch, and listen *more*. Ignorance may be comfortable bliss, but it's no way to know what you need to know if you want to make healthy decisions for yourself and for your family. And don't just get more news, get it from more than one source. Relying on only a single source means relying on only one set of editors and reporters to judge for you what's important and what's not and how the news should be presented. If they don't choose to report that new study on heart disease or the latest news on climate change, you just won't know about it. Or if the reporter writing the story on mercury in fish chooses to omit the fact that it's only a risk for the unborn children of pregnant women, you won't know. So the more sources you use, the more diverse your information will be, and the more likely it is that you might find stories or facts in one place that reporters or editors at another news source chose to leave out.

On the other hand, don't be a 24/7 news victim either. That will help counteract the Awareness/Ready Recall Effect, whereby the more easily a risk comes to mind, the more concerned we tend to be. When the sniper had everyone in the Washington, D.C., area scared back in 2002, people in that area might have made healthier judgments about the risk if they had turned off their TV or radio or computer, put down their smart phones, stopped reading the paper, and taken the dog for a walk.

Think about How You Think. Remember from Chapter 2 all those mental shortcuts we use to make decisions under conditions of Bounded Rationality, when we don't have all the information, or the time required to get all the information, or the smarts necessary to understand all the information, but we have to make up our minds? Remember how those mental shortcuts can sometimes interfere with making a rational choice? Well, just knowing how you think can help you think better.

Consider the first of the shortcuts we talked about, the Framing Effect, how the first way we hear about something colors how we think about that issue subsequently. When you're considering a risk issue, *try to frame it in a different way.* If, as in the case of building new nuclear power plants, the risk is framed in terms of past events like Chernobyl and Three Mile Island, ask yourself whether the design and operation of those plants are the same for the ones being proposed now. If the risk is framed as "chemical," reframe your thinking and ask yourself those specific questions about exposure and hazard. If the issue of mercury in seafood comes up in a way that emphasizes the risks involved, try to reframe the question of whether to eat seafood in terms of both the risks *and* the benefits.

Reframing is a good way to keep trade-offs in mind. Consider the news in 2007 about drug-coated stents, those metal devices that doctors put into clogged veins and arteries to open them up and keep them open longer than the bare metal kind. That reduces the need for follow-up procedures to reopen vessels that close up again, and since each procedure to place a stent carries risk, the fewer procedures that have to be done, the safer you are. But when the news media reported a study that suggested that patients with drug-coated stents might have a higher rate of blood clots than patients with bare metal stents, thousands of people started opting for bare metal stents to avoid the risk of the clots, forgetting the risk-reduction benefits of the drug-coated kind. (Research presented at an American College of Cardiology conference in March 2009 found that the clot risk of both is about the same.) They might have made more thorough decisions had they reframed a threat presented in terms of risk, in terms of its potential benefits.

This works the other way too. If a choice is framed in terms of benefits, like hormone replacement therapy (HRT) for postmenopausal women, *reframe the issue* and ask yourself about the risks. HRT may help you avoid those hot flashes and mood swings, but you have to compare that against the small possibility of raising your risk of heart disease, breast cancer, blood clots, and stroke.

Here's another reframing suggestion. Risks are often described in terms of how many people might be victims. So reframe the question and ask yourself, out of the total population at risk, how many *won't* suffer. If someone says, "The risk of dying in a fall for the average American is 1 in 20,000," reframe things so that you think about the 19,999 people who *don't* die, not just the one person who does.

The example of the drug-coated stents mentioned above also illustrates one of the dangers of the Categorization/Representativeness mental shortcut that we use to categorize partial information by comparing it against patterns into which the partial information seems to fit. The stent study was only one piece of evidence, but because of the Fallacy of the Small Sample, where we assume that what is true for one piece of evidence is true in general, many people made choices about their health using only this partial information and categorized it in a way that *seemed* to make sense but may have actually raised their risk.

What can you do? Just think about how you think. As with all the mental shortcuts that we use for snap decision making that can contribute to a Perception Gap, be aware of the danger of the Categorization Effect. Try to catch yourself at it, and ask yourself if you are jumping to conclusions based on incomplete information. Are you judging a risk book by its cover, without at least opening the book? Try not to rush to judgments; get into the habit of keeping an open mind and getting more information, to give the rational part of the Affective process more say in the choices you make.

To deal with the distorting effects of Anchoring and Adjustment, try to think about the absolute risk, not the relative risk in the context of some other value. Remember the example about Chernobyl used in Chapter 2, where two stories presented statistics about the overall death toll? The second sentence was the same in each, but the stories began with different initial values, different anchors.

1. "More than 5,000,000 people lived in areas contaminated by radioactive fallout from the Chernobyl nuclear accident. Considerable controversy remains over the lifetime death toll among all those exposed, with estimates ranging from 4,000 to more than 100,000."

2. "To date, authorities believe that 56 people were killed by the Chernobyl accident. Considerable controversy remains over the lifetime death toll among all those exposed, with estimates ranging from 4,000 to more than 100,000."

If you want to avoid the Anchoring and Adjustment Effect on how you think about the overall death toll from the Chernobyl accident, just take out the first sentence of both stories, the anchor that might distort how you adjust your thinking about the value in the second sentence, and just pay attention to the second sentence.

To avoid the distortions of Optimism Bias, remember the advice of psychologist Daniel Gilbert and avoid the "illusion of foresight," which leads us to see things through rose-colored glasses the further off in the future they are, and try "nexting," or thinking about the future as if it were tomorrow, which leads to more realistic judgments about how things might turn out.

Framing. Loss Aversion. Categorization. We *need* such mental tools to make quick judgments under conditions of Bounded Rationality. But being self-aware of how they are coloring our perceptions can help keep them from causing judgments that lead to a potentially harmful Perception Gap. And so can self-awareness about how specific Risk Perception Factors lead to judgments that feel right, but that raise your risk.

Understanding the Risk Response to Control the Risk Response. So now let's consider some ways to use what you learned about those Risk Perception Factors in Chapter 3 and about the social and cultural forces that feed our fears in Chapter 4, to reduce the dangers of the Perception Gap.

Remember Linda, who is still worried about radiation from the Three Mile Island accident in 1979, and who lives above some of the most uranium-rich/radon-producing bedrock in North America, but still hasn't had her own house tested for radon because "it's not a man-made thing"? Linda is at risk because of a Perception Gap. As a result of the psychological Risk Perception Factor that makes things scarier when they are Human-Made and less worrisome when they are Natural, Linda is probably being exposed to, and not doing anything to remediate, potentially carcinogenic levels of ionizing radiation.

But suppose Linda has learned that sometimes we're too afraid of some things, or not afraid enough of others, because specific Risk Perception Factors make some risks *feel* bigger or smaller, regardless of the scientific evidence, and Linda has learned that one of those factors is whether the risk is Natural or Human-Made, and she realizes, "Hey, that's *me* about radon!" Now Linda can ask herself the next question, the really important question, the question that can help her balance the emotional/instinctive part of the Risk Response system with more objective consideration of the factual evidence: "Does whether radon comes from a natural source or a human-made source have anything to do with how risky it is to me?" Linda can challenge her own thinking and reframe the risk by temporarily filtering *out* the Risk Perception Factor that is part of her Affective response so she can get a clearer view of the facts.

Consciously realizing which specific Risk Perception Factors may be making you more or less afraid can help you test your own thinking to see how much those factors, rather than the facts, are the basis for your fears. You can try this yourself. Pick some risk that you're worried about. Let's say it's that chemical bisphenol A (BpA) that we talked about earlier. Ask yourself which of the psychological Risk Perception Factors from Chapter 3 might be involved in your feelings about the threat from BpA. Make a list:

- It's Human-Made. That makes it scarier.
- It comes from an industry that most people don't Trust. That makes it scarier.
- We can't detect it with our own senses, which is a form of Uncertainty, adding further to the fear.
- It's imposed on you, not a risk you take by Choice. That makes it scarier.

Those components of the Affective response are all probably part of your concern about BpA. But now that you can see how they may play a role in your perception, just mentally put them aside for a second and ask yourself those separate questions about hazard and exposure. "What sort of actual harm does BpA do to

us? At what dose? Am I exposed? By what route? To how much?"
Ask yourself some other basic factual questions that you'd want the
answers to. "Is it a risk for *me* or for people in some other particular
subgroup? Is the likelihood of the risk big or small? How strong
or weak is the evidence?" It might take a little bit of homework to
answer these questions, but remember: *learn more = decide better.*

But more than just getting additional information, you have
identified and temporarily set aside the emotional/instinctive components of your Risk Response. That can help you see the facts a bit
more clearly. Your overall response will still include those Affective
factors—you only set them aside temporarily—but now the facts
can play a bigger role, and that should lead to a more informed and
healthier choice.

Now try it the other way. Pick some risk that you've heard about
that *doesn't* worry you personally too much, let's say the risk of
using your mobile phone while you drive. Go through the same
process. Make a list of the Risk Perception Factors that explain why
you feel the way you do about the risk:

- Certainly you feel that you have Control over things
  while you're DWP (driving while phoning), which
  makes it seem like less of a risk.
- You get a Benefit out of being able to connect to people
  by phone while you're driving, and that makes you play
  down the Risk in your mind.
- You are taking the risk Voluntarily. That makes it feel
  less risky.

Those are valid reasons why the risk you're taking doesn't feel all
that scary—and they help you understand the Perception Gap that
is increasing your risk! So now you can see both parts of the risk,
the one from the phone *and* the one from your feelings. Set aside
those feeling factors just for a moment and consider honestly that

it's dangerous to use your mobile phone while you drive, probably more dangerous than you're willing to admit, and see how your emotion might be clouding your reason and leading to a dangerous Perception Gap. (Do not do this exercise while you're driving!)

Are you concerned about nuclear power? Identify the Risk Perception Factors that might be contributing to those concerns— the risk is Human-Made, with high potential Pain and Suffering (cancer); it's not detectable or easy to understand, so there is high Uncertainty; if things go wrong, the result could be Catastrophic—and try to look at the facts about nuclear power without those Affective lenses coloring your view.

You aren't worried as much about heart disease as everybody says you should be? Ask yourself why. Perhaps it's because the risk factors for heart disease seem like the result of behaviors you choose, so the risk of heart disease feels Voluntary, or you think you can start dieting and exercising when you want to, so you have a sense of Control, or the risk is Chronic and seems like it involves less Pain and Suffering. Try to consider the scientific facts about your risk of heart disease *without* those factors, just for a moment.

You can apply this same suggestion to what you learned in Chapter 4 about the social components of the Risk Response. Consider the risk of nuclear waste. Among the many factors that make that risk scarier for many people is the social Stigma attached to it. Nuclear waste is so widely thought to be a big risk that the fears of the many tend to sweep others along. Few of us have probably actually looked into the facts of whether such waste can actually be handled, transported, and stored safely. We just take the group's word for it that it can't. So try to separate out what everybody else thinks and think for yourself. After all, it's *your* health you usually care about most.

Remember that we are tribal, and we tend to adopt positions that confirm the underlying worldviews of the social groups to which we belong. (Remember Cultural Cognition from Chapter 4, with its Hierarchists ↔ Egalitarians and its Individualists ↔

Communitarians? If you took the quiz back then, you have an idea of where you sit on those continua.) We are powerfully influenced by the leaders of our tribes. Take climate change. Al Gore is a tribal leader of one side. Rush Limbaugh proudly carries the banner for the opposite tribe. When Al and Rush speak, they're not just discussing the facts about climate change. They are also carrying their tribe's banner into the underlying culture clash that the disagreement over climate change is really all about. They selectively cite the facts that support their underlying cultural views about how society is supposed to be organized as it deals with issues like climate change.

If you just want to follow the leader who's waving the most appealing flag, fine. But remember, what feels fine may *not* be what is actually best for your health. If you want to think for yourself and make the most appropriate choice for *your* life, the challenge is to try to step outside the social pressure of your tribe(s) and think about the risk independently. This gets way back to the first suggestion: keep an open mind. This may not make you popular. But it may help make you *healthier.*

And remember, as you try to think for yourself, that risk issues are controversial and hit at the heart of powerful economic and political interests, so social advocates twist and spin and manipulate information about those risks to advance their own interests. This happens on both the right and the left and across a whole range of issues. Climate change serves as a particularly sinister example. In the name of economic gain or partisan political advantage, businesspeople and politicians have deliberately emphasized doubt about the mountains of evidence and overwhelming scientific consensus that global warming/climate change is not only real, but it's happening now. (My personal favorites are the people on the political right who dismiss concern about the effects of rising industrial production of CO_2 because it's something that we naturally breathe out of our lungs. This can only be a deliberate effort to sway public perceptions because I have too much respect for the intelligence of these people to think that they would say something so dumb out of simple ignorance.)

To counteract the manipulations of social forces that are constantly trying to control what you believe, just apply a little skepticism to the information you get about any risk. Who is the source? What might that source's financial or political motivation be? How fair does the source seem to be with the facts? How open-minded is the source about alternative points of view? (Remember, you have to be a little questioning even of sources with which you agree.) A dose of healthy skepticism about the honesty and validity of information on contentious risk issues will probably get you closer to the sort of independent thinking that should help you end up the healthiest.

⚡

Narrowing the Perception Gap between our fears and the facts, and doing a better job of getting risk "right," is no easy thing. It means thinking more carefully and more rationally, and that runs counter to the more powerful emotional and instinctive parts of the overall Affective Risk Response. But by understanding the social forces that influence our perception of risk, the specific psychological Risk Perception Factors that make threats feel more or less scary, and the underlying mental shortcuts that we use to make decisions about anything, we can at least begin to separate out those Affective inputs while we consider the facts a bit more clearly and carefully. Doing this won't make you perfectly rational. That's not possible, as Darwin realized. But by seeing how all those Affective influences color how you see the facts, you can give the rational part of the Risk Response system a bit more say in the choices you make, and hopefully, those choices will help keep you healthier and safer.

The motivation should be clear. Although our Affective Risk Response often gets things right, sometimes it gets things wrong.

That Perception Gap between our fears and the facts leads to dangerous personal choices. It can lead to dangerous chronic stress. And it can contribute to dangerous social choices that result in all sorts of policies that may feel right but that actually increase our risk. That is where we conclude, with some thoughts about how to apply our understanding of the risk response to the challenge of making smarter decisions as a society.

TOWARD HEALTHIER CHOICES AS A SOCIETY

So how is government supposed to be rational if we individual citizens are not? How can we expect rational policy that maximizes risk reduction with the most efficient use of public resources, from politicians who, to stay in power, bend to the will of their funders and their voters (usually in that order), when neither group is being purely rational about which policies will do the general public the most good? How can we expect government decision makers to rise above the pressure from advocates of myriad points of view and rationally consider only the facts in making risk-management decisions? How, under any democratic form of government, can we ignore the passions of the people even when those passions create a Perception Gap that promotes inefficient policy and raises our risk?

We can't. The ideal of perfectly rational government risk-management policy is no more achievable than the goal of perfectly rational personal risk perceptions. We are Affective as individuals, and we are Affective as a *group* of individuals acting socially through our government. But even more than you and I have to balance our feelings and the facts if we want to avoid the personal dangers of the Perception Gap, government has to think carefully if it is to make the most efficient choices about how to use limited resources to do the most people the most good. That's easy to say. The question is, how?

Some very bright people suggest using tools like cost/benefit analysis (CBA) to quantify all the aspects of a decision in dollar terms and see which choices yield the most bang for the buck based on the facts, not on our fears. The U.S. government already mandates this sort of analysis for any regulatory decision that could have more than $100 million worth of costs or potential economic benefits, measured by dollars spent compared with years of life saved (which are then converted into dollars). It's an approach to get more objective and less emotional about societal decision making. CBA has contributed to decisions like taking lead out of gasoline, putting defibrillators in public places to save people suffering sudden heart failure, and including information about trans fat content on food labels.

But CBA is just one source of information for regulators and politicians, who still have to deal with public pressure as they make their decisions. CBA can improve decision making, but it still has to compete against the influences that our values, instincts, and fears have on policy choices. Even with CBA, we are still prone to potentially dangerous societal Perception Gaps from policies based more on our feelings than on the facts.

Some people have suggested that we hand over the responsibility for risk-management policy making to technocrats, experts located in some special agency that is sheltered from the direct passions of the public, sort of the way the Supreme Court is, so that they can make more rational decisions using their superior knowledge and wisdom, in the public's best interest.

That was essentially the idea proposed by Supreme Court Justice Stephen Breyer in his 1995 book, *Breaking the Vicious Circle*. The key, to Breyer (a circuit court of appeals judge at the time he wrote it), was to reduce the direct influence that our Affective risk perceptions can have on risk-management decision making in order to improve the quality of those decisions. Breyer's proposal was what pioneering social psychologist Robert Zajonc was talking about in a groundbreaking speech on the power of emotion over reason when he said, "One might be able to control the expression of emotion but not the experience of it itself. It is for this very reason that law, science, sports, education, and other institutions of society keep devising ever-new means of making judgments 'objective.' We wish some decisions to be more independent of these virtually inescapable reactions."[12]

Many people might agree with the laudable goal of Breyer's rationalist ideal, more efficient risk-management policy making in the name of doing society the most good. But most would probably quarrel with the way he goes about it. (Then-Senator Joseph Biden called Breyer "presumptuous and elitist," and opposed his nomination to the Supreme Court, based in part on this proposal.) But even if you don't have a problem with Breyer's seemingly antidemocratic process, Zajonc was right. Our Affective perceptions, colored not just by the facts but by all the factors that this book has laid out, are "virtually inescapable." Breyer's ideal may be intellectually appealing, but it is realistically unachievable.

So what are we to do? How are we supposed to keep our fears (too high or too low) as individuals from growing into social pressure on policy makers to do things that feel right but that don't maximize efficient use of resources to protect public and environmental health? How do we keep the Affective Risk Response from creating a societal Perception Gap where popular but suboptimal policies *create* risk in and of themselves specifically *because* they are popular but suboptimal?

The findings of the scientists and thinkers whose work this book tries to summarize suggest one possible new approach. Why not consider all the components of our Affective Risk Response system, not just the facts, in a more comprehensive and realistic way of thinking through the pros and cons of various risk-management options? Essentially, why not factor our feelings and values *into* the cost/benefit analysis approach to figuring out which policy choices will do us the most good, instead of trying to factor them *out?* As described in the previous pages, from the innate wiring and chemistry of the brain up, human risk perception and behavior are Affective, a mix of reason and emotion and instinct. They are not, have never been, and really can never be *purely rational.* Isn't it wiser, then, *more rational,* that policy making should include rather than exclude the "virtually inescapable" Affective reality of human perception and behavior in order to develop realistic policies that maximize our well-being? If we agree that in the more complex modern world of risk in which we find ourselves, the Affective system sometimes gets things wrong, then instead of trying to make decisions that are "more independent of these virtually inescapable reactions," we should find ways to factor what we know about these inescapable realities of the Affective Risk Response *into* our thinking as we try, as a society, to think as carefully as we can about which policies will do us the most good.

Let me use an example to make this idea a bit more concrete. In a paper wonderfully titled "Cost-Benefit Analysis and the Pricing of Fear and Anxiety" University of Pennsylvania law professor Matthew Adler describes the way the U.S. Food and Drug Administration made its "medical gloves" policy.[13] That rule sets a limit for manufacturers on how many medical gloves out of each batch can be defective. Defects include things like letting liquids leak through or ripping open, which if you're a health-care provider dealing with somebody with a possibly infectious disease could make you pretty nervous. But it's impossible for manufacturers to make absolutely perfect gloves every time, so the FDA wanted to figure out how many defective gloves per batch it would allow. If a batch had more than that, it would have to be tossed out, and that costs money, so it wanted to calculate a policy that balanced the cost of batches of tossed defective gloves with the dollar benefit of gloves with no defects. The benefits would be infections and the related health-care costs *avoided* by gloves that don't fail.

It was easy to figure out the dollar value of the tossed gloves, and it was pretty easy to figure out the cost of all the medical care involved if a glove failed and a health-care worker got sick, the costs that could be avoided by perfect gloves. But the analysts also considered how much a defective glove costs when a health-care provider *freaks out* about a leak or a defect and, afraid of having been infected, orders blood tests to see what kinds of germs she may have picked up. Those tests cost money. *They are an objective, quantifiable way to measure the price the system pays for the worker's fear!* They are what in the cost/benefit world is known as a *revealed preference*, a behavior (ordering the blood test) that reveals our preference for safety and helps analysts put a dollar value on "riskiness" (like workers in riskier jobs demanding more pay or car shoppers paying more for cars with higher safety ratings).

It was a remarkably creative and insightful bit of policy making, because it recognized that defective gloves cause predictable behaviors *that are the result of people's feelings*, behaviors that can be quantified and converted into the objective economics useful for rational policy decision making. The FDA was able to think more comprehensively about the realities of how people perceive risk and how they behave. It factored in, not out, the Affective quality of the issue, and in the end, it set a more stringent limit on how many gloves per batch could be defective.

Think about all the other ways in which our Affective Risk Response leads to behaviors that reveal what we are more, or less, afraid of. People reveal their fears about natural disasters when they do or don't buy flood or earthquake or fire insurance. People reveal their worries in the reduced value they are willing to pay for property near a chemical factory or power line. They reveal their worries in the flu shots they do or don't get, the level of punitive damages jurors assess to companies whose products or behaviors harm somebody, or the increase in the number of people killed on the roads when driving goes up after a high-profile airplane crash makes the news. We do all sorts of things to stay safe that would allow policy makers to quantify our fears. And we do all sorts of things when our fears are low that would allow policy makers to quantify the effects when we're not worried enough, such as rates of skin cancer from the sun because so many people aren't worried enough to protect themselves, the number of bicyclists who are more severely injured in crashes because they aren't worried enough to wear helmets, and the costs to the health-care system and the economy because some of us don't worry enough about weighing too much. (A study published in May 2009 put the cost of obesity-related health care in the United States at an astounding $147 billion, 10 percent of all medical spending![14]). Those behaviors can be cataloged, their dollar implications can be quantified, and our fears, high or low, can be factored into policy making.

We can factor affect into cost/benefit analysis another way too. We can just plain ask people how much they would be willing to pay to reduce their risk, or how much they would pay to accept higher risk. (This is how cost/benefit analysis is done already.) Technocrats call this *expressed* preference, when they ask people, "How much would you be willing to pay to reduce your risk of premature death by 1 in 1,000?" or "How much would you have to be paid to accept an increased risk of premature death of 1 in 1,000?" The problem with this so-called Willingness to Pay (WTP) research is that it doesn't ask people about the *qualitative* characteristics of the risk. It doesn't specifically ask people how much their willingness to pay is influenced by the fact that the risk is Human-Made, is Catastrophic, involves Children, or that it's new, or kills people in a way that involves a high degree of Pain and Suffering. The WTP research *does* tell respondents what the risk is (air pollution or lead in drinking water or dying in a motor vehicle crash), but it *doesn't* specifically ask people how much the Affective nature of the risk matters to their answers. Like most methods of cost/benefit analysis, it's founded on economics. It overlooks the psychology that these pages have made clear matters so much in what people's preferences really are.

So what might be considered, by far smarter people than I, are specific ways to factor the key components of the Affective Risk Response system *into* the expressed preference method of finding out how much people would be willing to pay to reduce their risk, or what amount they'd be willing to accept to raise the risk. If we factor the feeling aspects of how we realistically perceive risk into the objective way of quantifying which policies will do us the most good, those policies should more accurately provide what society truly believes is the most health and environmental safety protection for the buck.

Some Ideas That Can Be Put into Practice Now

I'm sure there are all sorts of problems with what I've suggested. I think those challenges can be met, but that will take time. However, we don't have to wait. Even as we work to find ways to develop a more holistic, realistic sort of cost/benefit analysis, we can immediately begin to apply what we know about the Affective Risk Response in order to make better social risk policy.

First, and this one seems like a no-brainer really, government must realize that risk perception based on both the facts and our feelings is an intrinsic, *inescapable* driver of human behavior. Cartesian rationalists might wish this away intellectually, but it's how humans are. This is how we think, how we decide, how we behave. As Ralph Waldo Emerson said in his essay *Self-Reliance*, "Every man discriminates between the voluntary acts of his mind, and his involuntary perceptions, and knows that to his involuntary perceptions a perfect faith is due . . . he knows that these things are so, like day and night, not to be disputed." Rather than irrationally clinging to the goal of rationality, we can use what we know about this aspect of human psychology to understand the realities of human behavior in response to risk, and factor that into policy making. As Italian philosopher Nicola Abbagnano put it, "Reason itself is fallible, and *this fallibility must find a place in our logic* (my emphasis)." We can—we should—use what research has taught us about the logic of public perceptions to think logically about how people perceive things and how they behave, so that we can foresee those behaviors and account for them in how we protect public and environmental health.

The next step is for policy makers to look at each risk issue and understand not just the facts, but also the specific psychological factors that explain why we *feel* the way we do about that risk. A few pages back, I suggested that you do this with your personal perceptions: make a list of the Risk Perception Factors that might be influencing your perceptions and creating a Perception Gap. Government and social policy makers should do the same thing. That would help them predict how we feel and how we are likely to behave, and *that* knowledge can help produce policies that will do us the most good.

Here are a few examples.

Let's start with an example discussed earlier, cell phones and driving. As mobile phones proliferated, so did the number of people injured or killed by motorists who were yakking and driving instead of paying attention to their driving. Pressure mounted on governments around the world to solve the risk of cell phone use by drivers. The facts were pretty clear. The devices distracted a driver's attention because he couldn't use both hands to operate the vehicle and he couldn't use his head to pay attention. The facts were also absolutely clear that most of the problem was the mental distraction. The best solution for public safety was to ban the use of mobile phones by anyone operating a motor vehicle.

But even as legislators faced pressure to deal with this new risk, they quickly realized that people were actually saying, "Take the phone away from that *other* driver, the one who is *imposing* the risk on *me*." They weren't saying, "Ban *my* phone." And lawmakers were heavily lobbied by the mobile phone industry not to ban the use of cell phones at all. So they had to do something, but an outright ban, which made the most sense, would be politically unpopular.

Many jurisdictions around the world chose the compromise of allowing cell phone use by drivers only if the device is hands-free, a decision that took into account public and industry pressure, but that ignored a key factor in the way we perceive and respond to risk, the issue of Control. Suppose that as legislators were considering a law to allow the use of hands-free mobile phones while driving, one of them had realized, "Because we'll be giving people the *feeling* that using a hands-free device makes them safer, we'll be giving them the sense that they have taken some control over their risk, and some of them will be *less* careful, even though they will still be distracted, and there is a very real chance that we'll be making things *worse*, not better." Would they have made a different choice? I don't know. What policy might work better? Beats me. That's above my pay grade, and off-topic anyway. The point here is that if policy makers took the psychology of risk perception into account, they could have been more thoughtful about choosing options that accounted for public behavior and might have chosen policies that would do more to improve public health.

Let's consider another example, the ongoing problem of people not getting vaccinated against the flu under normal circumstances. (Years when new strains of flu raise the risk, or circumstances that cause the regular flu vaccine to be in short supply, are unique situations.) In the United States, an annual flu shot is recommended for 196 million people who are between 6 months and 19 years old or over 50. The federal government estimates that only 44 percent actually get the shot. That means that about 110 million people who are at high risk remain vulnerable to flu, and since influenza is infectious and spreadable, those who don't get flu shots remain potential spreaders of the disease and a risk to many more.

So it's in society's best interest that people in high-risk groups get vaccinated.

But they don't, and they don't *for predictable reasons.* "Regular" flu is Familiar. That makes it less scary. A flu shot is always available, except under extraordinary circumstances, and that gives us a sense of Control (we can get the shot and protect ourselves whenever we want), and that makes flu less scary. Flu symptoms are nasty, but not as high on the Pain and Suffering scale as those of many other diseases, and that makes flu less scary. For many busy people, the hassle of getting the shot outweighs the Benefit, so they play down the Risk in their minds. And Optimism Bias probably plays a role too. Every year we see lots of people who *don't* get the flu, so many of us figure, "It won't happen to me."

Those psychological realities won't change. The people who are in charge of the flu vaccination program need to understand that, and they need to change the rules so that more people get vaccinated. They have tried reducing the hassle of getting the vaccine by making flu shots widely available through easy-to-get-to local clinics or at work. And they've made it free. But that hasn't been enough. There is still a Perception Gap creating risk for society. So they might also consider a financial incentive for people who get a flu shot, maybe a discount off their next visit to the doctor, to shift the Risk/Benefit perception of getting vaccinated. Or they could simply *mandate* flu vaccination for people in high-risk groups, the way we already do with vaccinations for children (with appropriate exceptions available, as with childhood vaccination, so that people don't have an increased fear of flu vaccine because it is being imposed on them).

Again, specific policy ideas are complex questions, and the details are beyond my expertise. But a full understanding of Affective risk perception would make clear the specific psychological barriers to getting everyone vaccinated who should be, and those insights can be used to design and implement a more effective program.

Here's another example. Many people who are eligible for flood insurance in the United States, and who can afford it, don't buy it. Nationally, only about half the people who are eligible for flood insurance get it. Those who don't say that they are less worried, in part because floods are Natural; in part because they have lived through flooding before and come out all right (in other words, the risk is Familiar, which makes it less worrisome); and because they can move their furniture to the second floor, or evacuate, or put sandbags around their house, or do other things that give them a sense of Control. They like the Benefits of where they live so much that they play down the Risk in their minds. They also sometimes suffer from the Fallacy of the Small Sample type of Categorization Effect, thinking that if a bad flood happened recently, it's not likely to happen again for a long time. (Which doesn't make sense, since next year's weather is unlikely to remember what last year's weather did.) So they suffer serious losses, from which they might have financially protected themselves, because of their Perception Gap. And as it stands now, because it is failing to consider the risk perception psychology involved, the national flood insurance program is falling short of its goal of helping communities and economies recover from flood damage.

The psychological reasons for the Perception Gap about the risk of flooding, and indeed about all risks of "natural" disasters, won't change. So, in the name of social policy that would help communities recover from natural disasters, why not make flood insurance, or earthquake insurance, or insurance against wildfires and forest fires a default requirement for property ownership, the same way other forms of insurance are already required? (Some types of natural disaster–related insurance are already mandatory, but only in designated high-risk areas and only for certain types of loans.)

Let's wrap up this short list of examples with a biggie in every sense of the word.

People being overweight or obese is a huge problem around the developed world, a leading risk factor for the world's greatest killer, heart disease. Its causes are complex, but Affective risk perception surely plays a big part. The Benefit of eating what we want, and as much as we want, when we want, causes us to play down the Risk. Most of us believe that being overweight is Voluntary. Most of us think that we have some Control over the risk of being overweight. Just ask the diet industry. Heart disease is not perceived to involve as much Pain and Suffering as some other ways to die. Social factors play a large role in the overweight epidemic too. Remember those people in Moirans-en-Montagne, the French village where everybody freaked out about the mysterious fires that turned out to be the work of an arsonist? We tend to adopt the views, and the behaviors, of those around us, an effect that grows stronger the greater the population of people around us who are behaving that way. It is likely that many people accept being overweight because so many other people are.

Those inherent psychological factors about the risks of being overweight will not change. But, in the name of public health, we might adopt policies that will reframe how those factors affect our choices. To change the risk/benefit perspective on being overweight, for example, health insurance might be priced to encourage people to stay healthy more than to help them pay their bills once they get sick (where such incentives exist, they could be increased). Some employers are beginning to deny health benefits to workers who smoke. Why not tie health benefits to weight loss as well, making exceptions as necessary for those who have problems controlling their weight?

But closing the societal Perception Gap regarding the risk of being overweight will also require a new approach to another weapon in government's risk management arsenal. Indeed, helping society make healthier choices about the most efficient ways to deal with *any* of the risks we face will require much more effective risk communication.

Risk Communication—Much More Than Just the Facts

Back in the 1970s and early 1980s, people in the chemical and nuclear power industries, and the government regulators overseeing those industries, were frustrated at what they felt was a Perception Gap between people's fears and the facts. They felt that people were more afraid of chemicals and nuclear power than they needed to be. So they turned to the social sciences for advice on how to communicate the facts about those risks to calm people down. That was how the practice of risk communication began.

The idea was to educate people, to tell them what they needed to know (according to the communicators) so that they would make more informed, rational judgments about the risks of chemicals and nuclear power. "Give them the facts and help them to understand what we experts know," went the thinking, "and they'll think about things the 'right' way, as in . . . the way we *want* them to think."

This approach largely failed for several reasons, one of which was that it ignored the emotional and instinctive components of the Affective Risk Response system. It presumed that the facts alone would be enough, that sufficiently informed, people would be "rational." It assumed that people could be educated with cognitive messages, ignoring the powerful subconscious elements of risk perception. Worse, this "here are the facts, so you can be smart enough to get it right" approach essentially *denied* people's feelings, implying that if their perceptions didn't conform to the facts after those facts had been explained to them in easy-to-read graphics and clear simple language, then, well, they were *wrong* (with an implicit message of "If you don't get it now that we've explained it to you, you're just *dumb*" mixed in)!

Small wonder that this approach failed. What is amazing is that it persists. Many government and corporate efforts to communicate to the public about risk still focus on the facts, and fail to recognize and respect the emotional and affective lenses through which people will see those facts. For example, statistics are offered to help people understand many risks, with little regard for the widespread problem of innumeracy and with no regard for the psychological "Can It Happen to *Me*?" Risk Perception Factor (remember, one in a million is too high if you think, "I might be *the one*!"). Information about radon explains the science quite well but fails to take into account the fact that when people learn that radon is naturally occurring, many of them will worry less, regardless of what the rest of the information says about the danger. Information about the risk of being overweight or obese talks about all the choices that people can make to lose weight, failing to realize that when you give people choices and a sense that the risk they are taking is voluntary, their fear goes down, and so does the likelihood they will make those healthy lifestyle decisions. And pointing out that the problem is widespread has the counterproductive effect of implying that the behavior is socially acceptable because so many people are doing it.

Certainly, good information can help people make more informed choices. It's vital. But that information has to be framed in ways that respect and account for how people are going to hear it and use it. Just as policy makers should take into account what we know about the specific components of the Affective Risk Response, risk communicators should use that knowledge to design and implement risk communication efforts that don't just offer the facts, but offer them in ways that are most emotionally relevant.

Here is a simple example. Suppose the government wants people who are at high risk for radon exposure, like Linda in Pennsylvania, to test their homes for radon levels. The risk communication would explain what radon is, where it comes from, what the risks are, and what you can do about it—the basic facts. But since we know that people are less afraid of risks that are natural than of those that are human-made, maybe right after they describe radon as naturally occurring, the communications might also say something like, "Here's another thing to think of as you decide what to do about the risk of radon. Remember, even though you know in your *mind* that radon is natural, it's your *lungs* where this radioactive substance does its damage, and your lungs can't tell where the substance came from. To your lungs, it doesn't matter. Just because it comes from a natural source doesn't mean that it isn't just as dangerous as a similar radioactive substance that might have been human-made. In your lungs, they're identical." The facts are there, but they are framed in a way that attempts to respect and account for how people perceive those facts.

Here's another example. This one isn't about educating people about an issue like radon or encouraging people to get a flu shot, but about the importance of risk communication for more immediate threats to public health and safety. After the September 11 terrorist attacks, some officials said things like, "Live your normal lives, or the terrorists win." New York Mayor Rudolph Giuliani suggested that people "go to restaurants. Go shopping." President Bush suggested that they "get down to Disneyland." Suppose that instead our government leaders had realized that how they communicate is every bit as important for protecting the public from the effects of terrorism as preventing another attack or bringing the bad guys to justice. And suppose they knew what risk perception researchers have known for 30 years, that when people are afraid, they do things to give themselves a sense of control, and that sometimes our desire for control can lead to a dangerous Perception Gap. Suppose the officials thought more holistically about risk perception and the behavior those perceptions lead to and recognized that high awareness of the airplane attacks would mean that fewer people would be flying, which meant that more would be driving. That was all rather obvious, *if* officials were thinking about risk perception and communication as key tools for protecting public health. But they weren't.

Instead of telling us to shop or go to an amusement park, they might have said something like, "Live your normal lives, or the terrorists win. For example, while flying is scarier for all of us these days, if you are so worried about flying that you decide to drive because driving gives you that reassuring sense of control, just remember that driving is statistically much riskier than flying. So if you choose to drive instead of fly because it makes you feel safer, and you're hurt or killed in a car crash, you could say that you're a victim of the terror these attacks are intended to evoke. Please keep that in mind as you decide how to travel."

Would that have saved all those people who were killed on the roads in the months just after September 11? No. Might it have saved Sarah and some others? Probably. Were many of the excess deaths beyond what would have been expected for those months directly attributable to the fear caused by the September 11 attackers? Absolutely. Did the government fail to use risk communication, and an understanding of risk perception, to protect the American public from this aspect of terrorism? Sadly, yes.

On the other hand, there are the positive lessons learned from the way risk communication was handled in other cases, like the effort by the U.S. Food and Drug Administration (FDA) and Department of Agriculture (USDA) when the first mad cow was found in America in late 2003. All the psychological Risk Perception Factors pointed to possible overreaction. Though the risk had long existed elsewhere, now, in the United States, it was New. Beef eaters in the United States would now fear that "It Can Happen to *Me!*" as beef eaters had in country after country in Europe when the disease first showed up there. Uncertainty in the United States was high because science was still unsure of how bovine spongiform encephalopathy (BSE) got from cow to human. The suspected agent, a mysterious misshaped protein called a prion, was invisible and could not be detected, another form of unsettling Uncertainty. And the Awareness/Ready Recall Effect was high. Over the Christmas holiday, the American press led with the story for days.

But the public's response was surprisingly mild, and one big reason was what officials from the FDA and USDA did, and said. Crucially, they announced that even though muscle meat was not believed to be the way the disease got from cow to human, they were recalling all the meat that had been shipped from the processing plants that might have handled the carcass of the sick cow whose brain had been found to carry mad cow prions. Most important, they said that they were doing this "with an abundance of caution." In other words, they were going beyond what the scientific evidence suggested was necessary. They were going beyond what the law required. The actual physical risk was infinitesimal, but officials weren't saying, "The risk is low. There's nothing to worry about," as officials in many other nations had. They were recognizing that people might be afraid, and that fear itself was something that had to be respected as real, and managed as part of the overall government response to the risk of mad cow disease.

There is a vital lesson here. Risk communication is a result not just of what an agency or a company *says*, but also of what it *does*. Policies and actions "speak," particularly to the Risk Perception Factor of Trust. Trust is based on many things, but one of them is the competence and intent of the organizations that are supposed to protect us. If those people and agencies seem competent, honest, and truly concerned for public safety, they will be more trusted, and that will dramatically improve their ability to manage risk and avoid the dangers of a Perception Gap. It wasn't the words that the USDA and the FDA chose to describe their action, "abundance of caution." It was the action itself, pulling all that muscle meat from the market, going beyond what the law required in the name of public safety, that "spoke" about whether the government was doing all it could, all we'd want, to keep us safe. In part as a result of these risk communications actions and messages, beef sales in the United States were barely affected by the arrival of mad cow disease, an event that had badly damaged other nations' economies.

The importance of trust for the effectiveness of any government agency responsible for risk management bears emphasis. The precious, fragile asset of trust in the government agencies that are supposed to protect us can make all the difference in how we respond to a terrorist attack, a pandemic disease, a hurricane, or an outbreak of contaminated food. Trust in government will have a great deal to do with how afraid we are, or aren't, of new technologies, such as food made from cloned animals or the products of nanoscience. Trust in the agencies that are supposed to protect us will play a role in our medical choices, our lifestyle choices, how worried we are about environmental threats, and what we press the government to do about them. As the mad cow example illustrates, actions of government that respect and respond to the Affective nature of people's concerns, even when those concerns don't match the scientific facts, are a powerful way to build that trust.

Here is another example of this vital point, that risk communication is implicit in what government does, not just explicit in what it says. In Japan, the *hibakusha*, the survivors of the atomic bombing of Hiroshima and Nagasaki, are entitled to many special government benefits. Those who suffer from five diseases connected with radiation are also eligible for additional medical benefits. In 2001, the government established science-based standards to determine who qualifies, since many *hibakusha* who lived farther from the center of the explosions received practically no radiation dose at all, which made it much less likely that radiation caused their illness. Under that standard, 99 out of every 100 Japanese atomic bomb survivors who applied for special medical benefits were turned down.

Some of them sued the Japanese government, and those lawsuits got a lot of attention in the press. Remember the Fairness Risk Perception Factor! How fair did it seem to deny these people such benefits? Did the facts of proximity to ground zero and actual physical dose matter? Not much at all. Public outrage was widespread. Political pressure built on the government. Then-Prime

Minister Shinzo Abe, who was already in political trouble, created a new system under which any *hibakusha* who had those diseases, whether they were exposed to enough radiation to cause them or not, would get the special benefits.

It was a straight capitulation to fear and political pressure, and as a precedent for overall risk-management policy making, it was fraught with all sorts of problems. But we're only talking here about risk communication and how actions "spcak" to people's response to risk, and this one spoke loudly. The controversy ended. The lawsuits all but dried up. The financial cost to the Japanese government of the medical care was far less than the government stood to lose in court. And trust in the government was at least slightly improved. (Abe soon lost his job anyway, but for other reasons.)

Insert any grade school truism you want here: "Actions speak louder than words" or "It doesn't matter how you talk the talk. It matters how you walk the walk." The lesson is that as policy makers consider what actions to take to protect our health and safety, not just which words to use, they must consider the Affective Risk Response to the options they are considering, because in trying to manage risk, they are also managing public behavior, and that behavior will depend to a great degree on how government and corporate policies and actions "speak" to our perceptions.

There is one final point to make in this quick discussion of the importance of risk communication as part of overall risk management. It has to do a good job of communicating the facts that people want and need to know. To be effective, it has to reflect the perceptions and interests and concerns of the audience, the people that the communication is trying to reach. Stunningly, risk communication often includes only what the experts think people *ought* to know.

The problem is wisely addressed in the book *Risk Communication: A Mental Models Approach* by M. Granger Morgan, Baruch Fischhoff, Ann Bostrom, and Cynthia Atman. The first steps in this approach are to learn what the experts think that people need to know about the issue—the experts' "mental model" of the issue—and then to ask a representative sample of real people what they know, what they don't know, and what they *want* to know about the issue—the real world's "mental model" of the issue.

The messages that result from this more inclusive approach do a much more thorough and precise job of giving people the information most likely to help them make healthier choices.

The mental models approach also tests those messages to see if they actually help, and adjusts them if they don't. It recognizes a critical point, that risk communication can have a meaningful impact on how people behave, so it has to be done carefully, not in the ad hoc sort of way that a lot of government agencies do it now. In essence, the authors recognize that risk communication itself can lead to a Perception Gap, which can be dangerous. They write on page 4, "Poor risk communications can create threats larger than those posed by the risks that they describe. We should no more release an unproven communication on people than an unproven drug." Worldwide, there are efforts underway to improve government risk communication.

- European governments, recognizing the damaging societal Perception Gaps that arose from the way governments handled mad cow disease and a number of other risk controversies, have established risk communication programs and expertise that pay close attention to the Affective components of public perceptions.
- The International Atomic Energy Agency (part of the United Nations), which recognized that poor risk communication that failed to account for people's perceptions was a key factor in the long-term social/psychological/economic consequences of Chernobyl, is enhancing its risk communication assistance to member

states that have nuclear power programs or are thinking about starting one.

- The World Health Organization (WHO) has developed detailed guidelines for risk communication, which include close attention to the emotional and instinctive ways in which we respond to risk. So have the U.S. Centers for Disease Control (CDC). The WHO and CDC received widespread praise for their risk communication in the spring of 2008, when a new version of H1N1 influenza, "swine" flu, broke out in Mexico. Their communications helped publics worldwide take the risk seriously, but avoid more extreme reactions.

- The U.S. FDA, stung by a string of controversies that have shaken public trust in the agency, has convened a special committee of experts to develop better risk communication policies based in part on the Affective nature of our Risk Response. The FDA is also developing better ways for health-care providers to communicate the statistics of health risks, recognizing innumeracy as a risk in and of itself that has to be managed as part of the agency's mission to protect public health and safety.

These efforts at better risk communication are all part of the broader idea that underlies the entire second half of this chapter. Government is in the business of risk management, protecting human and environmental health. But it's not just protecting us from too many parts per million or defective medical gloves. To a great degree, we need careful thinking by government risk managers to protect us from ourselves when for reasons deeply embedded in our psyche we are too afraid or not afraid enough. That risk, the risk of the Perception Gap, the risk that can arise when our fears don't match the facts, has to be managed too. Government policy making and risk communication, built on an understanding of and respect for the Affective nature of our Risk Response, will help narrow the societal Perception Gap and produce social policy that will leave us all safer.

CLOSING THOUGHTS

In his groundbreaking book *Descartes' Error*, neuroscientist Antonio Damasio describes Elliott, a patient who had no problem making rational sense of information, but who nonetheless could not live a normal life. Elliott passed every standard psychological and intelligence test with flying colors. But he was dysfunctional as a person because he was missing one thing: his cognitive brain couldn't converse with his emotional brain. The wiring connecting his prefrontal cortex, the area of the brain behind the forehead that plays a key role in making decisions, had been damaged and could no longer connect with the areas of the brain involved with emotions. So Elliott couldn't make decisions about anything, because he could not place *a value* on one choice over another. One job over another, one place to live over another, even which time would be best for simple appointments—these choices involved judgments about which one was better. It was not a matter of facts alone. The choices between options called for a decision about which one *felt* better than the other, and Elliott could not tell. He could *think* about one choice being better than another, but he couldn't *feel* it, and without feelings, he could not decide.

It's an important lesson about how the human animal functions. The overwhelming evidence from Elliott, from Susan Napolitano, from Linda in Pennsylvania, from all those people who got behind the wheel of a motor vehicle instead of into an airplane after September 11, and from everybody else you've met in the preceding pages supports the view of Thomas Aquinas, who said, "Most men seem to live according to sense rather than reason." We are *Homo naturalis,* not purely *Homo rationalis.* We are Affective beings whose views of and responses to the world are shaped not just by what we know, but also by what we feel. Indeed, our perceptions and behaviors are often shaped *mostly* by what we feel. Scottish philosopher David Hume said, "Reason is, and ought only to be the slave of the passions, and can never pretend to any other office than to serve and obey them."

Yet somehow, in our Enlightenment confidence in the supreme power of rationality, some people think that we can make choices about risk simply by thoroughly gathering all the "sound science" about hazard and exposure and probabilities, coolly calculating the costs and benefits of the various options for dealing with the risk, and choosing what the facts will then clearly show us is the rationally "right" way to go. The facts will reveal the truth. Enlightenment pioneer Immanuel Kant said, "All our knowledge begins with the senses, proceeds then to the understanding, and ends with reason. There is nothing higher than reason."

Sorry, Professor Kant. Sorry, all you devotees of the myth of ideal rationality, all you believers in the supreme power of the human cortex to think and reason our way to "correct" choices. You bow before a false god. As Elliott's tragic circumstances warn us, all the facts in the world are meaningless, in the fullest and most precise meaning of that word, without the other components of Affect that help us judge which choices are better or worse, right or wrong, good or bad. We need our feelings to make sense of things, to judge pros and cons, risks and benefits, to decide among choices which one is right. Which one *feels* right. *Without Affect there is no truth, just meaningless data.*

Risk is not just a statistic. It is an idea and a feeling, a perception informed not just by the reasoning of the thinking cortex that humans have more recently developed, but by all the emotional and instinctive cortical systems that we have had since prehuman times, long before we developed the relatively recent ability to think and reason. We remain Affectives, not pure Rationalists. We need to heed the wisdom of Blaise Pascal, who observed, "We know the truth, not only by the reason, but by the heart." Pascal spent the first part of his life as a brilliant rational mathematician and scientist—tutored in part by rationalist Descartes ("I think, therefore I am") himself—and the second as a religious philosopher. An interesting shift in perspectives, and a telling metaphor for this book. Pascal's two-part life, and his observations about the truth from his masterwork *Pensées*, perfectly sum things up. Reason *and* Affect. Facts *and* Feelings. Thinking *and* Sensing. They are not separate. It's not either/or. It's *and*. We must understand that they are interwoven components of a single system that helps us perceive the world and make our judgments and choices.

Still, we should not accept the idea that simply because this is who we are, we should therefore simply accept our true nature and defer to its innate wisdom. That is more than simplistic. It's dangerous, because sometimes this system simply is not wise. As powerful as it is, the Affective system of perception is not perfect. Evolved to respond to simpler circumstances, it can make mistakes about more complex modern challenges, errors that get us into trouble. This book is full of examples.

So what are we to do? We can't function as perfect reasoning machines. Elliott teaches us that. Nor can we trust ourselves to always make the right calls when our reason is mixed with emotions and instincts not yet calibrated to handle the kinds of threats we now face. And we can't wait for evolution to work out the bugs, because we're pretty clearly mucking things up so badly, so fast, that there isn't time for that sort of patience.

What we *can* do to avoid the dangers that arise when our fears don't match the facts—the most rational thing *to* do—is to understand our Affective Risk Response system more intimately, and how each part shades our perceptions and colors our judgments, and use that self-evaluation to step back and think things through more carefully, more completely, and more honestly.

That holistic view of the Affective Risk Response system, an absolutely fascinating system whose components and details have been summarized in the pages you've just read, will let you know yourself a little better, think a little more carefully, and hopefully will empower you to make wiser, healthier choices for yourself, your family, and the tribes to which you belong.

Be safe.

ENDNOTES

INTRODUCTION

1. This story is drawn from an actual series of events in Needham, Massachusetts, in the late 1980s, on which I reported as a local TV journalist. Some details, including names, have been altered.
2. A good source for the overall idea of the affect heuristic is Paul Slovic, Melissa Finucane, Ellen Peters, and Donald G. MacGregor, "Rational Actors or Rational Fools: Implications of the Affect Heuristic for Behavioral Economics," *Journal of Socio-Economics* 31, no. 4 (2002), pp. 329–342.
3. www.who.int/mediacentre/news/releases/2005/pr38/en/index.html.

CHAPTER 1

1. For much more on this, see Joseph LeDoux, *The Emotional Brain* (New York: Simon & Schuster, 1996). LeDoux was one of the pioneers of neuroscientific research into the biological roots of emotion. This is a highly readable book on the biological basis of the risk response.
2. The 22-millisecond delay figure comes from a conversation with LeDoux.
3. Charles Darwin, *The Expression of the Emotions in Man and Animals* (New York: D. Appleton, 1872), p. 38.
4. Michael Davis and Paul Whalen, "The Amygdala: Vigilance and Emotion," *Molecular Psychiatry* 6 (2001), pp. 13–34.
5. James McGaugh and Benno Roozendaal, "Role of Adrenal Stress Hormones in the Forming of Lasting Memories in the Brain," *Current Opinion in Neurobiology* 12, no. 2 (2002), pp. 205–210.
6. E. Claparede, "Recognition and 'Me-ness,'" in *Organization and Pathology of Thought*, ed. D. Rapaport (New York: Columbia University Press, 1951), pp. 58–75.
7. Arne Ohman, Anders Flykt, and Francisco Esteves, "Emotion Drives Attention: Detecting the Snake in the Grass," *Journal of Experimental Psychology: General* 130 (2001), pp. 466–478.

8. Anna Pissiota, Örjan Frans, Åsa Michelgård, et al., "Amygdala and Anterior Cingulate Cortex Activation during Affective Startle Modulation: A PET Study of Fear," *European Journal of Neuroscience* 18, no. 5 (2003), pp. 1325–1331.

9. Ned Kalin, Steven Shelton, Richard Davidson, and Ann Kelley, "The Primate Amygdala Mediates Acute Fear but Not the Behavioral and Physiological Components of Anxious Temperament," *Journal of Neuroscience* 21, no. 6 (2001), pp. 2067–2074.

10. Arne Ohman, Anders Flykt, Daniel Lundquist, and Francisco Esteves, "The Face in the Crowd Revisited: A Threat Advantage with Schematic Stimuli," *Journal of Personality and Social Psychology* 80 (2001), pp. 381–396.

11. Paul Whalen, Lisa Shin, Sena McInerney, et al., "A Functional MRI Study of Human Amygdala Responses to Facial Expressions of Fear versus Anger," *Emotion* 1, no. 1 (2001), pp. 70–83.

12. Paul J. Whalen, Scott L. Rauch, Nancy L. Etcoff, et al., "Masked Presentations of Emotional Facial Expressions Modulate Amygdala Activity without Explicit Knowledge," *Journal of Neuroscience* 18, no. 1 (1998), pp. 411–418.

13. Ralph Adolphs, Daniel Tranel, Hanna Damasio, and Antonio Damasio, "Fear and the Human Amygdala," *Journal of Neuroscience* 15 (1995), pp. 5879–5891.

14. Nathalie Gosselin, Isabelle Peretz, Erica Johnsen, and Ralph Adolphs, "Amygdala Damage Impairs Emotion Recognition from Music," *Neuropsychologia* 45 (2007), pp. 236–244.

15. LeDoux, *The Emotional Brain*, p. 19.

CHAPTER 2

1. These figures come from a 2002 analysis by Joshua Cohen, at that time at the Harvard Center for Risk Analysis.

2. Herbert Simon, "Bounded Rationality," in John Eatwell, Murray Milgate, Peter Newman (eds.), *Utility and Probability* (New York: Norton, 1990), pp. 15–18.

3. Pioneers in the field of heuristics and biases include Daniel Kahneman, Amos Tversky, and Paul Slovic. For much more on this, see a good collection of academic articles in Daniel Kahneman, Paul Slovic, and Amos Tversky (eds.), *Judgment under Uncertainty: Heuristics and Biases* (Cambridge, U.K.: Cambridge University Press, 1982).

4. Antonio Regalado, *Wall Street Journal,* December 29, 2003.

5. A. J. Wakefield, S. H. Murch, A. Anthony, et al., "Ileal-Lymphoid-Nodular Hyperplasia, Non-specific Colitis, and Pervasive Developmental Disorder in Children," *Lancet* 351 (February 28, 1998), pp. 637–641.

6. There is a terrific Web site on John Snow and the foundation of epidemiology at www.ph.ucla.edu/epi/snow.html.

7. Daniel Kahneman and Amos Tversky, "Prospect Theory: An Analysis of Decision under Risk," *Econometrica* 47, no. 2 (1979), p. 268.

8. Nathan Novemsky and Daniel Kahneman, "The Boundaries of Loss Aversion," *Journal of Marketing Research* 42, no. 2 (2005), pp. 119–128.

9. Ross Roley, "Runner's Reluctance," on the Web site Baseball Analysts, http://baseballanalysts.com/archives/2007/11/runners_relucta.php.

10. David Romer, "It's Fourth Down and What Does the Bellman Equation Say? A Dynamic Programming Analysis of Football Strategy," National Bureau of Economic Research Working Paper No. 9024, June 2002.

11. Barbara McNeil, Stephen Pauker, Harold Sox, and Amos Tversky, "On the Elicitation of Preferences for Alternative Therapies," *New England Journal of Medicine* 306 (1982), pp. 1259–1262.

12. The EPA suggests that pregnant women not eat shark, swordfish, king mackerel, or tilefish, and eat only 12 ounces per week, or about two servings, of shrimp, canned light tuna, albacore tuna, salmon, pollock, and catfish. The complete EPA warning about fish consumption is at www.epa.gov/waterscience/fish/advice/index.html.

13. Gary Myers and Philip Davidson, "Maternal Fish Consumption Benefits Children's Development," *Lancet* 369, no. 9561 (2007), pp. 537–538.

14. Kahneman et al. (eds.), *Judgment under Uncertainty,* p. 14.

15. Sarah Lichtenstein, Paul Slovic, Baruch Fischhoff, et al., "Judged Frequency of Lethal Events," *Journal of Experimental Psychology: Human Learning and Memory* 4 (1978), pp. 551–578.

16. (1) The biggest risk is 1 in 10. (2) 1 in 1,000 = 0.1 percent. (3) 1 percent = 10 in 1,000. (4) With equal numbers on a single die that are odd and even, if 1,000 rolls don't come out pretty close to 500 heads and 500 tails, check the die.

17. Isaac Lipkus, Greg Samsa, and Barbara Rimer, "General Performance on a Numeracy Scale among Highly Educated Samples," *Medical Decision Making* 21 (2001), pp. 21–37.

18. The Problem of the Points: Imagine that Bob and Betty have each put up $100 and are playing a tournament of RISK. The first one to reach six

wins takes the $200. But when the score is 5-3, with Betty ahead, both of them are sick of playing RISK for the last 19 hours, and they agree to quit. How should they split the pot? Pascal and Fermat figured out that Betty needed only one more win, and Bob needed three. This led to the calculations of the odds of those future outcomes, which produced a formula for splitting the pot, but if I showed you the whole thing, your head would hurt.

19. Lance Forrow, William Taylor, and Robert Arnold, "Absolutely Relative: How Research Results Are Summarized Can Affect Treatment Decisions," *American Journal of Medicine* 92, no. 22 (1992), pp. 121–124.

20. David Armor and Shelley Taylor, "When Predictions Fail: The Dilemma of Unrealistic Optimism," in Thomas Gilovich, Dale Griffin, and Daniel Kahneman (eds.), *Heuristics and Biases: The Psychology of Intuitive Judgment* (New York: Cambridge University Press, 2002), pp. 334–347.

21. Dan Hurley, "Divorce Rate. It's Not as High as You Think," *New York Times*, April 19, 2005, www.divorcereform.org/nyt05.html.

22. Daniel Gilbert, *Stumbling on Happiness* (New York: Vintage Books, 2007).

23. Sarah Lichtenstein, Paul Slovic, Baruch Fischhoff, et al., "Judged Frequency of Lethal Events," *Journal of Experimental Psychology: Human Learning and Memory* 4, no. 6 (1978), pp. 551–578.

24. Neil Weinstein, "Unrealistic Optimism about Future Life Events," *Journal of Personality and Social Psychology* 39, no. 5 (1980), pp. 806–820.

25. Michael Scheier, Charles Carver, and Michael Bridges, "Distinguishing Optimism from Neuroticism (and Trait Anxiety, Self-Mastery, and Self-Esteem): A Reevaluation of the Life Orientation Test," *Journal of Personality and Social Psychology* 67 (1994), pp. 1063–1078.

CHAPTER 3

1. This story is adapted from a conversation with a ticketing agent at United Airlines two weeks after the September 11, 2001, terrorist attacks, relating the experience of a flight attendant friend.

2. Gerd Gigerenzer, "Out of the Frying Pan and into the Fire: Behavioral Reactions to Terrorist Attacks," *Risk Analysis* 26, no. 2 (2006), pp. 347–351.

3. Garrick Blalock, Vrinda Kadiyali, and Daniel Simon, "The Impact of 9/11 on Driving Fatalities: The Other Lives Lost to Terrorism," Social

Science Research Network, 2005, http://papers.ssrn.com/sol3/papers.cfm?abstract_id=677549.

4. Michael Sivak and Michael Flannagan, "Consequences for Road Traffic Fatalities of the Reduction in Flying Following September 11, 2001," *Transportation Research Part F* (2004), pp. 301–305.

5. Michael Kosfeld, Markus Heinrichs, Paul Zak, et al., "Oxytocin Increases Trust in Humans," *Nature* 435 (2005), pp. 673–676.

6. Thomas Baumgartner, Markus Heinrichs, Aline Vonlanthen, et al., "Oxytocin Shapes the Neural Circuitry of Trust and Trust Adaptation in Humans," *Neuron* 58 (2008), pp. 639–650.

7. Joel Winston, Bryan Strange, John O'Doherty, and Ray Dolan, "Automatic and Intentional Brain Responses during Evaluation of Trustworthiness of Faces," Nature Neuroscience (online), February 19, 2002.

8. Michael Mease, "Risk and Preventive Factors of Post-Traumatic Stress Disorder and Its Co-morbid Disorders," *Current Opinion in Psychiatry* 13, no. 6 (2000), pp. 587–589.

9. Jim Stimpson, "Prospective Evidence for a Reciprocal Relationship between Sense of Control and Depressive Symptoms Following a Flood," *Stress and Health* 22, no. 3 (2006), pp. 161–166.

10. Maria Livanou et al., "Beliefs, Sense of Control and Treatment Outcome in Post-Traumatic Stress Disorder," *Psychological Medicine* 32, no. 1 (2002), pp. 157–165.

11. Robert Saper, Stefanos Kales, Janet Paquin, et al., "Heavy Metal Content of Ayurvedic Herbal Medicine Products," *Journal of the American Medical Association* 292, no. 23 (2004), pp. 2868–2873.

12. Paul Whalen, "Fear, Vigilance, and Ambiguity: Initial Neuroimaging Studies of the Human Amygdala," *Current Directions in Psychological Science* 7 (1998), pp. 177–188.

13. "Ethics and SARS: Learning Lessons from the Toronto Experience," report by a working group of the University of Toronto Joint Centre for Bioethics, www.yorku.ca/igreene/sars.html.

14. No one is sure how West Nile virus got to the United States. It could have been carried in by a bird that managed to get to the United States from the Middle East. The strain that appeared was similar to one that was unique to Israel at that time, but the geography of the source is also unknown.

15. www.missingkids.com/missingkids/servlet/PageServlet?LanguageCountry=en_US&PageId=169. The number is 1-800-843-5678.

16. "Trends in Arrests of Online Predators," www.unh.edu/ccrc/index.html.

CHAPTER 4

1. Robert Cialdini, Richard Borden, et al., "Basking in Reflected Glory; Three (Football) Field Studies, *Journal of Personality and Social Psychology*, 34, no. 3, (1976), pp 366-375.

2. Dan Kahan, "Cultural Cognition as a Risk Determinant," Harvard Law School Program on Risk Regulation Research Paper No. 08-20, http://ssrn.com/abstract=1123807.

3. Dan Kahan, Donald Braman, Paul Slovic, et al., "The Second National Risk and Culture Study: Making Sense of—and Making Progress in—the American Culture War of Fact," *Harvard Law School Program on Risk Regulation*.

4. The story is well captured in Marc Poumadere and Claire Mays, "Fires in Moirans-en-Montagne," in *The Social Amplification of Risk*, ed. Nick Pidgeon, Roger Kasperson, and Paul Slovic (Cambridge, U.K., and New York: Cambridge University Press, 2003), pp. 209–242.

5. A lot of these ideas, and many more, were first brought together in Roger Kasperson, Ortwin Renn, Paul Slovic, et al., "The Social Amplification of Risk: A Conceptual Framework," *Risk Analysis* 8, no. 2 (1988), pp. 178–187.

6. Paul Slovic, "Perception of Risk: Reflections on the Psychometric Paradigm," in *Social Theories of Risk*, ed. Sheldon Krimsky and Dominic Golding (Westport, Conn.: Praeger, 1992), pp. 117–152.

7. Paul Slovic, James Flynn, and Mark Layman, "Perceived Risk, Trust and the Politics of Nuclear Waste," *Science* 254 (1991), pp. 1603–1607.

8. "Key News Audiences Now Blend Online and Traditional Sources," Pew Research Center for the People and the Press, August 2008, http://pewresearch.org/pubs/928/key-news-audiences-now-blend-online-and-traditional-sources.

9. Joseph Hibbeln, John Davis, Colin Steer, et al., "Maternal Seafood Consumption in Pregnancy and Neurodevelopmental Outcomes in Childhood (ALSPAC Study): An Observational Cohort Study," *Lancet* 369 (2007), pp. 578–585.

10. George Gerbner, Laurence Morgan, et al., "Growing Up with Television: Cultivation Processes," in J. Bryant and D. Zillmann (eds.), *Media Effects: Advances in Theory and Research*, 2nd ed. (Mahwah, N.J.: Lawrence Erlbaum Associates, Inc.), pp.43–47.

CHAPTER 5

1. Alison Holman and Roxanne Silver, "Terrorism, Acute Stress, and Cardiovascular Health: A 3-Year National Study Following the Septem-

ber 11th Attacks," *Archives of General Psychiatry* 65, no. 1 (2008), pp. 73–80.

2. Committee on Fluoride in Drinking Water of the National Research Council, *Fluoride in Drinking Water: A Scientific Review of EPA's Standards,* (Washington, D.C.: National Academies Press, 2006).

3. Susan Griffin, Kari Jones, and Scott Tomar, "An Economic Evaluation of Community Water Fluoridation," *Journal of Public Health Dentistry* 61, no. 2 (2001), pp. 78–86.

4. "Biological Effects of Ionizing Radiation (BEIR) VII, Phase 2," National Research Council of the National Academies of Science, www.nap.edu/openbook.php?isbn=030909156X.

5. Ali Mokdad, James Marks, Donna Stroup, and Julie Gerberding, "Actual Causes of Death in the United States, 2000," *Journal of the American Medical Association* 291 (2004), pp. 1238–1245.

6. Since electricity generation accounts for only 15 percent of human-made fine particle pollution in the United States, according to EPA Air Emissions Sources, Particulate Matter, www.epa.gov/air/emissions/pm.htm, we need to adjust the death toll numbers from particulates down so that they represent only the percentage of particle pollutants caused by power generation.

7. Anthony Leiserowitz, "Climate Change Risk Perception and Policy Preferences: The Role of Affect, Imagery, and Values," *Climatic Change* 77, nos. 1–2 (2006), pp. 45–72.

8. http://pewglobal.org/reports/pdf/252.pdf.

9. http://news.bbc.co.uk/2/hi/in_depth/7075759.stm.

10. Philippe Grandjean et al., "Cognitive Deficit in 7-Year-Old Children with Prenatal Exposure to Methylmercury," *Neurotoxicology and Teratology* 19, no. 6 (1997), pp. 417–428.

11. From the EPA: "Do not eat Shark, Swordfish, King Mackerel, or Tilefish because they contain high levels of mercury. Eat up to 12 ounces (2 average meals) a week of a variety of fish and shellfish that are lower in mercury. Five of the most commonly eaten fish that are low in mercury are shrimp, canned light tuna, salmon, pollock, and catfish. Another commonly eaten fish, albacore ("white") tuna has more mercury than canned light tuna. So, when choosing your two meals of fish and shellfish, you may eat up to 6 ounces (one average meal) of albacore tuna per week."

12. Zajonc's speech, "Feeling and Thinking, Preferences Need No Inferences," was given in 1979 at the meeting of the American Psychological

Association honoring him with the association's Distinguished Scientific Contribution Award. His ideas inspired a lot of the social science work that this book tries to summarize.

13. Matthew Adler, "Fear Assessment: Cost-Benefit Analysis and the Pricing of Fear and Anxiety," *Chicago-Kent Law Review* 79 (2004), p. 977, http://ssrn.com/abstract=466720.

14. Eric Finkelstein, Justin Trogdon, Joel Cohen, and William Dietz, "Annual Medical Spending Attributable to Obesity: Payer- and Service-Specific Estimates," *Health Affairs* 28, no. 5 (2009), w822–831.

INDEX

Absolute risk, 55–56, 176–177, 223–224, 230
Acetylcholine, 7–8, 10
ACSH. *See* American Council on Science and Health
Adler, Matthew, 240
The Advancement of Learning (Bacon), 135
Affective people, xv–xvi, 199, 214, 237
  knowing/feeling of, 260, 261
  reason and, 215–216
Affective Risk Response system. *See also* Risk response
  behaviors revealing fear in, 241
  expressed preference and, 242–243
  necessary understanding of, 262
  perceptions that make things worse, xvii–xviii, 66, 85, 187–188, 214–215, 240
  psychological/neurobiological components of, xvi, 112, 236
  rationality and, 249
  risk communication and, 250–251
  subconscious, 19, 148
  tools for protection and, xvii, 68, 70
  trade-offs and, 81–82, 84, 224–225, 228–229
Against the Gods: The Remarkable Story of Risk (Bernstein), 54
Airbags, media on, 175
All Quiet On the Western Front (Remarque), xi
AMBER. *See* America's Missing: Broadcast Emergency Response alert
American Council on Science and Health (ACSH), 181
America's Missing: Broadcast Emergency Response (AMBER) alert, 123
Amygdala, 2–7, 26, 194
  built-in fears and, 14–16
  cerebral cortex and, 2, 66
  Control and, 85
  damage to, 17
  fear beginning at, 4

*f*MRI of oxytocin and, 72–73
MRI/*f*MRI observation of, 16–17
oxytocin in, 71
Triple F response of, 2, 4–5, 7, 10, 12–14, 159, 194, 195
Amygdala, protection process, 7–14
  acetylcholine release, 7–8
  glucocorticoids release, 10
  glutamate release, 10–11
  hyper memory, 9–10, 50–51
  implicit memory storage, 9, 13, 194
  norepinephrine release, 9, 194
  sensory information increase, 8, 13
Anchoring/Adjustment, 45–48, 216
  death rates and, 46–47
  distortions of, 230–231
  nuclear power and, 47–48
  United Nations participation and, 45–46
  Wheel of Chance as anchor, 45–46
Anthrax, 86, 113, 192–193
Arachnophobes (spider-phobic), 15
Asbestos, mesothelioma and, 38
Atman, Cynthia, 255
Autism, 35–36
Awareness/Ready Recall Effect, 48–52, 139, 216, 228
  Categorization connection to, 49–50
  frequency/probability and, 50
  on journalists, 180
  mad cow disease and, 252
  media influence on, 51, 59, 180
  memory vividness and, 50–51
  sniper shootings and, 48–50
  society magnification of, 159

Bacon, Francis (Sir), 135
Basking in Reflected Glory (BIRG), 143
Belief adoption, society influence on, 159
Berkman Center for Internet and Society, 124
Bernstein, Peter, 54

Biases, 24
    confirmation, 225
    information skepticism of, 219
    of journalists, 181–182
Bierce, Ambrose, 1, 2
Biological system, of risk response, 17–20, 86
BIRG. *See* Basking in Reflected Glory
Bisephenol A (BpA), 33–34, 232–233
Blood chemistry, fight or flight response
    changes in, 195
Boston Globe, 87, 117–118
Boston University (BU), 78
    National Institutes of Health biological
        laboratory, 78, 131, 132–133
Bostrom, Ann, 255
Botulism, 60
Bounded Rationality, 21–63, 216, 218,
    228, 231
    Optimism Bias and, 61
    Simon on, 23–24
Bovine growth hormone, 151, 164
Bovine spongiform encephalopathy (BSE),
    30, 31, 252
Breaking the Vicious Circle (Breyer), 238
Breast implants, 76
Breyer, Stephen, 238
BSE. *See* Bovine spongiform encephalopathy
BU. *See* Boston University
Built-in fears, 14–20
    of dark, 14, 18
    of scared/angry faces, 15–17
    of snake/spider, 14–15
Bush, George W., 30, 75, 113, 251

Calories per thought (CPT), 24
Can It Happen to Me, 109–114, 136, 210,
    246, 250, 252
    anthrax, 113
    SARS and, 111–112
    September 11, 2001, 113–114
    West Nile virus and, 112–113
Cancer, 99, 199–203, 224
    celebrities survival of, 202
    death rate, 199
    ionizing radiation cause of, 205–206
    mesothelioma, 38
    NIH on research spending, 200
    Pain/Suffering from, 96–97, 201
    problems of probability and, 38
Catastrophic or Chronic, 105–109, 176, 242
    Chernobyl nuclear accident, 106, 207
    climate change and, 212
    definition of, 105

evolutionary psychology and, 108–109
plane accident, 105–106
Three Mile Island nuclear accident, 207
tribal influence and, 108, 109
tsunami, 108
Categorization, 32–39, 247
    Awareness/Ready Recall Effect connec-
        tion to, 49–50
    BpA and, 33–34
    distortions of, 230
    drug-coated stents and, 229–230
    Fallacy of the Small Sample, 35–37
    fluoride and, 204
    nuclear power and, 34
    Optimism Bias interaction with, 61
    Problems with Probability, 37–39
CBA. *See* Cost/benefit analysis
CBS Evening News, 99–100, 167
CCRC. *See* Crimes Against Children Re-
    search Center
CDC. *See* Centers for Disease Control
Cell phone usage. *See* Driving while phoning
    (DWP)
Centers for Disease Control (CDC), xviii, 22,
    199, 257
Cerebral cortex, 2, 66
CFA. *See* Consumer Federation of America
Chemical spill, media on, 169–171
Chernobyl nuclear accident, xix, 47–48, 206,
    208, 228, 230–231
    Catastrophic or Chronic, 106, 207
    risk communication for, 256–257
Children. *See also* Risks to Children
    abduction of, 119–120, 126–127, 164
    dental decay in, 204
    impaired growth rates of, 196
The China Syndrome, 51
Choice, 89–92
    cloned animals and, 90
    controversial facilities and, 91–92
    DWP and, 89
    heart disease and, 201
    lifestyle/obesity as, 189, 248
    nuclear power and, 91
Climate change, 146–148, 208–213, 235. *See
    also* Global warming
    Can It Happen to Me, 210
    Catastrophe and, 212
    Control and, 212
    conversation about, 135–142
    Cultural Cognition on, 211–212
    Framing Effect on, 212
    human/environmental harms from, 209

Human-Made forces and, 212
Kahan on, 148–150
Leiserowitz on, 210
Risk *vs.* Benefit and, 212
Risks to Children and, 212
Cloned animals, 90
Clustering, 38–39
Cognitive cortex
    rational risk analysis from, 4–5, 66
    thalamus and, 4
Cognitive dissonance theory, 182–183
Communitarians, 146, 212, 235
Confirmation bias, 225
Conscious awareness
    cerebral cortex and, 2, 66
    explicit memory and, 9–10
    fear and, 1–2
    for narrowing Perception Gap, 215–217
Consumer Federation of America (CFA), 90
Control, 62–63, 67, 136, 158, 174, 176, 191, 216
    amygdala alert for, 85
    anthrax and, 86, 192
    biological/chemical terrorist attack
        and, 86
    cancer, lack of, 201
    climate change and, 212
    DWP and, 88, 190, 245
    flood insurance, national and, 247
    H1N1 "swine" flu vaccination and, 86–87
    obesity and, 190
CORF. *See* Cutting Off Reflected Failure
Cosmetic pesticides, 152
Cost/benefit analysis (CBA), 238
    expressed preference in, 242–243
    revealed preference in, 241
    WTP in, 242
"Cost-Benefit Analysis and the Pricing of Fear
    and Anxiety" (Adler), 240
CPT. *See* Calories per thought
Crimes Against Children Research Center
    (CCRC), 124
Cronkite, Walter, 99–100, 167, 213
Cultural Cognition, xvii, 142–156, 216
    on climate change, 211–212
    Communitarians, 146, 212, 235
    criticisms of, 155–156
    Egalitarians, 146, 212, 234
    Hierarchists, 145, 212, 234
    Individualists, 145–146, 204, 212, 234
    society structure and, 144–145
Cultural Theory of Risk, of Douglas/
    Wildavsky, 144, 155–156
Cutting Off Reflected Failure (CORF), 143

Damasio, Antonio, 259
Darwin, Charles, 5–6, 69, 220, 236
Death causes
    cancer, 38, 96–97, 99, 199–203,
        205–206, 224
    chronic obstructive pulmonary
        disease, 99
    falls, 98–99
    heart disease, xviii, 96–97, 99, 105–106,
        199–203
    optimism and, 59–60
Death rates, 46–47
Decision making
    CBA for, 238
    without knowledge, 23
    mental shortcuts for, 23–26
    research on, 24–25
Decision-making tools
    Categorization, 32–39, 49–50, 61, 204,
        229–230, 247
    Framing Effect, 26–32, 43, 136, 172,
        174, 212, 216, 217, 228, 229
    Loss Aversion, 40–62, 136, 139, 147,
        159, 180, 190, 191, 216, 228, 230–231,
        246, 252
Depression, stress and, 197
Descartes' Error (Damasio), 259
Descartes, René, 225–226, 261
Douglas, Mary, 144
Dow Corning, 76
Drinking/Driving, 191
Driving death increase, after September
    11 terrorist attacks, xviii, 65–66, 67,
    187–188, 251
Driving while phoning (DWP), 22, 233,
    244–245
    Choice and, 89
    Control and, 88, 190, 245
    hands-free devices and, 245
    Optimism Bias and, 190
    Risk *vs.* Benefit and, 190
Drug-coated stents, reframing information
    on, 229–230
DuPont Columbia Award, 167
DWP. *See* Driving while phoning

Earthwatch Institute, 128
Eastern equine encephalitis (Triple E), 83,
    114
Ebola virus, 78–79
Economics, decision-making process and,
    24–25
Egalitarians, 146, 212, 234

Electric/magnetic fields (EMFs), 102–103
Emerson, Ralph Waldo, xiv, 243
EMFs. *See* Electric/magnetic fields
Emotion. *See also* Instinctive reaction, to fear
  power of, 239
  predictable behaviors as result of, 241
  Rationality *vs.*, 260
Emotional events, memory and, 8–9
Endowment Effect, 41–45
  Epicurus and, 41
  fish nutrient benefit and, 44
  health treatment choice and, 42–43
  mercury exposure and, 43–45
  value and, 41
Energy levels
  fear and, 12–14
  Triple F response and, 12–14, 195
ENN. *See* Environmental News Network
Environmental health, xviii, 94, 164
Environmental News Network (ENN), 181
Environmentalists, xv, xx
Epicurus, 41
Evolutionary psychology, 108–109
Explicit memory
  conscious awareness and, 9–10
  high level glucocorticoid impairment
    of, 10
  hippocampus and, 10, 11, 196
Exposure, 177–179
  how much matters, 178–179
  to mercury, 43–45, 175–176, 222–223
  to pesticides, 22, 164
Expressed preference, 242–243

Fairness, 130–131
Fallacy of the Small Sample
  of Categorization, 35–37
  drug-coated stents and, 229–230
  of MMR vaccine/autism, 35–36
Families (Howard), 135
FDA. *See* Food and Drug Administra-
    tion, U.S.
Fear, 4, 241
  built-in, 14–20
  conscious awareness and, 1–2
  factors, 65–133
  first/think second, 5–7, 163
  instinctive reaction to, 1–2
  irrational, xix–xx, 43
  of "it could kill me," 14
  memory and, 8–12
  neuroanatomy of, 193–194
  over reason, 5–7

  PTSD and, 87–88
  of radiation, xix, 95–96, 205, 207
  of social rejection/isolation, 14
de Fermat, Pierre, 54
Fight response, 2, 4–5, 194
Finland, nuclear power/waste in, 79–80
Fires, of Moirans-en-Montagne, 156–158,
    159
Fischhoff, Baruch, 255
Flavavirus, 115, 116
Flight response, 2, 4–5, 194
Flood insurance, national, 247
  Categorization Effect, 247
  Fallacy of the Small Sample and, 247
  Natural/Familiar/Control, 247
  Risk *vs.* Benefit and, 247
Flu vaccination, 245–246. *See also* H1N1
    "swine" flu vaccination; West Nile virus
  Can It Happen to Me and, 246
  Familiarity and, 246
  Optimism Bias and, 246
  Pain/Suffering and, 246
  Risk *vs.* Benefit and, 246
Fluoridation, 203–205
*f*MRI, 16–17, 100
  of oxytocin/amygdala, 72–73
Food and Drug Administration, U.S. (FDA),
    76, 240, 241
  risk communication of, 252–253, 257
  Trust of, 76, 253
Food, Irradiation of, 152–153
Framing Effect, 28–29, 43, 136, 172, 174,
    216, 217, 228, 229
  on climate change, 212
  as decision-making tool, 26–32
  mad cow disease and, 30–32, 172
Freeze response, 2, 4–5, 194
Frequency, Awareness/Ready Recall Effect
    and, 50
Funke, Karl-Heinz, 74

Genetic engineering, 94–95
Gerbner, George, 186
Gilbert, Daniel, 59, 231
Global warming, 128, 135–142
  Globescan survey on, 211
  Pew Global Studies survey on, 211, 212
Globescan survey, on global warming, 211
Glucocorticoids, 10
Glucose
  for brain power, 24
  for energy, 12–13
Glutamate, amygdala release of, 10–11

Goiania
    radioactive cesium at, 160–162
    social perception of, 161
Gore, Al, 75, 138, 235
Gray, George, 220
Greenpeace Web site, 95, 219
Groupthink, 163–166, 216
    environmental advocates and, 164–165
    Iraq invasion and, 163
    September 11 terrorist attacks and, 164
Guidant Corporation, 77–78, 174, 227
Gun purchase increase, after September 11
    terrorist attacks, 191–192

H1N1 "swine" flu vaccination, 86–87, 257
Hazard, 177–178, 219–222
Healthier choices, individual, 214–237
    Cultural Cognition influence remem-
      brance, 225–226
    get more information for, 218
    information from neutral sources,
      218–219
    innumeracy challenge and, 223–224
    news consumer, be a smarter, 226–228
    open mind for, 217
    practical tools for, 217–236
    risk questions and, 219–223
    take time for risk judgment, 217–218
    think about what you think, 228–231
    think for yourself, 225
    trade-offs and, 224–225
    understanding risk response, 231–236
Healthier choices, as society, 237–258
    CBA and, 238
    DWP and, 244–245
    flu vaccination and, 245–246
    medical gloves policy, 240–241
    national flood insurance, 247
    obesity, 248
    risk communication and, 249–258
    understanding psychological factors in
      risk perception, 244–248
    understanding risk perception, 243–244
Heart disease, 99, 199–203
    Catastrophic or Chronic, 105–106
    CDC on, xviii, 199
    death rate, 199
    Pain/Suffering and, 96–97
Herbal medicines, 93–94
Hierarchists, 145, 212, 234
Hippocampus
    explicit memory and, 10, 11, 196
    glucose and, 13

Hormone replacement therapy (HRT), 101, 164
    reframing information on, 229
Howard, Jane, 135
HRT. See Hormone replacement therapy
Human made chemicals, in blood, 28–29
Human made forces, 212
Hume, David, 260
Hussein, Saddam, 113–114

Immune system, 195–196
Implicit memory, amygdala storage of, 9, 13, 194
Individual Perception Gap
    anthrax and, 192–193
    DWP and, 190
    not worrying enough and, 189–190
    obesity, 189
Individualists, 145–146, 204, 212, 234
Individuals, risk of getting risk wrong as,
    187–198
Innumeracy, 52–56
    absolute/relative risk and, 55–56,
      176–177, 223–224, 230
    challenge of, 223–224
    problems with, 250
    statistical probability and, 54
Instinctive reaction, to fear, 1–2
Iraq invasion, Groupthink and, 163
Irradiation, of food, 152–153
Irrational fears/choices, xix–xx, 43

Jackson, Holbrook, 21
Jacob I Have Loved (Patterson), 214
John Birch Society, on fluoridation, 203
Journalists
    Awareness/Ready Recall Effect on, 180
    Biases of, 181–182
    Pain/Suffering and, 180
    personal experience and, 181
    vs. public servants, 183
    Uncertainty/Framed Effect and, 180
"Judged Frequency of Lethal Events," 59–60

Kahan, Dan, 144, 148–151, 156
Kahneman, Daniel, 25, 40
Kant, Immanuel, 260
Kennedy, John F., assassination of, 8
Know Your Chances: Understanding Health
    Statistics (Woloshin/Schwartz/Welch), 224
Knowledge, judgment/decision making with-
    out, 23

Lancet, 35, 36, 175–176
    fish nutrient benefit study by, 44

LeDoux, Joseph, 18, 215
Leiserowitz, Anthony, 210
Life Orientation Test, 61–62
Limbaugh, Rush, 225
Loss Aversion, 40–45
    Anchoring/Adjustment, 45–48, 216,
        230–231
    Awareness/Ready Recall Effect, 48–52,
        139, 159, 180, 216, 228, 252
    Endowment Effect, 41–45
    football coaches and, 42
    Framing Effect and, 43
    health risks and, 42
    Innumeracy, 52–56
    Optimism Bias, 56–62, 136, 147, 190,
        191, 216, 231, 246
    risk attention and, 43

Mad cow disease, 73–75, 172–173, 184, 227
    Awareness/Ready Recall Effect and, 252
    Can It Happen to Me, 252
    FDA/USDA risk communication on,
        252–253
    Framing Effect and, 30–32, 172
    risk communication for, 256
    Uncertainty and, 252
    Wall Street Journal on, 30–31, 32
    Washington Post, 31–32
Malaria, 83–84
Marburg virus, 78–79
Mass murder, 106–107
Massacre, 107
McClellan, Scott, 30
"The Mean World Syndrome" (Gerbner), 186
Media, 133, 166–186
    on airbags, 175
    Awareness/Ready Recall Effect and, 51,
        59, 180
    birth control/blood clots, 177
    cancer attention from, 201–202
    chemical spill story, 169–171
    competition of, 183–184
    defense of, 179–184
    on Guidant Corporation, 174
    hopeful aspects of stories by, 179–180
    information provision role of, 184
    on mad cow disease, 73–74, 172–173, 184
    on mercury risk, 175–176
    on MTBE, 177–178, 184
    New/Familiar Risk and, 115–116
    noteworthy accounts by, 179
    Risk to Children and, 122
    sensationalism by, 168

on SIDS, 184
simplistic limitation of, 183
source increase and, 227–228
story dramatization by, 167–168,
    171–172, 226–227
tools to protect from, 176–179
Media, tools to protect from
    Exposure/Hazard and, 177–178
    population at risk and, 177
    relative/absolute risk, 55–56, 176–177,
        223–224, 230
Medical gloves policy, 240–241
Medicines and Healthcare Products Regula-
    tory Agency (MHRA), 93–94
Memory
    explicit, 9–10
    of fear, 8–12
    glutamate for, 10–11
    hyper, 9–10, 50–51
    implicit, 9, 13, 194
    stress and, 196
    vividness of, 50–51
Mendel, Gregor, 94
Mental model approach, to risk communica-
    tion, 255–256
Mental shortcuts, for making decisions, 23–26
Merck pharmaceutical company, 76–77
Mercury, 224–225
    exposure to, 43–45, 175–176, 222–223
    hazard for, 221–222
Mesothelioma, 38
Methyl tertiary butyl ether (MTBE),
    177–178, 220
MHRA. See Medicines and Healthcare Prod-
    ucts Regulatory Agency
MMR vaccine, 35–36
Moirans-en-Montagne fires, 156–158, 159, 248
Monsanto Chemical Company, 162, 165
Morgan, M. Granger, 255
MRI, 16–17
MS. See Multiple sclerosis
MTBE. See Methyl tertiary butyl ether
Multiple sclerosis (MS), 82
Murder, 106
My Lai massacre, 107

National Cancer Act, 200
National Center for Missing & Exploited
    Children, 123–124
National Institutes of Health (NIH), 200
National Institutes of Health high security
    biological laboratory, at BU, 78, 131,
    132–133

"National Missing Children's Day," 120
National natural disaster related insurance, 247
National Research Council, U.S., on fluoridation, 203
Natural Resources Defense Council, 122
Natural/Human-Made Risk, 92–96, 137, 174, 216, 231–232, 247
   climate change and, 212
   environmental risk controversies and, 94
   genetic engineering, 94–95
   herbal medicines and, 93–94
   radiation and, 95–96
   skin cancer and, 190–191
   West Nile virus and, 92
Neurobiological components, of Affective Risk Response, xvi, 112, 236
Neutral sources, information from, 218
New York Times, 44, 86, 118, 174–175, 176, 180
The New Yorker magazine, 103
New/Familiar Risk, 114–119
News consumer, 226–228
NIH. *See* National Institutes of Health
Norepinephrine, 9, 10, 194
Nuclear power, 34, 79–80, 83, 95–96, 164, 205–208, 218. *See also* Chernobyl nuclear accident; Three Mile Island nuclear plant; Yucca Mountain nuclear waste
   Anchoring/Adjustment and, 47–48
   Awareness/Ready Recall Effect and, 51, 52
   Choice and, 91
   Kahan on, 149–151
   radiation risk of, 206–207
   regulatory/financial obstacles to, 207–208
   Risk Perception Factors for concern of, 234
Nuclear Regulatory Commission, 100
Nuclear waste
   in Finland, 79–80, 91
   Pain/Suffering and, 98
   Risks to Children and, 207
   in Yucca Mountain, 80, 91, 162

Obesity, 242
   Choice/Control and, 189, 190, 248
   Pain/Suffering and, 247
   Risk *vs.* Benefit, 248
   WHO on, 189
Online news, 182–183
Ophidiophobes (snake-phobic), 15
Optimism Bias, 58–62, 136, 147, 191, 216
   Awareness/Ready Recall Effect on, 61
   Bounded Rationality and, 61

Categorization interaction with, 61
   distortions of, 231
   DWP and, 190
   flu vaccination and, 246
   nature of risk and, 59–60
   short term *vs.* long term in, 58–59
   terrorist attacks and, 57–58
Oxytocin
   experiment with, 71–72
   social bonding and, 71

Pain/Suffering, 96–99, 176, 180, 216
   from cancer, 96–97, 201
   death from falls and, 98–99
   flu vaccination and, 246
   heart disease and, 96–97
   major threats to, 98
   nuclear waste and, 98
   obesity and, 247
   radiation and, 207
   WTP and, 242
Pardo, Bruce, 107
Pascal, Blaise, 54, 261
Patterson, Katherine, 214
Pensées (Pascal), 261
People magazine, 168
Perception
   psychology, on risk, 127–128
   of risk, xii–xiii, 67, 156–166, 243–248
   social, at Goiania, 161
   social influence on, xvii, 156–166
   that make things worse, xvii–xviii, 66, 85, 187–188, 214–215, 240
   voluntary risk and, 92
Perception Gap, xiii, 26. *See also* Societal Perception Gap; Individual Perception Gap
   closing of, xvii, 213
   conscious awareness for, 216–217
   dangers of, xvii–xix
   innumeracy contribution to, 56
   media and, 185–186
   number knowledge and, 53
   risk communication leading to, 256
   stress and, xviii, 193–198
Personification, 126–130, 158, 176, 226
   of airbag danger, 175
   of child abduction, 127
   of global warming, 128
   war photos and, 128
Pesticide exposure, 22, 164

Pew Research Center for the People and the Press, 167, 168, 182
    Global Studies on global warming by, 211, 212
Plane accident, 105–106
Policy making, fear quantified by, 242
Population at risk, 177
Post-traumatic stress disorder (PTSD), 87–88
Precautionary Principle, 103–104
"The Problem of the Points" (Pascal/de Fermat), 54
Problems with Probability
    blurring of time, 39
    cancer and, 38
    of Categorization, 37–39
    Clustering and, 38–39
    random coin toss, 37–38, 39
Protection, from news media coverage, 176–179
Pryor, Sarah, 120, 121, 125
Psychological components
    of Affective Risk Response, xvi, 112, 236
    of fear factors, xvii
PTSD. See Post-traumatic stress disorder
Public health, xviii, 38–39. See also Healthier choices, as society
Public servants, media vs., 183

Radiation, fear of, xix, 95–96, 205, 207
Radioactive cesium, at Goiania, 160–162
Radon, 250–251
Rational risk response
    from cognitive cortex, 4–5, 66
    Darwin and, 5–6
Rationality, xvi, xx. See also Bounded Rationality
    Affective Risk Response system and, 249
    economists and, 25
    Emotion vs., 260
    facts and, 249
    healthier choices as society and, 243–244
    Perception Gap and, 215–216
Reason. See Conscious awareness
Reciprocal altruism, 131
Relative risk, 55–56, 176–177, 223–224
Remarque, Erich Maria, xi
Representativeness, 174, 178. See also Categorization
    drug-coated stents and, 229–230
    fluoride and, 204
Revealed preference, 241
Risk, 260–261
    absolute/relative, 55–56, 176–177, 223–224, 230

    of BpA, 33–34
    communicator, trust and, 75
    controversial, 235–236
    creator, trust and, 76
    exposure, 222–223
    of getting things wrong as individuals, 187–198
    hazard, 177–178, 219–222
    involuntary nature of, 89
    nature of, optimism and, 59–60
    perception of, xvii–xviii, 67, 156–166, 243–248
    qualitative characteristics of, 20, 242
    statistical probability and, 54
    voluntary, 92
Risk: A Practical Guide for Deciding What's Really Safe and What's Really Dangerous in the World Around You (Gray/Ropeik), 220
Risk and Culture: An Essay on the Selection of Technological and Environmental Dangers (Douglas/Wildavsky), 144
Risk communication, 249–258
    Chernobyl and, 256–257
    emotional response and, 249–250
    facts for rational judgment and, 249
    of FDA, 257
    government, 256–257
    for H1N1 influenza, 257
    leading to Perception Gap, 256
    on mad cow disease, 252, 256
    mental model approach to, 255–256
    positive lessons from, 252
Risk Communication: A Mental Models Approach (Morgan/Fischhoff/Bostrom/Atman), 255
Risk Perception Factor, 147
    Can It Happen to Me, 109–114, 136, 210, 246, 250, 252
    Catastrophic or Chronic, 105–109, 176, 207, 212, 242
    Choice and, 89–92, 189, 201, 248
    climate change conversation using, 135–142
    conscious realization of, 231–236
    Control, 62–63, 67, 85–89, 136, 158, 174, 176, 190, 191, 192, 201, 212, 216, 245, 247
    Fairness, 130–131
    fear fluctuation, 68, 69
    individual perspective and, 69, 70
    Natural/Human-Made Risk, 92–96, 137, 174, 190–191, 212, 216, 231–232, 247
    New/Familiar Risk, 114–119, 246, 247

Pain/Suffering, 96–99, 176, 180, 201, 207, 216, 242, 246, 247
Personification, 126–130, 158, 175, 176, 226
principles behind, 68–70
Risk vs. Benefit, 81–85, 140, 190, 191, 212, 224–225, 246, 247, 248
Risks to Children, 119–126, 164, 175, 176, 207, 212
Trust, 70–81, 137, 174, 207, 216, 227, 253, 254
Uncertainty, 86, 99–104, 116, 136, 137, 159, 172, 176, 179, 180, 192, 203, 204, 207, 252
Risk response, xiv–xvii, 1, 158
Affective people and, xv–xvi, 199, 214, 215–216, 237, 260, 261
Anchoring/Adjustment and, 46–47
biological system of, 17–20
first minutes of, 3–4
memory and, 8–12
number knowledge and, 53
physiological changes of, 2
quiz for, 11–12, 21, 25, 26–27, 32, 37, 40, 42, 46, 47, 52–53, 71, 90, 96–97, 126–127, 130, 151–155, 210
rational, 4–6, 66
subconscious processes for, 19
subcortex and, 2–3
Risk vs. Benefit, 81–85, 140, 191, 247
associated risk and, 82–83
climate change and, 212
DWP and, 190
flu vaccination and, 246
malaria and, 83–84
MS/Tysabri drug and, 82
nuclear power and, 83
obesity and, 248
personal decisions and, 84–85
perspective and, 84
tanning and, 191
trade-offs between, 81–82, 224–225
Triple E and, 83
waste disposal facilities and, 83
Risks to Children, 119–126, 176
airbag danger and, 175
AMBER Alert for, 123
biological drive to protect, 121–122
child abduction, 119–120, 125–127, 164
climate change and, 212
nuclear waste and, 207
sexual exploitation, 123–124
Ropeik, David, 220

Sapolsky, Robert, 194
SARS. See Severe acute respiratory syndrome
Schroeder, Gerhard, 75
Schwartz, Lisa, 224
Self-Reliance (Emerson), 243
Sensationalism, 168
September 11 terrorist attacks, 8, 109, 113–114, 164
driving deaths increase and, xviii, 65–66, 67, 187–188, 251
gun purchase increase after, 191–192
stress and, 197
Severe acute respiratory syndrome (SARS), 111–112
Sexual exploitation, of children, 123–124
SIDS. See Sudden infant death syndrome
Simon, Herbert, 23–24, 37
Skin cancer, 190–191
Snake, fear of, 15
Sniper shootings, 228
Awareness/Ready Recall Effect and, 48–50
Control and, 88
Uncertainty and, 101
Social bonding
Catastrophes and, 108, 109
oxytocin and, 71
Social influence
on belief adoption, 159
of Groupthink, 163–166
on risk perception, xvii, 156–166
Stigmatization, 160
Societal Perception Gap, 189, 198–213
Affective Risk Response and, 239
cancer/heart disease, 199–203
climate change, 208–213
fluoridation, 203–204
nuclear power, 205–208, 234
from policies based on feelings, 238
Spider, fear of, 15
Statistical probability
of cancer/heart disease, 203
understanding risk and, 54
Stereotyping. See Categorization
Stigmatization, 160, 161–162, 178
of nuclear power, 207
of technology/substances/risk management, 162
of Yucca Mountain nuclear waste, 162
Stress, xviii, 87–88
biological effects of, 195–197
blood chemistry change by, 195
blood pressure increase by, 195
clinical depression and, 197

Stress (*continued*)
 digestion shutdown, 195
 fertility problems and, 196
 immune system suppressed by, 195–196
 impaired growth rates, of children, 196
 judgment impairment from, 197
 memory formation and, 196
 osteoporosis risk from, 196
 Perception Gap and, xviii, 193–198
Stumbling on Happiness (Gilbert), 59
Subcortex, 2–3
Sudden infant death syndrome (SIDS), 184

TCE. *See* Trichloroethylene
Terrorist attacks, 57–58
 of September 11, 2001, xviii, 8, 65–66,
  67, 109, 113–114, 164, 187–188,
  191–192, 197, 251
Thalamus, 3–5, 194
Three Mile Island nuclear plant, 51, 95–96,
 98, 99–100, 207, 228, 231–232
Trade-offs, 84
 reframing of, 228–229
 Risk *vs.* Benefit, 81–82, 224–225
 risk/risk, 225
Tribe, 108, 109, 234–235
 BIRG-ing/CORF-ing, 143
 cohesion/protection in, 143
 types of, 143
 unity of, 144
Trichloroethylene (TCE), xi–xii, 214
Triple E. *See* Eastern equine encephalitis
Triple F response, 159
 blood chemistry change by, 195
 energy levels and, 12–14, 195
 of fight/flight/freeze, 2, 4–5, 194
 glucocorticoid release and, 10
 physical, 7
Trust, 70–81, 137, 174, 216, 227
 Dow Corning and, 76
 of FDA, 76, 253
 in government, 254
 Guidant Corporation and, 77–78, 174
 mad cow disease and, 73–75
 Merck pharmaceutical company and,
  76–77
 of nuclear power, 207
 oxytocin and, 71–72
 of people/organizations, 75–81
 in process, 78–81

 risk communicator of, 75
 risk creator and, 76
 among social animals, 72
 subconscious judgment for, 73
 of USDA, 253
 withholding information and, 77–78
Tysabri drug, 82

Uncertainty, 99–104, 116, 136, 137, 172, 176,
 179, 180, 252
 anthrax and, 86, 192
 fluoridation and, 203
 hormone replacement therapy, 101
 "I can't detect it," 102, 204
 "I don't understand it," 102
 "Nobody knows," 102–103
 Precautionary Principle and, 103–104
 radiation and, 207
 sniper shootings and, 101
 society magnification of, 159
 Three Mile Island nuclear plant accident
  and, 99–100
United Nations, 45–46
U.S. Department of Agriculture (USDA),
 252–253

Vioxx medication, 76–77
Virginia Tech, murder at, 107

Wakefield, Andrew, 35–36
Wall Street Journal, 30–31, 32, 172, 173, 180
Washington Post, 31–32, 128, 173, 184
Weinstein, Neil, optimism study of, 60,
 62–63
Welch, H. Gilbert, 224
West Nile virus, 92, 112–113, 179
 CDC on, 117, 118
 New/Familiar Risk and, 114–119
WHO. *See* World Health Organization
Why Zebras Don't Get Ulcers (Sapolsky), 194
Wildavsky, Aaron, 144
Willingness to Pay (WTP), 242–243
Woloshin, Steve, 224
World Health Organization (WHO), xix,
 106, 189, 208, 257
World War II, 128, 159, 204
WTP. *See* Willingness to Pay

Yucca Mountain nuclear waste, 80, 91, 162

ABOUT THE AUTHOR

David Ropeik is an international consultant and widely sought-after public speaker on risk perception and risk communication. Ropeik is an instructor at the Harvard University Extension School's Environmental Management Program, and he taught risk perception and risk communication at the Harvard School of Public Health (2000–2006). He was a television journalist in Boston for 22 years and twice won the DuPont Columbia Award, one of the highest honors in broadcast journalism. He has written articles about risk perception for *The New York Times, The Washington Post, USA Today, LA Times, The Boston Globe,* and *Nova* among others.